Other books by Roy Andries de Groot

Feasts for All Seasons
The Recipes of the Auberge of the Flowering Hearth
Revolutionizing French Cooking
Cooking with the Cuisinart

PRESSURE
COOKERY
PERFECTED

Roy Andries de Groot

SUMMIT BOOKS   NEW YORK

Published by Summit Books
A Simon & Schuster Division of Gulf & Western Corporation
Simon & Schuster Building
Rockefeller Center
1230 Avenue of the Americas
New York, New York 10020

Designed by Irving Perkins
Manufactured in the United States of America
Printed and Bound by The Murray Printing Company
1 2 3 4 5 6 7 8 9 10

Library of Congress Cataloging in Publication Data

De Groot, Roy Andries, date.
   Pressure cookery perfected.

   Includes index.
   1. Pressure cooking. I. Title.
Tx840.P7D39   641.5'89   78-1076
ISBN 0-671-40006-1
        0-671-40038-X Pbk.

Photographs courtesy of National Presto Industries, Inc.

for Charlotte

who tasted the perfectly pressured cassoulet
and then struck the spark . . .

CONTENTS

Introduction

CONVENIENCE COOKING
WITH NATURAL FOODS

The Age of Machine Cuisine

This book is a response to an apparent demand by millions of American home cooks. About twenty years ago, they began rebelling against the many hours they had to spend in the kitchen every day preparing the essential family meals by the old-fashioned, classical cooking methods. Sensing this rebellion, the big food companies began offering their "convenience foods," TV dinners, preprepared main dishes, ready-sauced vegetables, just-heat-and-serve frozen specialties, dehydrated cups of soup, skillet dinners, instant breakfasts . . . For a while, they were a big success. Now, suddenly and dramatically, they are being rejected, equally in every part of the country and in numbers so large that there can be no mistaking the trend. Every recent consumer-attitude survey has reported it as a major change in American eating habits. It seems to be the start of a new era in American cuisine.

What is happening, clearly, is that there is a massive turning away from convenience packaged foods and a turning toward natural foods, fresh fruits and vegetables, fish just out of the sea and the healthy, nutritious elements of high-fiber, whole-grain bulk. We are shopping less and less in the frozen food cabinets, more and more at the produce counters. Distribution of natural foods is booming. The raising and marketing of fresh Chinese vegetables is now a one-hundred-million-dollar business across the country. But although we are rejecting "fast foods" and are turning back to cooking natural ingredients from scratch, we still want fast preparation in our kitchens and, for that, we are turning to our new kitchen machines.

Among these new tools, the one appliance which provides more dramatic timesaving than any other is the improved, modernized, streamlined, steam pressure cooker. It is at least three times faster than normal cooking, and it is just about twice as fast as the microwave oven. Here are some typical test results. . . .

	Normal Cooking	Microwave Oven	Pressure Cooker
Sauerbraten, 5 lb	4 hours	1½ hours	45 minutes
Veal paprika, 2 lb	1½ hours	30 minutes	10 minutes
Swiss steak, 2 lb	2½ hours	1½ hours	30 minutes
Chicken Provençal, 3 lb	1 hour	35 minutes	15 minutes
Sweet-sour shrimp, 1 lb	1 hour	40 minutes	10 minutes
Chinese meatballs, 1 lb	45 minutes	30 minutes	15 minutes

You Save Money as Well as Time

The main reason, obviously, why so many of us have turned away from the convenience packaged foods is their more than 50 percent rise in cost over the past two years. Food costs have become public enemy number one. Yet, when we bring home our fresh ingredients, chop and cut the vegetables in our Cuisinart chopper-churner, whip the eggs in our Whip-O-Matic machine, almost instantly grind dried herbs and spices in our little electric spice mill, quickly knead the dough for hot biscuits with our electric dough hook, then assemble the main dish in our pressure cooker, we can often set a meal on the table in under one hour at a cost of about fifty cents a serving. Those machines we received as Christmas gifts do, in fact, eliminate the drudgery from cooking. The convenience now comes from the machine instead of from the frozen package.

Fear of the Chemical Feast

Another factor that is motivating so many of us toward fast, superheated steaming of natural foods is the growing fear of chemical additives. Almost all of the most recent opinion research studies show that the public's attitude toward mass-produced, canned or packaged foods, which was about 72 percent favorable in 1967, went down to about 60 percent unfavorable in 1975. The Lewis Harris opinion survey of consumer attitudes issued in May 1977 shows a deep public distrust of the food industry. Consumers indicated by their answers to the survey questions that they resented soaring food prices, questionable products with poor quality and safety, false claims in advertising, misleading packaging and labeling. . . . Almost half the people questioned (precisely 45 percent) named the American food industry as most in need of consumer pressure toward reform—placing it higher on the public danger list than even the oil industry, electric utilities, the drug industry, used-car dealers and nuclear power plants.

The direct cause of this widespread distrust of the food industry clearly is the growing issue of health and nutrition. Now that so many of us have formed the habit of reading the legally required lists of ingredients on the can and package labels, we have come to believe, rightly or wrongly, that the colors of the foods are chemical, the flavorings are chemical and that many of the basic ingredients come from the laboratory instead of from the farm. We are being told, repeatedly, that the continuing rise in the cancer rate is increasingly linked to artificial food additives. We often seem to be eating chemical parodies of the real food products. Part of the new cooking movement is, certainly, a rebellion against the chemical additives.

A Return to Natural Tastes and Textures

The recipes in this book—although they are prepared at the speed of convenience foods—produce dishes with the natural tastes and textures of fresh foods. Nothing is more natural than fresh vegetables pressure-steamed to perfection in a few seconds. They have a kind of dewy springtime, freshly picked, flowery earthiness about them, as if they had just been harvested and you were eating them in the farm kitchen. Because they were cooked so quickly, with minimum liquid and in an enclosed, airtight space (which eliminates all oxidation), all the original nutrients in the vegetables are completely preserved. When you open up the lid, you are instantly immersed in the irresistible natural aromas.

Although the principles of superheated steaming in a sealed pot are almost three hundred years old—and American manufacturers have been making and selling pressure pots for use in the home for more than seventy years—the latest pressure cookers are something quite new. The earlier models had pressure regulators that were relatively inaccurate and unsophisticated. You had to read a small needle-pointer moving in a narrow slot, and your chances of misreading it depended on the angle of the light. When you wanted 15 pounds, you could easily get 18. And, if you forgot to turn down the heat at precisely the right moment, you might even have reached 20 pounds. That much overpressure disintegrated meat into fibrous strings, mashed chicken almost to a paste and instantly overcooked beans, pasta, potatoes, rice or vegetables to a soggy wetness.

No such dangers lurk around the new pressure cookers. Regulation of the various cooking pressures is by the use of different plug-in weights, which close down or open up the steam vent, so that the accuracy of the internal steam pressure is now held to plus or minus 2 percent. If you forget to turn down the heat, there is an audible warning as the pressure regulator begins to jangle-jiggle-juggle with an insistent signal. Today, there are locking devices on the lids which prevent the possibility of an accidental mistake. Electric controls automatically adjust the heat. The latest type of pressure cooker is altogether more efficient, more accurate in terms of the precise doneness of the food, more flexible in terms of a wider variety of ingredients that can now be successfully pressurized. Many of the recipes in this book represent a kind of breakthrough in the most advanced techniques of speed cooking.

• Most of the one-dish meal recipes in this book can be cooked within an average range of 5 to 30 minutes—with advance preparation of the natural ingredients running from 5 to 25 minutes—thus making it possible to prepare a meal, from the moment you walk into the kitchen to the moment of serving at table, in from 10 to 55 minutes.

• Natural ingredients with widely different textures and cooking times can be combined into the same cooking pot by using the Chinese technique of cutting the foods into pieces of different shapes and sizes (see page 26).

• Some of the recipes in this book are for entire meals—including meats, sauces, assortments of vegetables and desserts—all cooked together at the same time in a single pot in 15 minutes or less (see page 76).

• In almost every recipe, any advance preparations—browning, presoaking, saucing, sautéing, searing, etc.—are done in the pressure cooker, using it as an ordinary, open saucepan to minimize after-dinner cleanup.

• Each main-dish recipe includes a suggestion for a nutritionally balanced menu, with an appropriate American or imported wine.

• The book includes recipes for hearty main-dish soups—since pressure cooking uniquely draws out the glutinous richness of meats, bones and aromatic vegetables—several of them prepared and cooked in under 30 minutes (see page 52).

• One more special skill of the modern steam pressure cooker is the precision and speed of its cooking of the so-called legumes, the excellently nutritious and healthfully bulky dried beans, split peas and various lentils, etc. With the elimination of the normal hours of presoaking and slow simmering, most bean pots can be pressured to perfect doneness in about an hour to an hour and a half (see page 61).

• For vegetarians, the perfection of pressurized, lightning-cooked vegetables is a special joy, most of them cooked within a minute or two (see page 182).

• Another extraordinary and unique accomplishment of the pressure cooker is its ability to produce, at almost magical speed, egg custards of a feathery-fluffy lightness, impossible to duplicate by any other cooking method. There are recipes for main-dish, savory custards filled with meat, chicken, shellfish, cheese or vegetables, as well as sweet dessert custards filled with fruits, liqueurs, figs, nuts, etc., with complete preparation times averaging about 20 minutes.

• Other special desserts uniquely possible under steam pressure are the light and fruity steamed puddings which some of us still remember from the country kitchens of our grandmothers—fluffy assemblages of fruits, dates, figs, ginger, nuts (including Christmas Plum Pudding), which used to take so many hours of slow simmering that we had to drop them out of our busy, modern lives. Now the pressure cooker can bring them back, lighter, more perfectly textured, more refreshing, more fruity and nutty than ever—most of them prepared and steamed in about an hour (see page 219).

• Finally, if you come from Boston and remember the steamed breads, you can now pressurize Boston Brown Bread, or Cranberry Bread, or even Southern Corn Spoon Bread in an average of 5 to 15 minutes (see page 206).

And a Substantial Conservation of Energy

Obviously, if you cook your foods in such extraordinarily short (one-third to one-quarter of the normal) times, at lower heat settings to maintain the steam pressure, you are saving at least two-thirds to three-quarters of the watts of electricity or the cubic inches of gas you would normally consume for the standard methods of cooking.

A recently published professional report estimated a saving of up to three hundred hours for a family of four on the cooking range per year. Depending on what rate you pay for your energy supply, you can easily calculate what this means in terms of an annual saving of dollars.

This book, then, will encourage you to shop for the natural fresh foods, to eliminate additives and artificial chemicals from your family cuisine, to concentrate on the balanced elements of nutrition and to include the proper amounts of high-fiber bulk foods. Pressure cooking, in reality, returns the control of the family nutrition to you, the home cook. All this will be possible while maintaining superfast preparation in your kitchen. Finally, in terms of your family budget, this book offers just as much convenience in the kitchen as with the packaged "convenience foods," but without their inconvenient prices.

Chapter I

THE MACHINES THAT DO
THE MIRACULOUS WORK IN
YOUR KITCHEN

The Secret Is the Superheated Steam

The most modern method of automatic speed steam cooking—with the thermostatically controlled electric cookpot released by its manufacturers only this year—goes back, in terms of its scientific concept and principles, an almost unbelievable three hundred years! In 1679, a French engineer, Denys Papin, knowing the basic physical principle that steam trapped in an enclosed space would build up pressure that, in turn, would raise the temperature at which water boils, invented his "Marmite Chaudière à la Vapeur," loosely translated as a "Hot Steam Cookpot." Notice that he said nothing about pressure. It was the high temperature that he wanted, so that he could, as he put it, "use the heat of my pot to digest, dissolve and melt bones," so as to be able to prepare, easily and quickly, glutinously rich, country-farmhouse-style bouillons and soups. Perhaps because Papin's cookpot was awkward (one published report stated that the lid had to be screwed on) and was always in danger of ruining the food by overcooking, nothing more was heard of the idea until the beginning of the twentieth century.

The modern high-temperature pressure cooker would, of course, never have been possible without the isolation and production of aluminum in 1825 by the Danish physicist Hans Christian Oersted, followed, two years later, by the German chemist Frederick Wohler, who devised a simpler method of making it. Wohler's shining little lumps of aluminum were displayed at the Paris Exposition of 1855 as a "precious metal" priced at ninety dollars per ounce. (Today, it costs about fifty cents per pound.) Then, the French scientist Sainte-Claire Deville launched a research program supported by the Emperor Napoleon III and discovered that aluminum could be cheaply and easily extracted from a certain type of clay available in large quantities around the French town of Baux. Thus "bauxite" became virtually the second name of aluminum. At last, in

1886, the young American metallurgical student, Charles Hall, invented the mass-production system which created the corporate empire of ALCOA and made aluminum one of the most universal of the world's metals.

The first aluminum containers for food—mainly drinking cups and mugs—were made in Germany and displayed at the Columbian Exposition in Chicago in 1893. They were seen and much admired by, among the thousands of visitors, some German-born, small-town businessmen and engineers from Wisconsin. Who knows—perhaps it was German chauvinistic pride that made these men go back home determined to start up manufacturing companies for aluminum in Wisconsin. So much so that, today, some eighty years later, about 97 percent of all the steam cookpots and pressure cookers made in the United States still come from various parts of Wisconsin.

In 1895, a small aluminum company was founded in Two Rivers. In 1898, the owner of a leather tannery in Manitowoc on the Lake Michigan shore converted his small plant to the making of aluminum utensils. In 1905, on the western side of Wisconsin, in the town of Eau Claire, The National Pressure Cooker Company was formed to make large, fifty-gallon, "steam pressure retorts" for commercial canning of fruits and vegetables. In 1913, the Manitowoc Aluminum Company landed its first, huge order, from the Quaker Oats people, for double-boiler cookers in which to prepare oatmeal porridge—an order which ran, eventually, into more than a million units. In 1914, what is probably the first home pressure cooker was the Flex-Seal, designed and made by the Low Brothers of the southern Wisconsin town of Fort Atkinson. At about the same time, the National people in Eau Claire brought out the first, small, ten-gallon, home pressure canner to help with wartime victory gardens. During the 1914–18 war, all aluminum went to the Armed Forces. When Armistice came, there was a heavy backlog of demand for home pressure canners and fierce competition between the various manufacturing companies. One of them was the original Manitowoc converted tannery—now greatly expanded by mergers with other companies and a building program of new factories in and around Manitowoc. In 1918, they launched nationally their new trade name for all their aluminum products—still one of the important pressure cooker names today, Mirro. The name became so successful so quickly that the company finally decided that the trademark tail might as well wag the corporate dog and changed its name to become The Mirro Aluminum Company.

Meanwhile, the National people in Eau Claire were also expanding and, in 1939, they brought out their first small home pressure cooker under the trade name, Presto—the name that has become, almost certainly, the best known and biggest of all in the making of pressure canners and cookers. So much so that the company finally changed its name to become National Presto Industries, Inc. During the 1941–45 war, again, all use of aluminum for civilian cookware was stopped. By 1945, when the war ended and Mirro announced its small, home Mirro-Matic Pressure Pan, the national pent-up demand for pressure canners and cookers was tremendous. Eleven separate manufacturing companies were competing in the market. But it very soon became clear that the major sales battle was between Mirro and Presto. Within a few years, it was estimated that about forty-five million American homes were using pressure canners or cookers and that of these, 98 percent were either Mirro or Presto. The Mirro-Matic was all-aluminum. Presto introduced also, in addition to its aluminum, stainless-steel models. Since 1975, both Mirro and Presto have reported a new national upsurge in the demand for steam pressure equipment for the home as "more American families seem to be more eager than ever before to beat the high cost of processed foods."

The Current Mirro Machines

The special feature of almost all the Mirro-Matic pressure cookers is that each has an excellently designed, three-way control weight for the pressure and temperature of the internal steam during the cooking operation (either 15 pounds–250° F–121° C, or 10 pounds–238° F–114° C, or 5 pounds–228° F–109° C). These machines, therefore, are fully flexible and can be used to prepare any recipe in this book. The sizes available for normal family use begin with a small, 2½-quart pot, which will hold up to 7 cups of soup or stew and is designed for the preparation of meals for one or two people. Then there is a 4-quart pot, which will hold up to 11 cups of soup or stew; a 6-quart, to hold up to 16 cups, both of these for average families; and an 8-quart, holding up to 22 cups, for larger families. (These holding figures are based on the general rule that a pressure cooker should not normally be filled more than two-thirds full.)

If you are a regular-party-giving family and will want to double, treble or even quadruple the amounts of the recipes in this book, you should own one or more of the pressure canners, which will prepare large quantities of food at exactly the same speed as, say, a meal for one. This is one of the special virtues of the pressure cooker. Since nature's rule is that, inside the pot, steam pressure and temperature are always perfectly equalized, the smallest amount of food can be perfectly cooked in the largest pot. It doesn't matter in the slightest how much air space you have around your pork chop or chicken breast. So you need not hesitate about investing in one of the larger pots, designed for canning, but equally good for family cooking. There is a Mirro-Matic 12-quart, a 16-quart and a 22-quart. All units, of course, come in mirror-polished aluminum, but several of them, also, in a limited choice of colors: harvest gold or avocado green.

The Current Presto Pressure Pots

The smaller Presto cookers for home use come with a one-way control weight for the pressure and temperature of the internal steam in the pot (15 pounds–250° F–121° C), but if you will write to the Home Economics Department of National Presto Industries in Eau Claire, Wisconsin 54701, it will send you a

three-way replacement control weight which will give you the full range of variations needed for all the recipes in this book. The standard family Presto units come either in polished aluminum, stainless steel, or in the color of harvest gold. There is a 4-quart, to hold up to 11 cups of soup or stew, and a 6-quart, to hold up to 16 cups.

Then, among the larger Presto units, either for canning or for rapid preparation of home party meals in larger quantities, there is a 12-quart, a 16-quart and a 20-quart. All these, incidentally, have to have three-way pressure temperature controls (to give them the necessary flexibility for their alternative uses in canning), and this is provided, in some models, by a three-way control weight and, in others, by a pressure-gauge dial which gives a continuous reading of the internal condition of the steam. These larger models all come in the harvest gold color.

The Presto Breakthrough of 1978

At the beginning of the year, Presto made the sensational announcement of a completely new concept and design of superheated steam pot—a practical application of new engineering and gastronomic ideas—a machine so efficient and flexible that it has given us the means of substantially enlarging the breadth and scope of this book. The Presto research engineers and experimental cooks have rethought, retested, reviewed, refined and reordered their most basic thinking about the use of the superheated steam cookpot. First, there is the question of the look of the thing. In the past, almost all pressure cookers have been made with long, saucepan-type handles, obviously as a tool strictly for use in the kitchen. Clearly, it was thought that their noise, the hissing of the steam, the jiggling and rocking of the control weight, the general sense of internal pressure, made a standard pressure cooker generally unsuitable for the living room or dining room.

Presto has now changed all that. The new steam pot is designed as a casserole, with casserole handles, the body and handsomely curving "pagoda lid" in balanced, two-toned colors. The noises of steam and jiggling weight have been muted. This new casserole cookpot can certainly be used as a serving dish at the table.

The electrical and engineering changes also represent radical new thinking. An electrical heater is built into the bottom of the aluminum cookpot with a thermostatic temperature control that can be plugged into an electric outlet in any room. With the cooking heat conducted directly to the food through the metal body of the cookpot (instead of through an air-spaced contact with a stove-top burner), and with the temperature kept almost precisely constant by a thermostat (instead of by human control of the burner), the efficiency of the cooking can approach perfection. We have found this to be true, in our experimental use of the new machine in the course of writing this book, not only in terms of superheated steam cooking, but also when using the new cookpot without its lid, for quick browning and sautéing of meat, or as a saucepan for, say, the gentle completion of a sauce, or the rapid reheating and finishing of a soup or a stew. In summary, we firmly believe that this new unit is clearly the forerunner of a new generation of superheated steam cookpots, more generally flexible and useful than any that have been previously produced.

Two sizes of the new Presto machine will be in production and national distribution by the end of 1978: a 3-quart model to come first, and to be followed by a 6-quart.

Another Revolutionary Forward Step in 1978—Crisp Fried Foods from a Pressure Cooker

The latest of the new machines is from the Wear-Ever Aluminum housewares division of ALCOA and includes a brand-new function in terms of pressure cooking. A lid that closes and locks in quite a different way from all the standard types has multiple control vents which allow frying of foods under pressure, so that, among other things, near-perfect Southern-style fried chicken can be produced in about one-third of the normal cooking time. Now, as a kind of "breaking of the pressure barrier," crackly-crisp fried foods can come out of the pressure cooker as well as those that are boiled, braised, poached or steamed. During our experimental work with these new machines and our testing of the special recipes which follow in this book, we found a dramatic improvement in cooking foods by pressure frying. The pressure seems to force the natural juices to remain inside the pieces of meat or fish—not expanding and bubbling outward, but simmering inward, concentrating their flavors while softening the flesh. When we bit into the pieces of beef or chicken, for example, we found, inside the crisp crust, that the flesh was not only juicier and softer than usual, but seemed to have its natural flavor concentrated and magnified.

The new machines are called the Wear-Ever pressure fryer-cooker and will come in the two standardized sizes of 4-quart and 6-quart, operating at 5 pounds pressure and an internal temperature of 228° F (109° C). This means, of course, that they can also be used, with water instead of oil, as normal steam pressure cookers for virtually any of the recipes in this book. The special pressure-frying recipes for the Wear-Ever machines are Medallions of Round Steak on page 93, Fruit-Stuffed Pork Chops on page 114, Fried Chicken on page 140, Barbecued Chicken on page 142, Chicken à la Kievski on page 144, Crispy Fish Fillets on page 170 and Rolled Stuffed Flounder on page 171. *Warning:* These pressure-fried recipes can only be prepared in the specially designed Wear-Ever machines. No pressure frying should ever be attempted in a standard pressure cooker.

Other Available Pressure Cookers from Home and Abroad

The Revere Copper and Brass people have been designing and making pressure pans, off and on, for thirty years. Their two current units are 4- and 6-quart sizes, both with stainless-steel bodies and copper-clad bottoms. The problem with them is that they are fitted with only one-way control weights permitting only 15 pounds–250° F–121° C. This seriously limits their flexibility in terms of cooking many different kinds of foods, and makes them impossible for some recipes. Also, the bottoms of these units are slightly recessed—a fact that makes it difficult to use them on smooth-top, counter-type electric cooking stoves. One would hope that, in view of the sharply rising national demand for pressure cookers, Revere will soon redesign and modernize its otherwise excellent units.

Finally, just to remind us that the techniques of pressure cookery are in demand all around the world, we are now beginning to see the importation (still in small quantities, of course) of some of the best of the foreign designs, including the British Prestige and Tower machines, the French S.E.B., the Spanish Bra from Barcelona and the two Swiss models, the Duromatic from Zurich, and the Flexil from Thurgau—the latter designed to seal in the steam by metallic pressure of the lid without the use of a plastic or rubber gasket. There are, also, one is told by traveling housewares experts, other designs being produced in Germany, Italy, Eastern Europe, as well as Australia and Japan. It seems that pressure cookery is being "discovered" by busy cooks everywhere!

Chapter 2

THE BASIC TECHNIQUES OF THE PRESSURE COOKER

The Do's and Don'ts That Apply to All Makes and Models

You will realize, from the previous chapter, that each brand and type of pressure cooker, although based on universal scientific principles, is slightly different in design and operation. So the first essential is to read the how-to-use section of the instruction booklet for your particular unit. Follow these instructions carefully as to bringing up the steam pressure and reducing it. Beyond this, however, in terms of general cooking advice, you have to face the fact that some of these booklets are written with more intelligence and sophistication than others. In some of them, we think, there is a bit too much stress on all the things that could possibly go wrong. The modern steam pressure cookpot is about as dangerous as a pair of kitchen scissors. It is certainly possible to cut or stick yourself with scissors, yet no one suggests that you should wear a suit of armor while snipping a bunch of chives.

One national manufacturer, for example, states in its booklet: "Never use your pressure cooker as an ordinary saucepan . . . the only way to use your cooker with the cover on is as a pressure cooker." We do not agree. You will see, from the recipes in this book, that not only do we use the open cooker for advance browning and sautéing of the meats—a trick which saves dishwashing and also helps to provide superbly flavored natural sauces—but we also use the cooker with its lid on, without pressure, as a most efficient steamer of breads, dumplings and fruit puddings.

The Rules That Make It All Easy and Sure

After thirty years of experience with steam pressure cookers, we have developed our own basic rules, which apply, in general, to all makes and models. Let us go through the routine of a recipe, step by step.

THE USES OF THE INTERNAL RACK

Every steam pressure cooker currently on the market includes as standard equipment an internal, removable, metal rack which can be used to lift the food about 3/8 to 1/2 inch above the bottom of the pan. First, of course, if the recipe calls for you to brown or sauté the foods before pressurizing, you remove the rack. Then the recipe will tell you whether or not to put it back. You should understand the reason why. If the food is to be steamed only, making no contact with the liquid in the bottom of the pan, it is usually possible to have an amount of boiling liquid somewhere between 1/2 and 3/4 cup under the rack without its touching the food. But, if you are preparing a soup or a stew, where the pan may be half full and all the ingredients will be swimming in the liquid, then, obviously, there is no point in using the rack.

Another reason for the use or nonuse of the rack has to do with one of the fundamental facts about steam pressure cooking. Steam does not transmit aromatic flavors from one food to another. This is why, in a pressure casserole, you can cook, say, Brussels sprouts, carrots, onions and a delicate egg custard together in the same pan, with none of the separate flavors becoming intermingled. Fine, in this case. But that isn't always what you want. If we are preparing a rich beef stew and have gone to great pains to achieve a perfect balance of herb and spice flavors in the bouillon, we may want those flavors to be "injected" into the meats and vegetables. Fortunately, for our purposes, superheated liquid inside the pressure cooker *does* carry the flavors from one ingredient to another. So if you want the flavors of your ingredients to remain separated, use minimum liquid and insulate the foods from the liquid with the rack. If you want your flavors to mingle, do not use the rack so that your ingredients are in contact with the liquid.

WHAT KIND OF LIQUID—AND HOW MUCH—TO AVOID BURNING?

Every pressure recipe, of course, depends on a certain amount of boiling liquid to provide the superheated steam. Although the conventional pressure steaming liquid is usually water, excellent natural sauces follow automatically from the use of, for example, beef or chicken bouillon, various types of wine, tomato or other vegetable juices and, when a slight touch of sweetness is involved, orange or other fruit juices. The combinations and permutations are almost limitless. Give your imagination free rein.

As to how much liquid—this is where we disagree with some of the recipe writers who seem to be so afraid of the liquid boiling away, with resulting burning of the food, that they tend to put in too much liquid at the start. The inevitable result is soggy food. Our answer is to use the correct amount of liquid, coupled with a degree of alertness to avoid the dangers of boiling away and burning.

We put the food and the precise amount of liquid in the pressure casserole and turn up the heat high to bring the liquid as quickly as possible to a rolling boil. But do not wait for it to boil. At once check the lid to see that the vent pipe is open, put on the lid, make sure it is absolutely tight, put the pressure control weight on the steam vent and bring up the pressure for the particular recipe, according to the instructions for the machine you are using. The moment the pressure regulator signals, by hissing, jiggling or rocking, that the required pressure has been reached, start your timer and turn down the heat to maintenance level. (After a couple of tries, you will know your settings exactly, and they will always be the same on your particular pressure cooker.) With the new, automated models, you simply turn down the thermostatic control until the small pilot light goes out.

From this point onward, pressure cooking by superheated steam is the truly automated food preparation of the modern age. During the cooking, you have no intimate contact with the food. There is no taking off the lid to sniff, stir and taste. No agonizing about adding a little bit of this or that. If you have put in the right ingredients, in exactly the right proportions and have done the right things with them before you put the lid on, you will get the right result, exactly the same every time.

HOW MUCH FOOD TO PUT IN?

The sizes of pressure cookers are measured differently from those of ordinary saucepans. When you buy a 2-quart saucepan, you know that you can, in fact, get 2 quarts into it by filling it up almost to its brim. This is not true of a pressure pan, which must always have some space left at the top, under the lid, for the superheated steam. If you buy a 4-quart pressure cooker, the most that you can expect to get into it is 3 quarts—sometimes, with certain foods, only 2 quarts. This is a problem of pressure cooking which you must clearly understand.

The food should never be allowed to come up so high in the pan that it might get into and block the steam vent. For example, if you had filled the pot much too full of a thinnish soup, it might, during the pressure cycle, start spraying out through the vent even though the pressure regulator was in position.

(Incidentally, the immediate steps to be taken to avoid this becoming a messy business are perfectly simple. Throw a damp cloth or towel on top of the pressure cooker to catch the spray. Then turn off the heat, transfer the pressure cooker to the sink and run cold water over it to reduce the pressure. When the pressure is completely down, open it up, take out some of the soup and start over.)

But some other foods can be even more troublesome—especially those that are starchy, absorb liquid and expand during cooking, such as dried beans, cereal grains, lentils, split peas and rice. If you are preparing a thick soup, very solid, say with dried beans or lentils, the general rule should be for the pot to be no more than two-thirds full. Or, if you are soaking and cooking dried beans by themselves, or steaming a substantial quantity of rice, it is best for the pot to be half full.

Following these rules, in our thirty years of experience with pressure cookers, we have never had the slightest trouble.

DO YOU NEED MORE THAN ONE SIZE?

Again, there is a basic difference between pressure cookers and ordinary saucepans. In a reasonably well-equipped kitchen, you need several different sizes of saucepans, because it is often difficult, if not impossible, to cook a small quantity of food in a large saucepan. The food spreads out too thinly on the bottom and starts to burn. This is not true of the pressure cooker as long as there is the smallest quantity of liquid inside it. The interior is full of superheated steam, all at exactly the same temperature, so you can cook a very small amount of food in a quite large pot. We suggest that you always buy a size slightly larger than the minimum for your daily needs. At the same time, it is often very useful to have two, so that different kinds of foods can be prepared separately for the same meal. For example, an extra vegetable from Chapter 19 to go with a main meat dish, a steamed bread from Chapter 20, a custard soufflé dessert from Chapter 21, a steamed fruit pudding from Chapter 22.

If you are a one- or two-person family, you might start experimenting with the smallest, 2½-quart Mirro-Matic model, or the 3-quart Presto. Then, for more ambitious menus and parties, you might want to add a 6-quart size. If you are a larger family, you might begin with a 4-quart and, later, add an 8-quart. If you regularly give large parties, you might want to move up to the altogether bigger sizes, which range from 12 quarts up to 22.

COMBINING FOODS WITH DIFFERENT COOKING TIMES—
THE CHINESE ART OF CUTTING

In planning and preparing one-dish meals in a pressure cooker, you often have to combine ingredients with widely different cooking times. A 2-inch cube of veal, for example, needs just about twice as much time to cook perfectly as does the same-sized cube of lamb. Yet you might want to combine both of them in a stew. In an ordinary stewpot, the problem is solved merely by lifting the lid and dropping in the lamb at a later stage of the preparation. With pressure cooking, it is a time-wasting nuisance to have to depressurize, open up the lid, put in a new ingredient and then reestablish the pressure. Chinese cooks solved the timing problems for all their ingredients thousands of years ago by simply developing the fine art of cutting various foods into pieces of various shapes and sizes. For example, to return to the veal and lamb problem mentioned above, if you were to cut each of the veal cubes to half the size of each of the lamb cubes, then both meats would cook in the same time. This cutting can, of course, be done with a sharp kitchen knife, but we have applied this basic solution to the problem of pressure cooking with the help of that marvelously flexible tool, a Chinese cleaver. Chinese cleavers (which are now stocked by most kitchenware shops) come in different sizes and weights, but the edge of the blade is always razor sharp. We think the best all-round one is of carbon steel, medium size and medium weight.

Specific instructions for cutting the various ingredients are given in the recipes. Always stand close to the cutting board, looking down on top of it, so that you can watch each stroke of the blade. With your right hand, firmly grasp the handle and part of the back of the blade of the cleaver. With your left hand, hold and press down the food to be cut. The tips of your left fingers should be tucked slightly under, so that the first knuckles become the guides for the blade and the protection for the fingertips. First, practice straight-across slices of, say, a carrot or turnip. Then, learn to make thin, diagonal slices. Pile these one on top of the other, then cut them downward into julienne strips. Cut the strips crosswise into dice.

You will soon become so attached to your cleaver that you will be using it for every kind of small job, where the amount of food involved is small enough to make it hardly worthwhile to use a larger machine. Pivoting the cleaver on its point on the cutting board and using a rocking motion, you can quickly do small-quantity mincing. You can chop a little bit of meat with a straight up-and-down motion of the cleaver. You can flatten out slices of meat by beating them with the side of the cleaver blade. You can use the back of the blade, beating down in crisscross patterns, to tenderize tough cuts of meat. All these techniques have been worked into the recipes of this book to make sure that, when the cooking is completed and the one-dish meal is served, every part of it is perfectly done.

WHAT HAPPENS INSIDE THE COOKPOT WHILE THE STEAM IS UNDER PRESSURE?

Let us now assume that you have cut the food to the correct size, have added the requisite amount of liquid and have brought it up to the proper degree of pressure. What is now happening to your food inside the pot, while the pressure regulator continues to hiss, jiggle and rock, is based on a fundamental fact of nature. The temperature at which the liquid boils and becomes steam depends on the pressure on its surface. At sea level, as every schoolchild is taught, the pressure of the earth's atmosphere is 14.7 pounds per square inch and, at this pressure, water boils at 212° F, or 100° C. This is what happens when you cook in an open saucepan without a lid.

But if you now seal the pot with an airtight lid, the steam can no longer escape and pressure begins to build up inside. As this pressure rises, the temperature of the boiling point also rises. If you increase the internal pressure by 5 pounds per square inch, you raise the temperature of the boiling liquid and its steam to 228° F, or 109° C. If you go up to an extra 10 pounds per square inch, the liquid and steam temperature inside your pot goes up to 238° F, or 114° C. At 15 pounds per square inch above normal pressure, the maximum for our pressure cookers, the internal temperature is up to 250° F, or 121° C. At this superheated temperature—and with the steam pressure loosening its fibers—any protein meat, vegetable, or other food is cooked to edible perfection in one-third to one-fourth of the normal time. Under the combined superheat and pressure, tough protein meats become glutinously soft and bones release their internal juices into the bouillon for soup— all the normal cooking processes are more efficient and faster.

SHOULD I COOK AT 15 POUNDS, 10 POUNDS OR 5 POUNDS PRESSURE?

Some manufacturers have now standardized their units at 15 pounds only—with no regulator available for any other pressure. We do not go along with this degree of oversimplification. We think that selling a cooker with only one pressure is like selling a car with only one gear ratio, or a television set to receive only one channel. Each of the three different pressures has its particular use and value in terms of the perfect preparation of food. Therefore, in the recipes in this book, we shall suggest different pressures for the different jobs. But we shall also give you the opportunity to convert from one to another.

Admittedly, if you are in such a hurry that you want maximum speed above every other consideration of quality and texture in the meal, then almost every recipe can, at a pinch, be prepared at 15 pounds. When you choose a particular pressure, you are really deciding at what temperature your food is to be cooked. Just as you have always set your oven to a particular temperature for a particular dish, so you should choose the temperature of your pressure cooker. Use the highest pressure and temperature for fresh, frozen and dried vegetables, dried fruits, cereal grains, wheat pilaf, rice; these are basically starchy foods, to be cooked quickly with minimum liquid, the steam pressure reduced immediately at the end of the cooking time to preserve the colors, nutritive elements and textures of the food.

Use the middle pressure and temperature for meats, poultry and game, fish and shellfish, which are basically protein foods requiring less heat and slightly slower cooking. Here, the 10 pounds pressure keeps shrinkage to a minimum, holds in the juices and produces the best finished texture.

The lowest pressure and temperature (5 pounds) is much more limited in its uses, but is essential for the steaming of perfect custards, for steamed breads and fruit or nut puddings, which must first be encouraged to rise by a period of steaming without pressure and can then be "baked through" under minimum pressure and temperature.

A CONVERSION TIMETABLE FROM ONE PRESSURE TEMPERATURE TO ANOTHER

Although there is often an ideal pressure temperature for a particular food, almost every recipe can be instantly converted from one pressure temperature to another. (A very few recipes, involving highly delicate ingredients, or yeast-raised doughs, are limited to the lowest pressure temperature—see pages 174, 207 and 219.) But, for the rest, if you are in a hurry and want to speed up a dish, you can often save a lot of time by moving up from 10 pounds to 15 pounds. Or, if you have a Revere pressure cooker which works only at 15 pounds—or a

Wear-Ever, which works only at 5 pounds—here is how you can adapt any of the recipes in this book. Incidentally, you can also adapt standard recipes to pressure cooking. Take the basic cooking time in a top-of-the-stove pot or in a casserole in the oven and divide it by three. This gives you roughly the 15 pounds pressure cooking time. Then, you can adapt to other pressures and temperatures with this chart.

15 lb—250° F—121° C	10 lb—238° F—114° C	5 lb—228° F—109° C
1 minute	1½ minutes	2 minutes
2	3	4
3	4	6
4	5	7
5	6	9
6	8	11
7	9	13
8	10	15
9	12	17
10	13	19
11	14	21
12	16	23
13	17	24
14	18	26
15	20	28
16	21	30
17	22	32
18	24	34
19	25	35
20	26	38
21	28	40
22	29	42
23	30	44
24	32	45
25	33	47
26	35	50
27	36	51
28	37	53
29	39	55
30	40	57
32	42	60
34	46	65
35	47	66
37	49	70
39	53	75
40	54	76
42	56	80
45	60	85
47	63	90
50	67	95
53	70	100
55	73	104
60	80	114

IF THE HISSING STOPS DURING THE PRESSURE CYCLE AND
SOMETHING IS WRONG

If the hissing stops during the pressure cycle and the pressure regulator also stops its signaling movements, one or more of three things could be wrong. First (and most likely), your maintenance heat setting is too low to keep the liquid boiling inside the pot and there is thus a loss of steam pressure. Turn up the heat to see whether the normal hissing and signals can be restored. If not, the second possibility is that all your liquid has boiled away and no more steam is being formed. If so, within a minute or two, the food will start burning. We usually sniff around the pressure regulator. The slight smell of burning is unmistakable. We at once turn off the heat, depressurize the pot in the normal way (see below) and open up the lid to investigate. Almost invariably, we catch the problem quickly enough so that the bottom layer of food is not badly burned and does not have to be discarded. We add the requisite amount of extra liquid and start over. The third possibility—which, in fact, has never happened to us, but about which we have been warned in instruction booklets—is a blockage of the steam vent. If it did ever happen to us, we would at once turn off the heat, transfer the entire pressure cooker to the sink, run cold water over it to reduce the pressure and when we were quite sure that the pressure was completely down, open up the lid and investigate.

WHEN THE COOKING IS COMPLETED—REDUCING THE PRESSURE
IMMEDIATELY OR GRADUALLY

When the timer rings and the cooking is done, the normal procedure is to reduce the internal pressure immediately to prevent any possibility of overcooking. The conventional method is to transfer the entire pressure cooker to the sink and run cold water over it to reduce the pressure. We have developed another method which is altogether faster and simpler. We arm ourselves with a pair of heatproof mitts. We turn off the heat and at once firmly grasp the pressure regulator and lift it very slightly. There will at once be a heavy hissing of steam as it escapes around the regulator. (On some of the newest models, this fast method of releasing the steam is allowed for in the design of the control weight. It can, without being lifted at all, be pushed slightly sideways, where it rests in a safely balanced position at a 45-degree angle, while the steam hisses out all around it.) Usually within less than thirty seconds, the hissing dies down and we remove the regulator entirely. There is gentle hissing through the steam vent for perhaps 5 seconds more and then silence to indicate that all steam under pressure has escaped. The lid is ready to be opened.

On the latest models of pressure cookers, and on all units manufactured from now on, an added safety lock prevents the lid from being opened as long as there is any remaining pressure inside. A small valve in the lid is pushed up by the internal pressure, and this valve, in turn, snaps a locking device on the lid which prevents it from being turned to open. This safety feature is now required on all new units.

Some recipes in this book, however, call for the postcooking pressure to be reduced not immediately, but gradually of its own accord, as the pressure cooker cools. This usually takes, roughly, from 3 to 5 minutes and there is a very good reason for the delay. If, for example, you have been pressure-cooking a very thick soup filled with solid ingredients—such as the Yankee Bean Stew on page 69—and the pressure were to be reduced immediately and suddenly, there would be a considerable turbulence, a fierce boiling and bubbling within the soup at the moment when the pressure went down. This turbulence might have sufficient force to burst open the beans and, possibly, disintegrate the other ingredients, thus spoiling the texture of the soup. Solid and thick soups, therefore, should have their pressure reduced gradually.

Also, if you have been steam-cooking a large and solid piece of meat such as the Real Rhineland Sauerbraten on page 87, and were to reduce the pressure suddenly, there might be quite forceful changes in the texture of the flesh. The fibers might tend to separate with a kind of miniature inner explosion of the protein cells, driving air in between the flesh and the bones, slightly disintegrating the muscle tissues and the fat. All of this would adversely affect the overall solid texture of the meat as it is carved. Here, again, gradual depressurizing is the better way. Each recipe in this book indicates the best way to reduce the pressure for each particular dish.

The Practical Organization of the Recipes

Immediately below the title of each recipe, you will find the following basic information, designed to help you to decide whether the particular recipe fits into your available time slot, your basic ingredients at hand and the menu you have in mind.

1. To serve how many people? We estimate the number of people rather than the number of servings, since we regard the latter figure as often grossly misleading. For example, four gluttonous people sitting down to dine might each have seconds and thirds, thus consuming 12 servings. Yet a recipe that is marked as being good for "12 servings" might normally be expected to fill the needs of at least 8 or 10 people. We prefer to assume that reasonable people, these days, are aware of the health hazards of overeating, so that the average of the "seconds" will be half-servings. Thus, if we say that a particular recipe is "for 4 people," we mean, in practical terms, 6 average servings.
2. Then we give you the actual cooking time under pressure and, if you will add to this your own estimate of how long it will take you to prepare the ingredients, you will have a reasonably clear idea as to how long it will take you to prepare this dish, from starting in the kitchen to serving at table. This time estimate is based on the use of the best pressure for the particular food, but, in case you are forced to speed up, we often give you alternative times at other pressures.

3. In the brief introduction to the recipe, we warn you of any necessary advance preparation or unusual requirements.
4. The ingredients lists include shopping hints and notes on sources of some ingredients.
5. At the beginning of the procedure text of each recipe, we indicate the size of the pressure cooker required, always with the proviso that a larger size can be used without any detrimental effect on the preparation of the recipe.

A Note on the Metric Conversions in This Book

Metric equivalent measurements are given in all these recipes, not simply as a meaningless kowtow to the "new movement," but as a serious contribution to good cooking and good shopping. As a nation, we are now committed to join the rest of the world in the metric system. Most of our liquor and wine bottles are already metric. So are many of the packages we buy at the supermarket.

In your kitchen, you need to learn only a very few new units, plus a few new temperatures. The unit of weight is the gram and a thousand of them make a kilogram, which is just over 2 pounds. Very soon you will be ordering a 4-pound beef roast as 2 kilograms. The unit of liquid is a liter, which is just over a quart. The prefix "deci-" means a tenth part of any of these units, "centi-" means a hundredth part and "milli-" means a thousandth part. In this book you will find the following metric abbreviations using these units: g (meaning gram), kg (meaning kilogram), dl (meaning deciliter), and ml (meaning milliliter).

As to temperature, the Celsius, or Centigrade, thermometer, which runs from water freezing at 0 degrees to water boiling at 100 degrees, seems to us to be much more logical than the old Fahrenheit system, where you had to remember that water froze, for some entirely inexplicable reason, at 32 degrees and boiled at 212 degrees. We now readily remember that body blood heat (when we touch the liquid in a pan with the tip of our finger) is 37 degrees C, that the proper "keep warm" temperature for dinner plates so that they will not burn your hand when you lift them is 60 degrees C and that a "keep warm" temperature for waiting food is, on the average, 72 degrees C.

It is all much simpler and less bewildering than the way things are now. We have avoirdupois ounces and pounds, fluid gallons, quarts, pints, "fluid ounces" (different from solid ounces), bushels, pecks, "dry quarts" (which are 16 percent more than liquid quarts) and so on, almost ad infinitum. What a relief just to remember grams, liters and meters!

A Note on the Menus

At the end of each main-dish recipe, there is a suggested, nutritionally balanced menu. It is designed to be planned and prepared roughly within the time limitation set by the main dish. Sometimes the extra, accompanying foods are simple, raw ingredients, involving no more effort than shopping and setting them out on serving platters. Other menus include, as an opening course, or a dessert, a recipe from another part of the book. The basic aim of each menu is simplicity—spending no more time than is involved in the preparation of the main dish.

A Note on American and Imported Wines

Each of our menus also includes specific suggestions for an accompanying wine which will uplift and magnify the pleasure of the particular food. We refuse to be dogmatic. We give alternative choices—of an American or an imported wine; of a more expensive, luxurious type; or of a simple, especially good-value, everyday wine. The most remarkable development of the last ten years has been the rise in excellence and prestige of the wines of California, which now takes its place as one of the major wine-producing areas of the world. There are rare (and expensive) California wines which are, in every way, the equals in quality of the greatest of Europe. But the special skills of the California producers—in the true American tradition—are as large-scale producers of inexpensive wines of such an excellence of quality for price that they have no equals anywhere else in the wine world. Any reader of this book who religiously follows our suggestions from beginning to end will taste a wide and comprehensive sweep both of the best American wines and of the best (and best value) labels currently being imported from France and other countries.

Chapter 3

BASIC RECIPES: BOUILLONS AND STOCKS

The Richness of Natural Preparation

There is something quite wonderful about bouillons, consommés, soups and stocks made from the original bones and flesh—not from cans, dehydrated cubes or packaged powders. In the old way, it took hours of slow simmering. In the new, pressure way, the job is done in something between 20 and 30 minutes. And what a job! Pressure seems to draw out of the bones and meats (whether they be red beef, light lamb or veal, chicken, goose or fish) the last essence of gelatinous richness, the final measure of character and color—far more efficiently than any amount of normal simmering. There is not a single one-dish meal in this book, not a single sauce, soup or vegetable casserole, that will not be dramatically improved if you use one of these stocks as the cooking liquid in place of drab, dull water. Our first, fixed rule is to avoid using water whenever possible. A dry white wine is better. A rich stock is usually better still. With the recipes that follow, you can make a supply at any time and it will keep in a covered jar in the refrigerator for at least two weeks. Or you can freeze it into ice cube trays or other containers and keep it up to a couple of months. Also, you can serve these restorative and strengthening bouillons as they are, perhaps garnished with a paper-thin slice of lemon and/or finely chopped chives or scallions, in a cup or mug as an excellent midmorning, midafternoon or midnight snack—or as the first course of a dinner, lunch or supper menu. Don't pass over this chapter. It is one of the most important in the book.

All-Purpose Rich Brown Beef Stock
Makes about 2 quarts (2 liters)
  (see page 34 for best method of storage)
Cook under pressure at 15 lb for 30 minutes
  (or at 10 lb for 40 minutes)

2½ lb (1.1 kg) nicely meaty, beef marrow bones, or other bones, sawed into pieces by your butcher
1 veal knuckle—also sawed into manageable pieces
2 lb (1 scant kg) lean beef soup meat, either short ribs, bottom round or shin, cut into 1-inch (2.5 cm) cubes
1 whole clove garlic, peeled and finely minced
2 medium yellow onions, peeled and coarsely chopped
1 tsp freshly squeezed lemon juice
1 tsp grated lemon rind
2 medium carrots, scraped and cut lengthwise into eighths
1 tsp whole coriander seeds
The white part of 1 leek, carefully desanded and chunked
1 stalk celery, with its leaves, chopped
Enough fresh parsley, leaves and stalks, chopped, to fill ¼ cup (60 ml)
Enough fresh thyme leaves, chopped, to fill 1 Tbs, or 1 tsp dried
Enough fresh marjoram leaves, chopped, to fill 1 Tbs, or 1 tsp dried
1 whole bay leaf
5 whole cloves
Salt, to your taste, about 2 tsp
12 whole black peppercorns
½ cup (1.25 dl) dry white wine

For this recipe you will need a pressure cooker with a minimum capacity of 6 quarts. Put the bone and knuckle pieces into it and add enough cold water just to cover them. Bring it rapidly to the boil, then, as soon as bubbling begins, pour away this first water and wash the bones under running cold water. (This is the professional chef's trick for quickly cleaning the bones so that during the later boiling they will not give off any bitter scum. It also helps to clarify the finished bouillon.) Rinse out your pressure cooker and return the bones to it, now adding all the other ingredients. Pour in 2 quarts (2 liters) of cold water—always start from cold, to extract the fullest flavor from bones and meat—making sure that all the solids are well packed down and are covered by the water to at least an inch. Also make sure that the pot is not more than ⅔ full. Put on the lid, bring up the pressure to 15 pounds and keep it cooking for exactly 30 minutes.

When the timer rings, turn off the heat and reduce the pressure immediately. Then open up the pressure cooker so that the air can get to it, and let it cool until you can handle it easily. Skim the liquid in the pot, carefully strain all the solids out of the liquid and store the bouillon in the refrigerator. The lean meat will be fairly well washed out, but can sometimes be used, thinly sliced, to provide some meaty texture to a green salad.

All-Purpose Golden Chicken Stock
Makes about 2 quarts (2 liters)
  (see page 34 for method of storage)
Cook under pressure at 15 lb for 30 minutes
  (or at 10 lb for 40 minutes)

3 lb (1.4 kg) chicken bones and meat (see opposite)
3 medium carrots, scraped and cut lengthwise into eighths

This is as universally useful as the preceding beef stock. In fact, we almost always keep a regular supply of both. You can be quite flexible about the chicken. It can be a 3-pound bird, cut up, or 3 pounds of backs and wings, or other parts, such as giblets, gizzards, necks. We once made quite a good version from 3 pounds of hearts alone. And if you have the leftover

The white parts of 2 leeks, carefully
    desanded and chunked
2 stalks celery, with leaves, chopped
The meat of 8 macadamia nuts, grated
3 cloves shallots, peeled and finely
    minced
1 clove garlic, peeled and finely minced
2 tsp fresh lemon juice
1 tsp grated lemon rind
1 tsp whole coriander seeds
2 tsp ground turmeric
Salt, to your taste
12 whole black peppercorns
2 whole cloves
½ cup (1.25 dl) dry white wine

carcass of a roast chicken, by all means throw that in, to add a nice toasted flavor.

For this you will need a pressure cooker with a minimum capacity of 6 quarts. Put the chicken pieces into it and pour in 2 quarts (2 liters) of cold water. (Always start from cold, to draw out the maximum character and flavor.) Make sure that the pressure cooker is no more than ⅔ full. Bring it up to the boiling point fairly slowly and skim the surface carefully to eliminate any bitter elements released by the chicken. Now add all the rest of the ingredients, put on the lid, bring up to 15 pounds pressure and cook for exactly 30 minutes.

When the timer rings, turn off the heat and reduce the pressure immediately. Then take off the lid and let the air get into the pot. As soon as the stock is cool enough to handle, skim off all the fat, strain the solids out of the liquid and store the bouillon in the refrigerator. The chicken meat will be fairly well washed out, but, as with the beef, it can sometimes be used, thinly sliced, to provide a meaty texture to a green salad.

Multipurpose Asparagus Bouillon

Makes about 2 quarts (2 liters)
    (see page 34 for storage)
Cook under pressure at 15 lb for 25 minutes
    (or at 10 lb for 33 minutes)

2 lb (1 kg) fresh asparagus spears, washed
    and with the scales removed
1 large Bermuda onion, peeled and
    chunked
Salt, to your taste
Freshly ground black pepper, to your
    taste

This can often be used in place of the beef or chicken bouillons and it also makes a most excellent "cup a soup," garnished with crispy, undercooked tips of the asparagus.

For this you will need a pressure cooker with a minimum capacity of 6 quarts. Remove the woody bottoms of the asparagus stalks by breaking them off by hand. As you bend them, they will snap at exactly the right spot. Throw away the woody bottoms. Cut off about an inch (2.5 cm) from each of the tips and store them in a covered jar in the refrigerator. Put what is left of the main stalks into the pressure cooker. Pour in 2 quarts (2 liters) of cold water and bring it quickly up to the boiling point. Add the onion, put on the lid, bring the pot up to 15 pounds pressure and let the bouillon cook for exactly 25 minutes.

As soon as the timer rings, turn off the heat and reduce the pressure immediately. Open up the lid, let everything cool until you can handle it easily, then strain the aromatic bouillon from the solids, thoroughly squeezing them out before discarding them. At this point stir in salt and pepper to taste. Bring the bouillon once more to the boil, stirring it occasionally, without pressure. It is now ready to use or store. If you want to serve it as a drinking bouillon on its own, bring it back to the boiling point once more and poach the asparagus tips in it for hardly more than 7 to 10 minutes, so as to keep them crisp. Garnish each cup with three or four tips.

All-Purpose Quick Fish Court-Bouillon

Makes about 3 quarts (3 liters)
Cook under pressure at 15 lb for 25 minutes
   (or at 10 lb for 33 minutes)

About 2½ lb (1.1 kg) mixed, fresh, firm-
   fleshed fish (including, whenever
   possible, cod, small flounder,
   halibut, eel, etc.), all cleaned, scaled
   and washed, but with heads and
   bones
2 cups (5 dl) dry white wine
1 medium carrot, scraped and sliced
The white part of a medium leek,
   carefully desanded and chunked
1 medium yellow onion, peeled and
   chunked
2 cloves garlic, peeled and sliced
1 whole bay leaf
3 good sprigs fresh parsley
Enough fresh tarragon leaves, chopped,
   to fill 1 Tbs, or 1 tsp dried
Enough fresh leaves of thyme, chopped,
   to fill 1 Tbs, or 1 tsp dried
6 whole black peppercorns
Salt, to your taste

This is the perfect broth to use for boiling a lobster, or steaming a mess of clams, to dribble into a crab soufflé, or to add to a fish sauce. The French word *court-bouillon* means, literally, "short bouillon"—a bouillon made for a specific purpose in a very short time—in contrast to "fish stock," which used to simmer all day on the back of the stove and was, therefore, always "in stock."

For this, you will need a pressure cooker with a minimum capacity of 6 quarts. Put into it 2½ quarts (2½ liters) of cold water, and quickly bring it up to boiling. At that moment, add all the fish, plus all the other ingredients except the salt. Stir and taste the bouillon, then add salt to your taste. Put on the lid, bring the pressure up to 15 pounds and cook for exactly 25 minutes.

As soon as the timer rings, turn off the heat and reduce the pressure immediately. Let everything cool, then strain the bouillon from the solids, discard the latter and store the bouillon in the refrigerator. This fish bouillon, of course, cannot be held as long as the beef or the chicken. In fact, it is best to make it fresh for each special use. (If you are lazy, or extremely pressed for time, it is possible—although with a large taste compromise—to replace this fish *court-bouillon* with bottled clam juice!)

Multipurpose Aromatic Mushroom Bouillon

Makes about 2 quarts (2 liters)
   (see page 34 for storage)
Cook under pressure at 15 lb for 20 minutes
   (or at 10 lb for 26 minutes)

Two ½-oz (14 g) packages dried wild
   mushrooms, broken up—they come
   from France, China, Italy or Spain,
   but also now packaged in the U.S.
   Northwest
1 lb (450 g) fresh, white, button
   mushrooms, sliced
2 quarts (2 liters) beef or chicken bouillon
   (page 35, or use canned bouillon)
10 cloves shallots, finely minced
2 tsp whole caraway seeds
Salt, to your taste
Freshly ground black pepper, to your
   taste

This stock has the same uses as the preceding bouillons. It, too, makes a memorable "cup a soup," often garnished with paper-thin slices of fresh, raw, button mushrooms.

For this you should have a pressure cooker with a minimum capacity of 6 quarts. Put everything into it except the caraway seeds. Stir the bouillon, taste it, then add salt and pepper, as pleases you. Put on the lid, bring the pressure up to 15 pounds and cook for exactly 20 minutes.

When the timer rings, turn off the heat and reduce the pressure immediately. Open the lid and stir in the caraway seeds. Do not strain this bouillon, but use it as is for cooking, in sauces, or for moistening mashed potatoes. The flavor will improve for several days if it is kept, tightly covered, of course, in the refrigerator.

Chapter 4

BASIC RECIPES: SAUCES

Luxurious Accompaniments to One-Dish Meals

Most of the time, the pressure cooker makes its own natural sauce during the cooking. If, for example, you brown pieces of chicken in oil at the bottom of the pot (see page 125) and then add a little wine for the pressure-poaching of the chicken, both this wine and the chicken juices will commingle with the brown frying glaze on the bottom of the pan to produce a superb natural sauce. It would be a crime to thicken it with butter, cream, eggs or flour, which would dilute and dull the natural deliciousness of the flavor. But sometimes an extra sauce does add a touch of luxury to a dish, so here are a few which we enjoy regularly and repeatedly. Some of them are made in the pressure cooker; others require no pressure and can be simmered in an ordinary saucepan. Still others need no cooking at all and are simply whipped together in a mixing bowl. All of them serve a multiplicity of purposes for a variety of dishes.

Glutinous Italian Beef and Tomato Spaghetti Sauce alla Bolognese
Makes about 2 quarts (2 liters)
(keeps refrigerated, or frozen, almost indefinitely)
Cook under pressure at 15 lb for 15 minutes
(or at 10 lb for 20 minutes)

6 Tbs (90 g) butter
½ lb (225 g) chicken livers
¼ cup (60 ml) top-quality Italian olive oil
¼ lb (115 g) sliced ham, finely chopped
2 medium carrots, scraped and finely chopped
2 sticks celery, with leaves, finely chopped
3 medium yellow onions, peeled and finely chopped

Perhaps this is the world's most famous sauce. Once upon a time, to get it really rich and rib-sticking, we followed the recipe of an Italian mama and simmered it slowly, slowly in a bright copper pot for two days. Now we get exactly the same luscious luxury in our pressure cooker in 15 minutes! We first made it thirty years ago when our children were seven and ten. They loved it so much, they demanded it four times a week. Very recently, we gave this recipe to our friends Myra and John, who feed nine-year-old Jessica. John says: "Jessica has such a crush on your sauce, she demands it every day and we make a gallon of it every weekend." The world changes, but the taste of a good thing remains eternal.

1 lb (450 g) chopped or ground, entirely lean beef, preferably chuck or bottom round

28-oz (780 g) can imported Italian peeled plum tomatoes, drained

About two 6-oz (170 g) cans imported Italian tomato paste

1½ cups (3.75 dl) good Italian red wine, preferably Chianti

2 cloves garlic, peeled and finely minced

½ oz (14 g) package imported dried wild mushrooms, broken up, but not soaked

½ cup (115 g) seedless golden raisins

⅓ cup (80 ml) Parmesan cheese, coarsely grated

Enough fresh leaves basil, chopped, to fill 2 Tbs, or 2 tsp dried

1 Tbs dried oregano

1 tsp good meat extract, perhaps Bovril

Salt, to your taste

Freshly ground black pepper, to your taste

Freshly ground nutmeg, no more than two grinds

Enough fresh parsley leaves, chopped, to fill ⅓ cup (80 ml)

For this sauce you will need a minimum 6-quart pressure cooker. Set it, without its base rack, onto medium-high frying heat, and melt in it 2 tablespoons of the butter. As soon as it is nicely hot, quickly sauté the chicken livers only until they are just stiff enough to chop. Take them out with a slotted spoon, chop them coarsely on a cutting board, and set aside. Now put into the still-hot pressure cooker the oil and, as soon as it is hot, quickly sauté the ham until it is nicely browned. Now add the carrot, celery and onion, sautéing them until just golden. Put in the beef, stirring it around and breaking it up with a wooden spoon, until it has lost its redness and darkened. Add the chopped chicken livers, gently working them in for not more than a couple of minutes, then add the tomatoes. Dilute one of the cans of tomato paste with the red wine and work in. Finally stir in, one at a time, the garlic, mushrooms, raisins, grated Parmesan, basil, oregano and meat extract. Mix everything thoroughly and taste it, especially judging the degree of saltiness. Then add salt as needed, plus pepper and no more than two grinds of nutmeg. Bring it all up to boiling, put on the lid, let the pressure come up to 15 pounds and cook for exactly 15 minutes.

As soon as the timer rings, turn off the heat and reduce the pressure immediately. Stir in the parsley and the remaining 4 tablespoons butter. Now adjust the thickness of the sauce. If it is a bit too thick, work in, tablespoon by tablespoon, more red wine; if a little too thin, thicken it with tablespoon after tablespoon of more tomato paste. Serve with more grated Parmesan cheese over very hot, chewily undercooked, lightly butter-tossed lasagna, spaghetti or tagliatelli.

A Good and Healthful Menu

Black and green olives
Pasta with Sauce alla Bolognese
    with a crusty Italian long loaf
A green salad
Italian Fontina cheese with fresh fruit
Coffee or tea

The Ideal Wines

Luxurious

An Italian red "Chianti Classico"
    or
A California red Barbera from Sonoma

Everyday

An Italian red Valpolicella from the Venice region
    or
A California Chianti from Mendocino

Basic English Apple Sauce
Makes about 1½ pints (7.5 dl)
   (stores perfectly in the refrigerator)
Cook under pressure at 15 lb for 8 minutes

1 whole fresh lemon for its rind
¼ cup (60 ml) sweet apple cider
6 large, firm, tart apples; we prefer Rome
   Beauties, but Greenings will also do
One 2-inch (5 cm) cinnamon stick
¼ cup (60 g) diced citron
Superfine-grind white sugar, to taste
¼ tsp ground cinnamon (optional)
2 Tbs (30 g) butter
Freshly ground nutmeg, to your taste

Some cooks frown on the practice of pressurizing apples for sauce. We disagree. We find that the high heat which develops inside the cooker brings out the flavor and gives a marvelous, gelatinous, almost syrupy richness to the finished sauce. This is because the pectin is drawn out from the seeds and skins. We eliminate the normal tendency of apples to froth by enclosing them in a covered pan inside the pressure cooker. The excellence of the final result will surprise you.

Do not oversweeten these apples. If you keep them tart, they will be a memorable accompaniment, garnish or sauce, to cut the richness of all kinds of luxurious meats or birds: in place of mint jelly or mint sauce for lamb, in place of orange sauce for duck, or as the classically superb accompaniment to English-style roast goose. Apples are also an ideal accompaniment to pork. Try this sauce with the pork loin on page 111, or the spareribs on page 108.

You will need a minimum 3-quart pressure cooker and a 3½-cup metal baking pan to fit inside the cooker with about ½ inch space all around. With a sharp potato peeler or a French lemon "zester," thinly scrape or slice off the yellow outer rind of the lemon. Mince the rind finely and soak it, in a small bowl, with 2 tablespoons of the cider. Carefully peel the apples, keeping the pieces of skin as large as possible, or in a fairly wide, continuous strip. Then slice the apples, without coring them, into ⅜-inch-thick (1-cm-thick) disks. Liberally butter the baking pan and layer the apple slices neatly in it. Bury the cinnamon stick between the layers. Also add half the citron and the minced lemon rind with its soaking cider. When all the apples are in and every corner of the pan is filled, carefully lay the pieces of apple skin, cut side down, on top, overlapping the pieces so as to form a kind of inner sealing lid. Wet everything down with the remaining cider, cover the pan completely and tightly with aluminum foil. Pour ¾ cup hot water into the pressure cooker, put in the base rack and set the baking pan on it. Put on the lid, bring the pressure up to 15 pounds and cook for exactly 8 minutes.

When the timer rings, turn off the heat and let the pressure reduce gradually of its own accord, usually in about 5 minutes. With a small pair of kitchen tongs, pick out the apple peelings and discard them. They have given up their nutty oils. Pick out the cinnamon stick (wash it under cold water, dry it and keep it for later reuse). Now stir into the fluffy-light apples—at the same time mashing them coarsely—as much sugar as your taste desires and, if you wish, the extra cinnamon. Also beat in, preferably with a wooden fork, the remaining chopped citron, the butter and a grind or two of nutmeg.

Delicate and Gentle Mustard Sauce
Makes about 5 cups (1.25 liters)
(keeps well in the refrigerator)
Cook without pressure for about 5 minutes

11 Tbs (160 g) butter
2 medium yellow onions, peeled and
    finely minced
2 Tbs cornstarch
1½ cups (3.75 dl) heavy cream
½ cup (1.25 dl) dry white wine
1 cup (225 g) superfine-grind white sugar
2 Tbs mustard, preferably imported
    French Dijon
1 egg yolk, lightly beaten
½ cup (1.25 dl) tarragon white wine
    vinegar
Salt, to your taste
Freshly ground black pepper, to your
    taste

Served hot, this is an excellent accompaniment to beef, pork, duck, turkey, or fried fish. Cool, it uplifts a plate of cold cuts, or can be beaten into the dressing for a supper salad. Try it with the flank steak on page 85, the sirloin on a string on page 89, or the rolled, stuffed flounder on page 171.

Choose a sauté pan that will easily hold about a quart of liquid. Set it on medium frying heat and melt 4 tablespoons of the butter in it. When it is hot, sauté the onions until they are just gilded. Then work in 1 tablespoon of the cornstarch. Next, stir in 1¼ cups of the cream and the wine. Bring it up to boiling and let it just simmer, stirring continuously, for 1 minute. Meanwhile, in a smallish mixing bowl, blend together the sugar, mustard and the remaining quarter cup of cream. Now work this mixture, carefully and gently, into the hot sauce in the sauté pan. When it is all thoroughly amalgamated, take the pan off the heat and, using a balloon wire whisk, beat in the egg yolk. Next, beat in the remaining butter one tablespoon at a time. Finally, blend the remaining cornstarch into the vinegar and add to the sauce, tablespoon by tablespoon, until you have exactly the flavor and thickness you want. Do not necessarily use all the vinegar. Taste and add salt and pepper, as pleases you, but too little rather than too much. Reheat the sauce and serve it hot, or allow it to cool to room temperature, or refrigerate it in a tightly lidded storage jar.

Almost-Perfect Garlic Sauce
Makes about 2 cups (½ liter)
(improves with keeping in the refrigerator)
No cooking at all

12 cloves garlic, peeled and mashed to a
    paste, either by hand in a mortar, or
    instantly in one of the new
    supermachines
The freshly squeezed juice of 4 lemons
2 tsp salt
About 1½ cups (3.75 dl) of the very best
    quality, first-pressing virgin olive
    oil, preferably imported from
    Provence

When we taste it on the tip of our tongue, we think it is absolutely perfect, but we don't dare to call it that because we don't believe that perfection exists in this bad old world. Try this with the Scottish Fish Pie on page 168.

In a mixing bowl, vigorously beat together the garlic, lemon juice and salt. Using a wooden spoon with a beating motion, begin to work in the olive oil, tablespoon by tablespoon, until you have a sauce of exactly the consistency, strength and thickness you want. Store it in a tightly lidded jar in the refrigerator. You should not heat this because the garlic oils would evaporate. This, to our peasanty taste, is the greatest and most universal of all sauces. It speaks every language and links all peoples. Shake the jar before pouring it out. If you want to be fussy, strain it before using. We never do.

Multipurpose Sweet-Sour Honey-Lemon Sauce for Pressured Vegetables

Makes about 2 cups (½ liter)
   (keeps well in the refrigerator)
No cooking at all

8 Tbs (115 g) melted butter
1 cup (2.5 dl) good, strong honey
The freshly squeezed juice of 2 lemons
1 Tbs red paprika, preferably top-quality,
   imported, medium, Hungarian

When fresh vegetables are pressure-cooked in hardly more than a minute, they come to table with a wonderful natural sweetness that somehow is matched and accentuated by this delicately sweet-sour sauce with a deep orange color. Use it sparingly. Dribble only a few drops over the small heaps of vegetables on your plate. We keep a regular supply of the sauce in our refrigerator and heat up as much as we need for the current meal. Try it with the Steam-Baked Zucchini on page 205.

Melt the butter, but do not overheat it. Pour it into a warmed mixing bowl, add all the other ingredients and beat them into a proper marriage with a balloon wire whisk.

A Menu Note

Try this sauce on crisply undercooked flowerets of broccoli, or on a side dish of baked carrots, with finely minced onion, moistened with a tablespoon or two of rich brown beef stock, chopped parsley, a pinch or two of ginger and some of this sauce dribbled over the top. Broccoli or carrots done in this way go excellently with corned beef, a beef roast, or a baked rack of lamb—a very little of this sauce goes well over creamed onions with a pork and veal meat loaf, or grilled steak, or broiled fish.

Fiery-Hot North African Pili Pili Red Pepper Sauce

Makes about 2 cups (½ liter)
First marinate peppers 1 week
Cook at 15 lb pressure for 2 minutes

24 small, finger-shaped, dried hot red
   peppers
2 Tbs salt
2 Tbs sugar
About ½ cup (1.25 dl) tarragon white
   wine vinegar
About ½ cup (1.25 dl) good olive oil
2 tsp ground coriander seeds
2 tsp ground whole cumin seed
1 cup (2.5 dl) beef bouillon (see page 35,
   or use canned)
Freshly ground black pepper, just a few
   grinds
Red cayenne pepper, a few pinches

This is for you if you happen to love red-hot Mexican *chiles habaneros*, Indian hot curry, Chinese Szechuan cooking, or any of the other great dishes of the world which fill your mouth with fire. It is one of the classic sauces of Morocco, where red pepper is called *flefla*, while paprika is *filfillah* and black pepper is *filfil*. Obviously, then, the name of this sauce is Moroccan slang for a mixture of black and red peppers. It keeps virtually forever in the refrigerator. It could not possibly go bad— no bacteria could live for even one second in its searing fire! Naturally, you use only a drop or two on rice, on barbecued pieces of beef or lamb or in a salad dressing or sauce.

You will need a minimum 2½-quart (or slightly larger) pressure cooker, without its base rack. First, wash the red peppers in cold water, remove any stalks and tear each pepper slightly open, so that the vinegar will be able to get inside. Put them

1 Tbs freshly squeezed lemon juice
Enough fresh parsley leaves, chopped, to
    fill ⅓ cup (80 ml)
2 cloves garlic, peeled and finely minced

into a 1-pint mason jar, interleaving them, as you put them in, with the salt and sugar. Just cover them with enough of the vinegar, and stir thoroughly to dissolve the salt and sugar. Then pour on top a layer of oil just about ½ inch (1.2 cm) thick to seal the peppers from the air while they are marinating. Screw the top tightly on the mason jar, put it in the refrigerator and forget it for about a week. The longer you leave it, the more fiery the mixture will become. In Tunisia, this is called *harissa* and is the base for a number of different sauces.

When the marination is complete and you are ready to make the final sauce, empty the entire contents of the mason jar into a hand mortar or an electric blender and pound or whirl it to disintegrate the peppers. The objective is to make a thin paste, and if you have too much liquid, add a tablespoon or two of bread crumbs. You store this base in the refrigerator and use only a teaspoon or two of it each time you make your pili pili sauce.

Put into your pressure cooker the ground coriander and cumin plus the beef bouillon, then bring it gently to the boil without the lid. Work into it a few grinds of black pepper and 2 or 3 pinches of red cayenne. Now stir in, teaspoon by teaspoon, enough of the red pepper base paste to make the sauce absolutely as peppery hot as you can grin and bear it—usually, to our taste, about 3 teaspoons. When you have it the way you want it, stir in the lemon juice and an extra tablespoon of oil. Heat it to boiling, put on the pressure lid, bring it up to 15 pounds and cook for exactly 2 minutes.

When the timer rings, turn off the heat and reduce the pressure immediately. Stir the sauce thoroughly, and add, at the last moment, the parsley and the garlic. If, at any time, the sauce becomes too peppery hot, it can be slightly softened by working in more lemon juice and oil. Pili pili sauce can be served either warm or cold. Store it, of course, in the refrigerator in a tightly lidded jar. Do we need to repeat that you should serve it only a drop or two at a time!

An Aromatic Marinade for Bland and Tough Meats

Makes about 10 cups (2½ liters)
No cooking at all

2 bottles of a good, full-bodied, strong
    red wine—preferably a not-too-
    expensive Burgundy
10 medium yellow onions, peeled and
    sliced
10 whole cloves
12 cloves shallots, peeled and chopped
4 cloves garlic, peeled and minced
1 cup (2.5 dl) cognac
1 cup (2.5 dl) top-quality olive oil

If you have ever tried to concoct a low-budget meal with a chuck or flank steak, you know how tasteless and tough these so-called "cheaper cuts" can be. But they can be greatly improved—both as to flavor and tenderness of texture—by being thoroughly steeped for a few hours, or even a day or two, in an aromatic and penetrating wine marinade. The important herbs for improvement of the meat are bay leaves and thyme. The minimum marination should be for about 12 hours—overnight in the refrigerator—but, for very tough meats, it can sometimes be for three days, or more. Turn the meat over at least three times every day, so that all sides of it are kept thoroughly moist. Sometimes, finally, some of the marinade can be

Enough fresh leaves thyme, chopped, to
   fill ½ cup (1.25 dl), or 8 tsp dried
4 whole bay leaves, crumbled

used in the pressure-cooking of the meat, or even, strained, in the sauce.

Mix all these ingredients together in a large bowl. Let them live together for about an hour or two, to develop and mingle their flavors, then put in the meat to soak. (See recipe on page 93.) Note especially that there is no salt in this marinade, since salt would tend to seal the pores of the meat and prevent the penetration of the aromatic flavors.

Chapter 5

BASIC RECIPES: HOT APPETIZERS

Dramatic and Easy Canapés Before the Meal

The pressure cooker makes it a fast and simple job to prepare hot canapés, which always seem to us to express hospitality— in terms of something specially prepared for the guests—much more than cold bits out of cans or frozen packages. One of the best, earthy, peasanty platters to provide for the opening of a party is the traditional French mound of hot sausage chunks accompanied by an aromatic potato salad. Potatoes and sausages can be cooked together in one pressure cooker. This French recipe is the first, below, followed by others from the Chinese and other ethnic sources, as well as some of our own inventions.

Another, almost-ready-made way of launching a party is to order, from your local Chinese restaurant, a takeout supply of those extraordinary little Chinese wrapped canapés called *dim sim*. Each is about a single bite, filled with an aromatically cooked morsel of meat, fish or vegetable, enclosed in various shapes of rice dough coverings and all colorfully decorated. They are always meant to be hot-steamed just before serving, and the pressure cooker is virtually the ideal instrument for this job.

Hot Sausages with French-Style Lyonnaise Potato Salad
For a party of 12
Cook under pressure at 15 lb for 5 minutes
(or at 10 lb for 7 minutes)

3 to 4 lb (1½ to 2 kg) mixed boiling
   sausages (see opposite)
12 small-to-medium, fluffy, boiling
   potatoes
4 Tbs (60 g) butter

When we have a few days' notice of a party, we send a mail order to one of the wonderful, old-time sausage shops in Milwaukee (perhaps Usinger's or Weisel's), asking them to send us a box of mixed sausages: beef-garlic and smoked-beef franks, Milwaukee knackwurst, Polish sausage, smoked bratwurst, pork sausage, etc. They come protected by dry ice and seem to be able to reach any part of the country in about

¾ cup (1.85 dl) dry white wine

10 Tbs top-quality olive oil

2 Tbs imported tarragon white wine
vinegar

1½ tsp mustard, preferably imported
French Dijon, plus more to serve

1 tsp salt

Freshly ground pepper, to your taste

1 Tbs various fresh herb leaves, chopped
(optional, see opposite)

Enough fresh parsley leaves, chopped, to
fill 1 cup (2.5 dl) fairly loosely

three or four days. A mound of these sausages—with their varieties of colors, aromas, flavors, shapes and sizes—accompanied by piles of creamy potatoes, makes a memorable show of farmhouse abundance and earthy plentitude.

For 12 people you will need a minimum 8-quart pressure cooker or divide the recipe in half and use a 4-quart pot.

Cut the sausages into ¾-inch (2 cm) chunks, halve them lengthwise, and reserve. Wash and peel the potatoes, then cut them into ⅜-inch (1 cm) slices and set aside in a bowl of water. Set your pressure cooker on medium-high frying heat and quickly melt in it the butter. As soon as it is hot, lightly brown the sausage chunks in batches, as you can fit them in, removing each finished batch and setting aside. Do not over-brown the sausage chunks, or the subsequent pressure steaming may overcook them. When all are browned, put them all back into the pressure cooker in a level layer, hiss the wine over them and set the base rack on top of them. On it, neatly arrange the potatoes. Put on the lid, bring the pressure up to 15 pounds and cook for exactly 5 minutes.

Meanwhile, lightly beat together in a mixing bowl the ingredients of the dressing for the potatoes: the oil, vinegar, 1½ teaspoons of the mustard, and salt plus pepper, to taste. If you have any fresh herb leaves (say, either basil, chive, marjoram, tarragon or thyme), finely chop enough to fill 1 tablespoon and beat into the dressing. This last is optional—do not substitute dried herbs. Also have ready a warmed, flat serving platter.

As soon as the timer rings, move quickly to avoid letting the food cool down. Turn off the heat and reduce the pressure immediately. Carefully remove the potato slices, to avoid breaking them, and arrange them neatly, slightly overlapping, around the edge of the hot serving platter. Remove the base rack and lift out the sausage pieces with a slotted spoon and arrange the chunks in the center of the platter, spearing them, if you wish, with toothpicks. Give a final beat to the dressing and dribble it, quite lavishly, over the potatoes. Sprinkle fresh chopped parsley on the potatoes. Serve to each guest on a small, warmed plate, with a fork, and pass extra mustard for the sausages.

A Note on the Accompanying Drinks

Remember that this is a peasanty opening to a meal and should be served with peasanty drinks. Not, for example, with an expensive champagne, or an extra-fine, subtle sherry. It goes excellently with ice-cold glasses of a dry white wine of strong character: say, a California Pinot Chardonnay, or a French Sancerre, a Campari with soda, or some other aromatic Italian vermouth, or one of the famous-name aperitif drinks. Your guests will be in a festive mood by the time they move to the dinner table.

Chinese Cucumber Submarines

For 4
Cook under pressure at 15 lb for 10 minutes
(or at 10 lb for 13 minutes)

½ lb (225 g) boneless, entirely lean veal,
    chopped or ground
1 whole egg, lightly beaten
2 slices good, boiled ham, with a little fat
    but not too much, finely diced
4 fresh button mushrooms, finely diced
2 Tbs cornstarch
Up to 2 Tbs dry sherry
1 tsp salt, to your taste
3 cucumbers, each about 3 to 4 inches (7.5
    to 10 cm) long and 1½ inches (3.75
    cm) in diameter, peeled
¾ cup (1.85 dl) dry white wine
2 Tbs light soy sauce

Surely these days everyone knows that a submarine is not just a dangerous warship. It is also almost any kind of long, narrow sandwich. Here is the neatest of all edible submarines: a cucumber with its central seeds scooped out and replaced by an aromatic meat filling. After briefly cooking the whole cucumber and the meat, you cut it into bite-sized appetizer chunks. The combination of the warmly juicy, refreshing outer ring of cucumber with the savory filling is a fine balance of flavors and textures. Scooping out the cucumber is relatively easy with a smallish knife with a narrow blade and a small teaspoon with a longish handle.

For this you will need a minimum 6-quart pressure cooker. First, in a mixing bowl, thoroughly blend together the ingredients for the filling: the veal, egg, ham, mushrooms, a tablespoon each of the cornstarch and sherry, plus about 1 teaspoon of salt, to taste. The mixture should be stiff enough to hold together, but not so stiff that it will be difficult to push into the cucumbers. You may soften it by adding a dash or two more sherry. Set aside this stuffing while you bore into the cucumbers.

Cut off one end of each cucumber and carefully scoop out the central seed core, working from one end and leaving the other end closed. Now gently stuff the meat filling into this cavity, firmly pushing it all the way down, so that the cucumber is fairly tightly filled. When it is full, cover the open end with a small square of foil. Set the base rack into the pressure cooker, pour in the wine, put in the cucumbers, standing up on their uncut ends (the points of the cucumbers fit neatly into the holes or slots of the rack and they lean against the walls of the pot). In this way, no juice from the stuffing is lost. Put on the lid, bring the pressure up to 15 pounds and cook the cucumbers for exactly 10 minutes.

As soon as the timer rings, turn off the heat and reduce the pressure immediately, cut each cucumber into 1-inch (2.5 cm) lengths and keep them hot in an oven at 160° F (70° C) while you quickly finish the sauce. In a small bowl, mix the light soy sauce with the remaining tablespoon of cornstarch. Take out the base rack from the bottom of the pressure cooker and smoothly work the soy-cornstarch mixture into the hot wine, heating it up and stirring continuously, until it thickens to the consistency of light honey. Dribble some of this sauce over each cucumber chunk and serve hot, with small forks.

Chinese Beef-Rice Baby Meatballs

For 4

Cook under pressure at 15 lb for 6 minutes
(or at 10 lb for 8 minutes)

1 lb (450 g) chopped or ground beef
4 scallions, white bottoms and green tops minced
1 tsp finely minced fresh ginger root (or ½ tsp ground ginger if fresh is not available)
2 whole eggs, lightly beaten
¼ cup (60 g) water chestnuts, finely minced
2 tsp sugar
4 Tbs dark soy sauce
Up to 3 Tbs dry sherry
1 cup (225 g) standard rice, soaked for 30 minutes in warm water
¾ cup (1.85 dl) dry white wine
3 Tbs vinegar
2 to 3 drops Tabasco
1 clove garlic, minced
2 Tbs light soy sauce
1 tsp sesame seed oil

If you know Chinese food and have a Chinese grocery in your neighborhood, you can prepare this recipe in the Chinese way with "glutinous sticky rice" and fresh ginger root. This type of rice will need only 20 minutes of soaking and 2 minutes less cooking time at 15 pounds. It is important to set the rice-covered balls in the pressure cooker at least ¼ inch apart, to allow for the expansion of the rice.

Use a 6-quart or smaller pressure cooker and, if necessary, cook the meatballs in batches. In a mixing bowl, lightly but thoroughly work together the beef, scallions, ginger, eggs, water chestnuts, and 1 teaspoon of the sugar. Now dribble over and blend in the dark soy sauce and up to 2 tablespoons of the sherry. You should have a mixture that remains just firm enough for the balls to hold together. Dip your hands in warm water and shape the mixture into balls about the size of cherry tomatoes. Spread the cup of rice out evenly on a tray and roll each ball into the rice until it is fully covered. Put the base rack in your pressure cooker, pour in the wine and arrange the balls about ¼ inch (7 mm) apart. Put on the lid, bring up the pressure to 15 pounds and cook for exactly 6 minutes.

Meanwhile, prepare the sweet-sour sauce. In a mixing bowl, blend together the vinegar, Tabasco, garlic, light soy sauce, sesame seed oil, the remaining tablespoon of sherry and the final teaspoon of sugar. Taste and adjust the flavor by adding a tiny bit more of any or all of the ingredients. Reserve the sauce until the balls are ready.

When the timer rings, turn off the heat, reduce the pressure immediately, take out the balls and dribble the sauce over them, then serve them at once, hot.

Chinese Pork-Stuffed Mushrooms

For 4

Cook under pressure at 15 lb for 5 minutes
(or at 10 lb for 7 minutes)

18 fresh mushrooms, with well-shaped, nicely white, medium-sized caps, wiped clean
½ lb (225 g) boneless, chopped or ground, lean pork
2 Tbs cornstarch
1 Tbs dry sherry
2 Tbs dark soy sauce
Salt, to your taste

For this you will need a minimum 4-quart pressure cooker. Separate the mushroom stems from the caps and set the caps aside. Trim off any dried ends from the stems, then slice them across into tiny disks and reserve them. In a mixing bowl, lightly work together the pork, 1 tablespoon of cornstarch, the sherry, 1 tablespoon of soy sauce, plus about 1 teaspoon of salt, or more, to your taste. Brush the inside of each mushroom cap with sesame seed oil, then lightly fill each one with the pork stuffing to form a smooth, raised mound. Do not press or squeeze it hard, or you will make it too heavy and solid. Put the base rack into the pressure cooker, pour in the

3 Tbs sesame seed oil
1 cup (2.5 dl) dry white wine
About 1½ tsp sugar

wine, set the mushrooms in neat circles (there may be more than 1 layer), put on the lid, bring the pressure up to 15 pounds and cook for exactly 5 minutes.

As soon as the timer rings, turn off the heat and bring down the pressure immediately, take out the mushrooms and reserve them warm in an oven at 160° F (70° C). Remove the base rack from the pot and prepare the sauce. Liquefy the remaining tablespoon of cornstarch, in a small mixing bowl, with the remaining tablespoon of soy sauce plus 1 tablespoon of the hot wine. Stir this mixture, tablespoon by tablespoon, into the remaining hot wine in the bottom of the pressure cooker. Heat the mixture up, stirring continuously, until it thickens to the consistency of light honey and becomes translucent. At the same time, stir into the sauce the mushroom stem disks and about 1 teaspoon of sugar, or more, to your taste. Dribble this sauce over the mushrooms and serve them at once, nicely hot.

Chinese Pot-Poached Duck Squares
For about 12
Cook under pressure at 15 lb for 25 minutes
(or at 10 lb for 33 minutes)

A duck of about 3½ to 5 lb (1.5 to 2.25 kg), thawed out in advance if frozen, then cut up, bones and all, into 1½-inch (3.75 cm) cubes—your butcher can do this for you in a couple of · minutes with his professional band saw, even if the bird is frozen—or you can do it yourself, after thawing, using a sharp Chinese cleaver
1 cup (2.5 dl) dry white wine
10 Tbs dark soy sauce
¼ cup (60 ml) dry sherry
4 scallions, white bottoms and green tops, minced
2 tsp sugar

This is a gorgeously earthy and informal beginning to a meal. You can try forks or toothpicks, but the guests will end up using their fingers to bite the duck meat off the bone. You could try to formalize the whole thing by boning the duck in advance. Quite apart from the extra trouble, we think that the peasanty informality is much more fun.

Assuming that your duck is already cut into cubes, put the cubes on top of the base rack, into your minimum 4-quart pressure cooker. If you have a 2½- or 3-quart pot, cook the duck in two batches, using ½ of the cooking liquid ingredients for each. Pour in the wine, soy sauce, sherry, scallions and sugar. Then put on the lid, bring the pressure up to 15 pounds and cook for exactly 25 minutes.

As soon as the timer rings, turn off the heat, reduce the pressure at once and check one of the duck cubes for doneness. The flesh should come away easily from the bone. If not, if the duck was a bit old, continue the pressure cooking for another 5 minutes. It should, eventually, be about as tender as chicken, but with a pinkish red color and a wonderfully aromatic taste. Serve the pieces, hot, on small warmed plates, each piece dribbled with a teaspoon or so of the sauce from the pot.

Tiny Cocktail Marinated Mushrooms

For 4
Cook under pressure at 15 lb for 4 minutes
(or at 10 lb for 5 minutes)

24 small button mushrooms, well-shaped,
    nicely white, left whole, but with
    any dried stem ends trimmed off
5 cloves garlic, peeled and finely minced
2 Tbs good olive oil
1 tsp dried oregano
2 pinches red cayenne pepper
1 Tbs light soy sauce
1½ Tbs dry vermouth
¼ cup (60 ml) dry white wine

Don't worry about the amount of garlic—only a small taste of it actually gets into the mushrooms.

Put all ingredients into a minimum 4-quart pressure cooker. Put on the lid, bring the pressure up to 15 pounds and immediately turn off the heat. Let the pressure fall gradually, of its own accord, usually in about 4 minutes. Serve the little mushrooms at once, hot, speared onto toothpicks.

Quick Terrine of Veal with Mushrooms

For 8
Cook under pressure at 10 lb for 30 minutes
(or at 15 lb for 22 minutes)

4 Tbs (60 g) sweet butter
3 medium yellow onions, finely chopped
Enough stalks celery (usually about 5) to
    fill 1 cup (2.5 dl) when diced
1 lb (450 g) fresh mushrooms, wiped
    clean and fairly thinly sliced
2½ lb (1.1 kg) boneless, entirely lean,
    chopped or ground veal
2 cloves garlic, finely minced
1 cup (2.5 dl) bread crumbs, preferably
    fresh and homemade
Enough fresh parsley leaves, chopped, to
    fill 1 cup (2.5 dl)
2 whole eggs, lightly beaten
¼ cup (60 ml) cognac or Armagnac
Freshly grated nutmeg, to your taste
Salt, to your taste
Freshly ground black pepper, to your
    taste

This is a superfast version of that most basic form of good eating: a French-style terrine or, in more down-to-earth language, a meat loaf. It is multipurpose. You can serve it hot in slices as an appetizer, or it is equally good cold the next day. It will make sandwiches or snacks—or a cold-cuts main dish for lunch or supper, garnished with small pickles and salad greenery.

Set a minimum 6-quart pressure cooker on medium-frying heat, melt in it the butter and, when it is hot, lightly sauté the onions and celery until they are just gilded. Add the mushrooms and continue sautéing them until their water is evaporated and the hissing in the pot dies down. Put the veal into a large mixing bowl and add to it the sautéed vegetables from the pressure cooker. Also work into it, lightly and gently, the garlic, bread crumbs, parsley, eggs, cognac, 3 or 4 grinds of nutmeg, plus salt and pepper, to taste. Now, finally, adjust the thickness of the mixture. It should have the texture of thickish mud. To thicken it, add more bread crumbs. To thin it, add a dash or two more cognac.

In an 8-quart pressure cooker, you will be able to cook the mixture in two batches. In smaller cookers, there will have to be three or more batches. Choose the largest, ovenproof china, round soufflé dish that will fit into your pressure cooker with at least ¾ inch (2 cm) to spare all around. Lightly butter the inside of the soufflé dish and fill it with the meat mixture up to ½ inch (1.25 cm) from the top edge. Tightly cover the soufflé dish with aluminum foil. Set the base rack inside your pressure cooker, pour in 1 cup of water, place the soufflé dish on the rack, put on the lid, bring the pressure up to 10 pounds and cook for exactly 30 minutes.

When the timer rings, turn off the heat, reduce the pressure immediately and check the terrine for doneness. A plunge thermometer should show an internal temperature of about 160° F (70° C) at the moment when the terrine is precisely done. (If you don't have a thermometer, you will have to cut open the terrine at its center and see that it is thoroughly cooked through. If not, give it another 5 minutes of pressure.)

Clam-Stuffed Cherry Tomatoes

For 4, or divide in half for 2
Cook under pressure at 15 lb for 2 minutes
    (or at 10 lb for 3 minutes)

18 fresh clams in their shells, scrubbed
    clean under running cold water
½ cup (1.25 dl) dry white wine
18 not-too-small cherry tomatoes
The freshly squeezed juice of 2 lemons
Salt, to your taste

This is a dramatic and excellent appetizer. You can shorten the preparation time considerably if you rope in some extra pairs of hands for the repetitive jobs of pulling the clams out of their shells and scooping out the centers of the tomatoes. (Incidentally, although no use is made in this recipe of the clam-flavored wine left in the bottom of the pressure cooker after the cooking, this marvelous liquid should be strained and saved for a future sauce or soup.)

Put the clams into a minimum 6-quart pressure cooker [if using a smaller pressure cooker, cook in 2 batches, using ½ cup (1.25 dl) of wine for each], without the base rack, pour in the wine, put on the lid, bring the pressure up to 15 pounds and cook for exactly 2 minutes.

As soon as the timer rings, turn off the heat and bring down the pressure immediately. All the clams should have opened and, using a pair of tongs, you can lift out each open shell, scoop out the clam with a spoon and discard the shells. Now, using a small sharp knife and a spoon, make a slit in the stem end of each tomato and scoop out enough of the inside flesh so that a hot clam can be securely popped into the space. Repeat with all the tomatoes. Dribble a few drops of lemon juice onto each clam-in-the-hole, lightly salt and serve at once, impaled on toothpicks.

Chapter 6

ONE-DISH-MEAL SOUPS

Hearty and Healthful for Lunch or Supper

One of the special joys of pressure cookers is the marvelous way in which they make creamy soups. The precisely controlled pressure technique seems to draw out the full-flavor essences from meats and vegetables in a way that is unequaled by any other method of cooking or type of kitchen pot. In fact, the pressure cooker combines and concentrates the glutinous elements of the natural juices, so that the finished soup is often the smoothest, most velvety, most nourishing and satisfying liquid that you have ever spooned into your mouth. Such a soup, with its cubes of meat and vegetables, plus, perhaps, a crispy loaf of bread, some good butter and a salad, can make an ideal, superfast main dish for an informal family lunch or supper—or even, in our case, for a simple party meal when close friends come in unexpectedly on short notice. The soups that follow, in short, are our lifesavers in terms of ease and speed of preparation, with no compromise as to health and satisfaction in the eating.

This chapter concentrates mainly on the hearty, solid soups. When you want a light, clear bouillon, you should turn to Chapter 3 on page 34.

Cream of Fresh Green Asparagus with Cubes of Lamb

For 4
Cook under pressure at 10 lb for 14 minutes
(or at 15 lb for 11 minutes)

8 Tbs (115 g) sweet butter
1½ lb (675 g) boneless, entirely lean, young lamb, preferably from the leg, cut into ¾-inch (2 cm) cubes
2 medium yellow onions, peeled and thinly sliced

This memorable soup is an essence of the flavor joys of asparagus. Sometimes we feel that it is even better than eating the fresh asparagus itself. This supreme vegetable of spring is here teamed with the prime meat of spring, the young lamb.

Use a pressure cooker with a minimum capacity of 6 quarts. Set it on medium-high frying heat, without its base rack, quickly melt in it 4 tablespoons of the butter and, when it is

2 lb (1 kg) fresh asparagus, usually about
    2 dozen medium spears, washed,
    trimmed, scraped and scaled
4 Tbs all-purpose white flour
2 cups (5 dl) dry white wine
Salt, to your taste (usually about 1 tsp)
Up to 1½ cups (3.75 dl) milk, for thinning
Up to ⅔ cup (1.6 dl) heavy cream
3 egg yolks
Enough fresh leaves rosemary, chopped,
    to fill 1 Tbs, or 1 tsp dried
Freshly ground black pepper, to your
    taste (usually about ½ tsp)
Up to ¼ cup (60 g) filbert nutmeats,
    coarsely chopped

hot, sauté the lamb cubes until they are just golden—usually in about 4 to 6 minutes. (If you insist on your lamb being well done, you can hiss in a tablespoon or two of bouillon and continue cooking until this liquid is completely evaporated.) Then, with a slotted spoon, take out the lamb and set aside. Put the sliced onions into the hot butter and let them sizzle gently until they are wilted. Cut about 2 inches (5 cm) from the tip of each asparagus spear and hold the delicate green pieces aside for their special garnishing purpose. Break off the woody bottoms of the asparagus, as described on page 36. Cut the remaining good parts of the asparagus stalks into 1-inch (2.5 cm) pieces and stir these into the sizzling onions. Make sure that the asparagus is thoroughly coated with hot butter. Leave it to sizzle with the onions for 5 minutes. Then, carefully and smoothly work in the flour. Next, turn the heat full on and hiss the white wine into the pressure cooker, ¼ cup by ¼ cup, stirring continuously. Then add 3 cups (7.5 dl) of water and stir in about 1 teaspoon salt, or more, to your taste. Put on the lid, bring the pressure up to 10 pounds and cook for exactly 14 minutes. Meanwhile, cut the reserved asparagus tips into ¼-inch (7 mm) disks and again set them aside.

As soon as the timer rings, turn off the heat, reduce the pressure immediately and check the soup. The asparagus stalks should be very soft and cooked out. If not, give them another 3 or 4 minutes of pressure. Also, if the liquid of the soup is now too thick, add some of the milk, tablespoon by tablespoon, to thin it to your liking. Now purée the entire contents of the pot by passing them through a Cuisinart chopper-churner (or one of the similar machines), electric blender, food mill or by hand through a sieve. Afterward, pass the puree through a fairly fine strainer to get rid of the strings of the stalks.

Now put the cream into the empty pressure cooker (off the heat, naturally) and, with a wire whisk, beat into it the egg yolks. Begin adding, ¼ cup by ¼ cup and beating continuously, a total of about 2 cups of the still-hot puree. Then pour in the rest of the puree, with the lamb cubes, the bits of the asparagus tips and the rosemary. Taste, add salt if needed, and about ½ teaspoon pepper. Heat it all up to just below boiling, stirring steadily with a wooden spoon, and hold it at that temperature for about 4 or 5 minutes, to complete the cooking of the lamb and the tips. Finally, just before serving, melt in, one by one, the remaining 4 tablespoons of butter, stirring thoroughly and scraping the bottom and sides of the casserole. Work in more milk, if necessary, to adjust the thickness. Ladle out into hot soup bowls, making sure that each diner gets a fair share of the lamb cubes and the crispy-chewy, bright green asparagus tips. Sprinkle each serving with chopped filberts, which not only provide a nutty flavor, but are also high in healthy fiber.

A Good and Healthful Menu   Cream of Fresh Green Asparagus with Cubes of Lamb
Hot biscuits
Salad of lightly cooked green beans tossed with oil and
vinegar
Cheese and fruit
Coffee or Darjeeling tea

The Ideal Wines   *Luxurious*

A French château red from the Graves district of Bordeaux
or
A California red Cabernet Sauvignon from the Napa Valley

Everyday

A French regional red Médoc from Bordeaux
or
A California red Cabernet Sauvignon from Sonoma

Beef Boil with Cornmeal-Cheese Dumplings

For 4
Cook under pressure at 15 lb for 10 minutes
    (or 10 lb for 13 minutes)
Steaming of dumplings an extra 15 minutes

For the Beef Boil

4 Tbs (60 g) salt butter
1½ lbs (675 g) boneless, entirely lean,
    beef stew meat, perhaps chuck or
    bottom round, cut into 1-inch
    (2.5 cm) cubes
¼ cup (30 g) all-purpose white flour
1 quart (1 liter) beef bouillon (see page
    35, or use canned)
2 cups (5 dl) dry white wine
8 medium carrots, scraped and cut into
    1-inch (2.5 cm) chunks
4 stalks of celery, with leaves, the stalks
    finely sliced and the leaves finely
    minced
12 small, white, boiling onions, peeled,
    left whole
Enough fresh thyme leaves, chopped, to
    fill 2 Tbs, or 2 tsp dried
Salt, to your taste, about 2 tsp
Freshly ground black pepper, to your
    taste

This method for preparing dumplings in the same pressure cooker in which the meat is cooked is a new technique. It allows a fluffy-light starch ingredient to be introduced into the one-dish menu without your having to use any other pan or pot. Once you have mastered this basic method for dumplings, you can switch to any other dumpling recipe (see pages 80 and 127).

Use a large pressure cooker of at least 6-quart capacity. Set it, without its base rack, onto medium-high frying heat and melt the butter in it. Quickly and lightly coat each cube of beef with the flour. Drop them, in batches if necessary, into the hot butter and sauté them until they are nicely browned, usually in 4 to 5 minutes. Next, hiss in the beef bouillon and wine. Also add the carrots, celery, onions, thyme, plus about 2 teaspoons of salt and pepper to taste. Stir thoroughly, put on the lid, bring up to 15 pounds pressure and cook for exactly 10 minutes.

Meanwhile, prepare the dumpling dough. Sift together into a mixing bowl the cornmeal, flour, baking powder and salt. Stir in the grated cheese, ¼ cup of the parsley and the scallions. In a separate bowl beat together the eggs, milk and melted butter. Work these liquids gently and slowly into the dry ingredients. You may add a dash or two more milk, if you wish, but do the minimum of mixing and keep the dough quite stiff.

For the Dumplings

1 cup (225 g) medium yellow cornmeal
¼ cup (30 g) all-purpose white flour
1 tsp double-acting baking powder
½ tsp salt
¼ cup (60 ml) sharp Cheddar cheese,
   grated
Enough fresh leaves of parsley, chopped,
   to fill ½ cup (1.25 dl)
Enough scallions, minced, to fill 2 Tbs
2 eggs, lightly beaten
½ cup (1.25 dl) milk
1 Tbs (15 g) butter, melted

As soon as the timer rings, turn off the heat and reduce the pressure immediately. Then turn the heat on, again, and adjust it so that the liquid in the now-opened cooker is gently simmering. Use a long-handled metal tablespoon to drop in the dumplings. Dip the spoon into the hot liquid, then dip it at once into the dough and bring out a spoonful which should slide easily into the bubbling liquid. Do not crowd the dumplings. They must have room to expand. You will not use all the dough for the first batch of dumplings. You can cook more later. As soon as the first batch is all in, put back the pressure cooker's lid, but just rest it on top, without turning it into the locked position. Do not put on the pressure control weight. Leave the central vent open. Let the dumplings steam inside this enclosed space for about 12 to 15 minutes. The first time you make these dumplings, it might be well to check them for doneness by sticking in a wooden pick or a shiny metal knitting needle. If it comes out clean, the center of the dumpling is perfectly done. You will soon get to know the precise timing, give or take a minute, in your cooker on your stove. Take out all the dumplings with a slotted spoon and place them on a hot serving platter. Ladle out the soup and float a couple of dumplings on each serving. Sprinkle the remaining chopped parsley on top, for color. When you need a second batch of dumplings, bring the soup just back to boiling, drop in more dumplings and proceed as before.

A Good and Healthful Menu

Tiny Cocktail Marinated Mushrooms (see page 50)
Beef Boil with Cornmeal-Cheese Dumplings
Salad of sliced avocado and Bibb lettuce with oil and vinegar
Baked apples
Coffee or Earl Grey tea

The Ideal Wines

Luxurious

A French red Musigny from Burgundy
      or
A California red Pinot Noir from Monterey

Everyday

A French red Côte de Beaune-Villages from Burgundy
      or
A New York State "Lake Country Red"

Cucumber Cream with Sliced Ham

For 4
Cook under pressure at 5 lb for 3 minutes
*   (or at 10 lb for 2 minutes)*
*   (or at 15 lb for 1 minute)*

4 Tbs (60 g) sweet butter
1¼ lb (550 g) thinly sliced, lean boiled
    ham, the slices then cut into ½-inch
    (1.25 cm) squares
4 medium cucumbers, peeled and diced,
    seeds left in
2 medium yellow onions, peeled and
    finely chopped
1 quart (1 liter) clear chicken bouillon (see
    page 35, or use canned)
The grated outer rind of half a lemon
Salt, to your taste
Freshly ground black pepper, to your
    taste
2-oz (60 g) can water chestnuts, finely
    slivered
Up to ¾ cup (1.85 dl) light cream
1 cup (2.5 dl) sour cream
Enough fresh chives, chopped, to fill 2
    Tbs, or 2 tsp dried
Enough fresh dill leaves, chopped, to fill
    2 Tbs, or 1 tsp dried
About 2 Tbs paprika, preferably bright-
    red, medium-sweet Hungarian

This is equally good ice cold at the peak of summer heat, or bubbling hot during the ice storms of winter.

Use a minimum 4-quart pressure cooker. Set it, without its base rack, onto medium-high frying heat, melt in it the butter and, when it is hot, quickly sauté the ham squares until they are lightly gilded. Turn off the heat, remove the ham with a slotted spoon and set it aside. Put into the pressure cooker the cucumbers and onions, and sauté them in the butter for 3 or 4 minutes. Now turn up the heat and add the chicken bouillon, lemon rind, with salt and pepper to taste. Put on the lid, bring the pressure up to 5 pounds and cook for exactly 3 minutes.

As soon as the timer rings, turn off the heat and reduce the pressure immediately. Puree the entire contents of the pot by passing it through a Cuisinart chopper-churner (or one of the similar machines), an electric blender, a food mill or by hand through a sieve. Put the puree back into the pressure cooker and stir in the ham and water chestnuts. Reheat, uncovered, to just below simmering, then stir in ½ cup of light cream and the sour cream. Reheat the soup, adjusting the thickness with more light cream, if necessary. Serve at once in hot bowls with sprinklings of bright green chives and dill on top, plus a few pinches of bright-red paprika.

A Good and Healthful Menu

Cucumber Cream with Sliced Ham
    A crusty French loaf
Salad of avocado, watercress and large dice of sharp Cheddar
    cheese with oil and vinegar
A fruit tart
Coffee or Formosa oolong tea

The Ideal Wines

Luxurious

A French château red from the Médoc district of Bordeaux
    or
A California red Zinfandel from the Napa Valley

Everyday

A French château red of the Saint-Emilion district of Bordeaux
    or
A California red Merlot from the Napa Valley

Cream of Mushroom with Dice of Pork

For 4
Cook under pressure at 10 lb for 10 minutes
  (or at 15 lb for 8 minutes)

¾ cup (1.85 dl) dry white wine
¾ lb (340 g) fresh mushrooms, wiped
  clean, then caps and stems trimmed
  and diced
4 Tbs (60 g) sweet butter
1½ lb (675 g) boneless, entirely lean,
  fresh pork, cut into large dice
2 medium carrots, scraped and thinly
  sliced crosswise
1 stalk celery, with leaves, stalks finely
  sliced, the leaves minced
1 medium yellow onion, peeled and
  thinly sliced
3 Tbs all-purpose white flour
1 quart (1 liter) milk
Enough fresh parsley leaves, chopped, to
  fill 2 Tbs
Salt, to your taste
Freshly ground black pepper, to your
  taste
¼ cup (60 ml) heavy cream, eventually to
  be whipped stiff
2 Tbs paprika, preferably bright-red,
  medium-sweet Hungarian

The earthiness of mushrooms seems somehow to fit exactly with the farmyard character of the flesh of the pig.

Use a pressure cooker of at least 4-quart capacity. With its base rack in position, pour in the wine and add the diced mushroom caps and stems. Put on the lid, bring the pressure up to 10 pounds and cook for exactly 10 minutes.

As soon as the timer rings, turn off the heat, reduce the pressure immediately, empty the mushrooms and wine into a storage bowl and reserve. Remove the base rack from the pressure cooker and set it over medium-high frying heat. Melt in it the butter and, as soon as it is hot, quickly sauté the dice of pork until they are nicely browned, usually in about 4 to 5 minutes. Remove the pork with a slotted spoon and set it aside. Next, quickly sauté in the hot butter and fat the carrots, celery and onion. When these vegetables are just gilded, sprinkle over them and work in the flour. When all the flour has combined with the butter, turn up the heat to its highest and begin adding the milk, ¼ cup by ¼ cup and stirring continuously. When you have the first cup thoroughly worked in, you can add the rest of the milk more quickly. Now adjust the heat so as to keep the soup just below the boiling point. Add the dice of pork and spread them around by stirring. Strain the aromatic wine from the mushrooms into the soup and also add the parsley. Puree the mushrooms by passing them through a Cuisinart chopper-churner (or one of the other, somewhat similar machines), an electric blender, a food mill or by hand through a sieve. Stir this puree into the soup, then taste it, adding salt and pepper as needed. Whip the heavy cream. Serve this excellent soup in hot bowls, with a little mound of whipped cream floating on the surface nicely colored by a sprinkling of the red paprika.

A Good and Healthful Menu

Cream of Mushroom Soup with Dice of Pork
  Crisp crackling corn bread
Salad of boiled sliced potatoes with watercress dressed in oil
  and vinegar
Brandied or glacéed chestnuts
Coffee or jasmine tea

Luxurious

The Ideal Wines

A French château red from the Pomerol district of Bordeaux
  or
A California red Cabernet Sauvignon from the Alexander Valley

Everyday

A French red regional Saint-Emilion from Bordeaux
  or
A California red Gamay Beaujolais from the Napa Valley

Oxtail in Red Wine

For 4
Marinate oxtail overnight
Cook under pressure at 10 lb for 40 minutes
*   (or at 15 lb for 30 minutes)*

1 large beef oxtail, cut at the joints by
    your butcher
2 big cloves garlic, peeled and sliced
1 fresh lemon, peeled, seeded, and thinly
    sliced, all juice carefully saved
4 medium yellow onions, peeled and
    sliced
1 bay leaf
2 cups (5 dl) strong red wine
¼ lb (115 g) salt pork, washed and diced
4 medium carrots, scraped and quartered
    lengthwise
The white parts of 2 leeks, carefully
    desanded and cut into 1-inch (2.5
    cm) chunks
Half a smallish head of cabbage, either
    hand or machine shredded
½ tsp ground cloves
1 tsp freshly ground black pepper
3 cups (7.5 dl) beef bouillon (see page 35,
    or use canned)
Salt, to your taste

This is a dramatic example of the speedy nature of the pressure cooker. We love oxtail soup—a marvelous, one-dish, glutinously satisfying stew. It used to take us a good part of a day to prepare it, including at least 3 hours of slow simmering. Now we can do it at any time in just over 1 hour.

Use a pressure cooker of at least 6-quart capacity. Wash the oxtail chunks and put them into a largish, covered, refrigerator storage bowl. Interleave the oxtail with the garlic, lemon slices, onion and the bay leaf, crumbled. Then thoroughly moisten the mixture with the red wine and set it in the refrigerator. Gently stir it around last thing at night and, again, first thing in the morning to make sure that everything keeps wet.

When you are ready to start preparing the meal, set the pressure cooker on medium-high frying heat and quickly sauté the diced salt pork. As the bits become crisp, take them out and drain them on a paper towel. Wipe the chunks of oxtail dry (reserving the marinade) and sauté them in the hot pork fat for 3 or 4 minutes. Then hiss in the marinade, with all its solids. Also add the carrots, leeks, cabbage, ground cloves, pepper, beef bouillon, with salt to taste. Stir everything together, put on the lid, bring the pressure up to 10 pounds and cook for exactly 40 minutes.

When the timer rings, turn off the heat and let the pressure reduce gradually, of its own accord, usually in about 4 to 5 minutes. It is best to serve this in open soup plates, so that the diners can dig the meat off the oxtail bones with forks and spoons (or, informally, with fingers!). Sprinkle some of the crisp pork bits over each serving.

A Good and Healthful Menu

Black and green olives
Oxtail in Red Wine
    A crusty French loaf
Salad of orange segments, paper-thin slices of purple onions
    and watercress dressed with cumin, oil and vinegar
A fruit tart
Coffee or tea

The Ideal Wines

Luxurious

A French red Chambertin from Burgundy
    or
A California red Cabernet Sauvignon from Sonoma

Everyday

A French red regional Burgundy
    or
A California red Grignolino from the Napa Valley

Quick New England Clam, Oyster and Shrimp Chowder

For 4
Cook under pressure at 15 lb for 4 minutes
    (or at 10 lb for 5 minutes)

¼ lb (115 g) salt pork, washed and diced
3 medium yellow onions, peeled and
    coarsely chopped
3 medium potatoes, peeled and diced
1 quart (1 liter) light cream, or half-and-
    half
18 medium shrimp, shelled and deveined
18 fresh oysters, shucked, their juice
    carefully saved
18 clams, shucked and coarsely chopped,
    or, as a compromise, 2 medium cans
    of minced clams with their juice
6 Tbs (90 g) sweet butter
Salt, to your taste
Freshly ground black pepper, to your
    taste
Oyster crackers, optional
Enough fresh parsley leaves, chopped, to
    fill 3 Tbs
1½ Tbs paprika, preferably imported,
    medium-sweet Hungarian

This is the most ancient and classic of all one-dish meals. In our fast way, with this ideal balance of shellfish, it seems better than ever. Pressure cooking tends to toughen the delicate fishy flesh, so we first prepare the rich broth, then just simmer the shellfish for a few last moments before serving.

Choose a pressure cooker of at least 4-quart capacity. Set it, without its base rack, on medium-high frying heat and quickly sauté the salt pork and onions until they are just gilded, usually in 3 or 4 minutes. Now turn the heat up to full, add the potatoes and hiss in the cream. Stir it all around, put on the lid, bring up the pressure to 15 pounds and, as soon as it reaches full pressure, at once turn off the heat and let the pressure reduce gradually of its own accord, usually in 4 to 5 minutes.

Set the cooker back on simmering heat (now without its lid), bring it up to the gentlest bubbling and add the shrimp. Stir them around, bring the liquid back to the gentlest bubbling and simmer the shrimp for precisely 3 minutes. Add the oysters and simmer them for exactly 1 minute more. Add the clams and continue simmering for exactly another minute. Quickly melt in the butter and add the reserved oyster juice. Taste, adding salt and pepper as needed. Stir thoroughly and bring everything back to just below the boiling point. Serve at once in hot bowls, with small oyster crackers sprinkled on top of the soup and a few sprinklings of the bright green parsley and red paprika for attractive coloration.

A Good and Healthful Menu

Terrine of Veal with Mushrooms (page 50)
New England Clam, Oyster and Shrimp Chowder
    Oyster crackers
Mixed green salad vinaigrette
Chocolate cake
Coffee or tea

The Ideal Wines

Luxurious

A French white Puligny-Montrachet from Burgundy
    or
A California Champagne Blanc de Noir from the Napa Valley

Everyday

A French white Riesling from Alsace
    or
A California white Folle Blanche from the Napa Valley

German Lentil Stew with Knackwurst

For 4
Cook under pressure at 15 lb for 20 minutes, plus 6 minutes
(or at 10 lb for 26 minutes, plus 8)

1 cup, about ½ lb (225 g) jumbo lentils
1 ham bone, chopped or sawed into large
    pieces with some meat on them—or a
    smoked knuckle
2 smoked ham hocks, also chopped or
    sawed into halves or quarters,
    according to size
1 small yellow onion, peeled, stuck with
    four whole cloves
1 bay leaf, crumbled
1 tsp whole coriander seeds
1 clove garlic, peeled and minced
2 cups (5 dl) clear chicken bouillon (see
    page 35, or use canned)
2 cups (5 dl) dry white wine
1 cup (2.5 dl) heavy cream
Enough fresh leaves parsley, chopped, to
    fill 2 Tbs
As many as possible of the following
    herbs, 1 Tbs fresh or 1 tsp dried:
    Fennel leaves
    Marjoram
    Savory
    Thyme
Salt, to your taste, depending on the
    saltiness of the ham and hock
Freshly ground black pepper, to your
    taste
6 good, fat, all-beef knackwurst
    sausages—best, whenever possible,
    from a German butcher
About 1 cup (2.5 dl) sour cream
Enough fresh chives, minced, to fill 2
    Tbs, or 2 tsp dried
The same amount of fresh dill

In this recipe the saving of time by the pressure cooker is particularly dramatic. The presoaking of the lentils is eliminated, and the traditional 3 hours of simmering is cut to less than half an hour. The glutinous essences of the ham bone and hock are drawn out to enrich the soup in a way that was never possible by the old techniques.

Use a large pressure cooker of at least 6 quarts. Put into it the lentils, ham bone pieces, ham hocks, onion stuck with cloves, bay leaf, coriander and garlic. Then pour in the chicken bouillon and wine. Put on the lid, bring up the pressure to 15 pounds and cook for exactly 20 minutes.

When the timer rings, turn off the heat and let the pressure reduce gradually, of its own accord, usually in 4 to 5 minutes. Stir the contents of the pot gently but thoroughly with a wooden spoon and add the cream, parsley, as many other fresh herbs as possible (fennel, marjoram, savory, thyme), with salt and pepper to taste. Stir once more and push in the knackwurst around the cooker. Put back the lid, bring the pressure back up to 15 pounds and continue cooking for exactly 6 more minutes.

When the timer rings again, turn off the heat, let the pressure reduce gradually of its own accord, then the dish is ready to serve. If you prefer, you may pick out the ham and hock bones, cutting the meat off them and returning it to the soup, discarding the bones. Or, if the meal is informal, you can give your guests the pleasure of picking the bones. Ladle the soup into large, hot bowls, decorating each serving with dollops of sour cream and good sprinklings of bright green chives and dill.

A Good and Healthful Menu

Clams on the half shell
German Lentil Stew with Knackwurst
    Broiled filled tomato halves
Bananas baked with rum
Coffee or Lapsang souchong smoky tea

The Ideal Wines

Moderately Priced

A German white regional Bernkasteler Riesling from the Moselle
A California White Riesling from Monterey

Chapter 7

ONE-DISH BEAN POTS

From Boston Baked Through French Cassoulet

to Yankee Bean Stew

Boston Baked Beans may be America's most famous Sunday-night supper pot, but it is only one of hundreds from around the world. Almost every country seems to have its fabulous bean pot—from the white bean *Cassoulet* of southwestern France, the Mexican *Frijoles Negros de Olla*, Italian *Fasoeil al Furn Piemontese*, the *Feijoada* of Brazil, Israeli *Cholent*, the *Fabadas Asturianas* of Spain, Arab *Ta'Amia*, *Barbunya Fasulyasi* of Turkey, to the Mogul *Kutta Dhall* of India. The reason for this worldwide popularity is, of course, that dried beans are always an inexpensive bargain and are exceedingly good for you. They are, after all, the seeds of plants containing the basic spark of new life. They are high in fiber, good for energy, contain important quantities of B vitamins (especially the valuable thiamine), as well as calcium, a lot of iron, a good balance of protein and amino acids for body building and repair.

The trouble with dried beans is that they always take so many hours to soak and so many more hours to simmer in the pot. All this is now changed with the pressure cooker. In most recipes, presoaking can be eliminated and cooking time is cut to about a quarter of the old method in the classic bean pot. We generally add meats and vegetables to make our one-dish meals even more nutritious.

A Practical Note   In the recipes which follow, you will find that the ingredients include quite large amounts of liquid, usually beef or chicken bouillon. This is required by our revolutionary pressure cooker technique of eliminating altogether the old-fashioned day-before or overnight presoaking of the dried beans. Now, in the recipes in this chapter, we do the soaking and the cooking of the beans in a single, relatively quick operation. Since each little bean, however, can be regarded as a tiny sponge, they do need to soak up a large amount of liquid. Also, different batches of even the same type of bean bought at different times may vary in degrees of dryness (and hence thirstiness), so that they will soak up varying amounts of liquid. So we believe that it is always better to have a little too much liquid than too little, to avoid the danger of the pressure cooker running dry and burning on the bottom. If, when you open the lid after the beans have been perfectly pressure-cooked, you find that there is still some liquid left in the bottom of the pot, just drain it off into a heatproof storage jar and hold it for some later use. The great advantage of our unique method of pressure-cooking dried beans is that they are never given the chance of soaking up just plain old water, which adds nothing to their flavor, but, instead, are filled, like little sponges, with the aromatic beef or chicken bouillon. We believe that, once you have tasted a bean pot prepared in our way, you will never want to go back to the old, slow, presoaked method. (Incidentally, also, do not be surprised by the wide variations in the amounts and the timings of the following recipes. Every variety of dried bean is as different from every other as chalk is from cheese, and each has to be prepared in its own special way if you are to get the best flavor and texture results from it. One kind of dried bean simply cannot be substituted for another kind.)

Our Modified Boston Baked Beans with Soy

For 2
Cook under pressure at 15 lb for 50 minutes
(or at 10 lb for 67 minutes)
Oven baking for about 30 minutes

½ cup (115 g) dried marrowfat beans, sometimes called Great Northern or white haricot
½ cup (115 g) dried soybeans, or, if unavailable, simply double the amount of the marrowfat
1 medium yellow onion, peeled and quartered
½ lb (225 g) salt pork, the salt washed off under running cold water, the pork then cut into 1-inch (2.5 cm) cubes
Up to 5 cups (1.25 liters) clear beef or chicken bouillon (see page 35, or use canned)
3 Tbs dark, unsulfured molasses
2 Tbs brown sugar
2 tsp dry mustard
1 bay leaf, to be crumbled
Enough leaves fresh thyme, chopped, to fill 2 tsp, or ½ tsp dried
Salt, to your taste

Boston purists may shudder, but we add the almost-magical soybean to our version of this famous dish. Not only does it give a fine nutty flavor, but it is a superb nutritional element—with seven times as much pure protein as the standard marrowfat beans, five times as much valuable fiber, four times as much calcium and four times as much iron. Bravo soy!

You will need a pressure cooker of at least 3-quart capacity and also a bean pot (or other lidded pot) of the same size to go into the oven. Mix the marrowfat and soybeans, wash them under running cold water, pick them over and put them into the pressure cooker without its base rack. Dig the quartered onion and the cubes of salt pork into the beans, spreading them around, here, there and everywhere, then pour in the first 4 cups of bouillon. Put on the lid, bring the pressure up to 15 pounds and cook for exactly 50 minutes. Meanwhile, mix together the molasses, brown sugar, mustard, and thyme, with the bay leaf crumbled between your fingers.

When the timer rings, turn off the heat and let the pressure reduce gradually of its own accord, usually in 4 to 5 minutes. Set your oven to 350° F (175° C) and put the bean pot into it for 3 or 4 minutes to warm up. When it is quite warm, but still not too hot to handle, take it out of the oven and, using a slotted spoon, transfer into it all the solid contents of the pressure cooker. Pour the molasses mixture over the top. Finally pour in just enough more bouillon to come up to the top surface of the beans. Bake in the oven uncovered, for about 30 minutes, or a little bit longer, if you can spare the time. In fact, the longer the better. Finally, taste and add salt, as needed, depending on the saltiness of the pork. The beans should have absorbed most of the liquid and should not be swimming in a soup. If there is too much liquid, turn the oven up to 400° F (205° C) and continue baking the pot for as long as may be necessary to evaporate the excess liquid, usually from 5 to 15 minutes. Serve at once on very hot plates, preferably accompanied by Boston Brown Bread (see page 207).

A Good and Healthful Menu

Our Modified Boston Baked Beans with Soy
   with Boston Brown Bread
Salad of diced cucumber, onion slices, radishes and lemon-juiced sour cream
Fresh fruit
Coffee or tea

The Ideal Wines

Luxurious

An Italian red Chianti Riserva from Tuscany
   or
A California red or Pinot Noir from Sonoma

Everyday

An Italian red Chianti from Tuscany
   or
A California red Barbera from the Napa Valley

The Great French Cassoulet of Toulouse

For 6
Cook under pressure at 10 lb for 45 minutes, plus 45, plus 10
   (or at 15 lb for 34 minutes, plus 34, plus 8)

2 cups (450 g) white haricot beans, Great Northern or marrowfat
3 medium yellow onions, peeled and chunked
6 whole cloves
6 Tbs (90 g) goose fat, salt butter or alternative
¾ lb (340 g) boneless lean beef, lamb or veal, cut into 2-inch (5 cm) chunks
½ lb (225 g) smoked pork chops
½ lb (225 g) slab reasonably lean smoky bacon
2 Tbs all-purpose white flour

This is the magnificent bean pot of Southern France—the festive equivalent to the U.S. Boston Baked Beans. It makes a marvelously informal party dish, especially for a grand buffet. The choice of meats is quite flexible, according to what is available at your local butcher: chunks of lean beef or lamb, fresh or smoked pork chops, good frankfurters or knackwurst, aromatic peperoni or salami sausage. . . . The preserved goose is a French specialty, often available at fancy food shops. You should have a minimum of three different kinds of meat or poultry.

You will need a minimum 8-quart pressure cooker. Pick over the beans and discard any cracked ones. Put 2 quarts (2 liters) of fresh cold water into the pressure cooker, without its base rack. Heat up quickly to boiling, adding the chunked on-

2 Tbs tomato paste
3 medium yellow onions, peeled, whole
3 bay leaves, to be crumbled
Enough fresh parsley leaves, chopped, to
    fill ¼ cup (60 ml)
Enough fresh tarragon leaves, chopped,
    to fill 2 Tbs, or 2 tsp dried
Enough fresh leaves thyme, chopped, to
    fill 2 Tbs, or 2 tsp dried
3 cloves garlic, peeled and minced
5 cups (1.25 liters) beef bouillon (see page
    35, or use canned)
Salt, to your taste
Freshly ground black pepper, to your
    taste
10-oz (280 g) can French preserved
    goose—not absolutely essential
½ lb (225 g) garlic sausage

ions and cloves. As soon as the water starts bubbling, dribble in the beans through your fingers slowly enough so that the water does not go off the boil. Put on the lid, bring up the pressure to 10 pounds and cook for exactly 45 minutes.

When the timer rings, turn off the heat and let the pressure reduce gradually of its own accord. Drain off and discard the water, putting all the solids into a storage bowl. Clean out the pressure cooker, set it over medium-high frying heat, melt in it the fat or butter and, when it is hot, quickly brown the chunks of fresh meat, batch by batch, plus the pork chops and the slab of bacon. During the frying, lightly sprinkle each piece with the flour. Finally, pack all the pieces back in the pot and add to them the tomato paste, whole onions, crumbled bay leaves, parsley, tarragon, thyme, garlic, 3 cups of the beef bouillon, with salt and pepper to taste. Put on the lid, bring the pressure up to 10 pounds and cook for exactly 45 minutes.

When the timer rings, turn off the heat, reduce the pressure immediately and put the bean mixture back into the cooker. With a wooden spoon, very gently but thoroughly mix everything in the pot. Do not crush the beans. Now gently bury in them, in different places, the pieces of preserved goose (if being used) and the garlic sausage. (All meats in a cassoulet should be in fairly large pieces, to be cut up at serving. You can, if it is more convenient, cut the larger sausages in half as you put them in.) Add the final 2 cups of beef bouillon and heat up the liquid to gentle boiling. Put on the lid, bring the pressure back up to 10 pounds and cook for exactly 10 minutes more.

When the timer rings, turn off the heat and let the pressure reduce gradually of its own accord. Open up the pot and you are ready to serve, preferably with a slotted spoon, leaving the juices at the bottom. They will be absorbed during later reheating. This kind of bean pot can be kept warm for hours and actually improves with the keeping and reheating.

A Good and Healthful Menu

Crisp slices of iced cucumber, lightly salted
The Great French Cassoulet of Toulouse
Salad of celery hearts and sprigs of watercress without dressing
Fresh fruit
Coffee or tea

The Ideal Wines

Luxurious

A French red Vougeot from Burgundy
    or
A California red Petite Sirah from Monterey–Santa Clara

Everyday

A French red regional Beaune from Burgundy
    or
A California red Zinfandel from Paicines in San Benito

Beef Boil with Cornmeal-Cheese Dumplings

Superspeed Sautéed and Poached Chicken with Broccoli and
Carrots and a Dessert of Steamed Fresh Pears Stuffed with
Coconut, Dates, Walnuts and Maple Syrup

Quick San Francisco Crab Cioppino

Beef Pot Roast with Mixed Fruits and Olives

Steam-Baked Zucchini with Mushrooms and Scallions, Sweet Potatoes with Apricots, Pears and White Grapes, French-Cut Green Beans as They Do Them in Provence and Young Carrots Candied with Maple Syrup

Cream of Fresh Green Asparagus with Cubes of Lamb, and Basic
Pressure Cooker Farmhouse Bread Without Pressure

Authentic Georgia Hopping John

For 2
Cook under pressure at 15 lb for 30 minutes plus 15 plus 4
*   (or at 10 lb for 40 minutes plus 20 plus 5)*

½ cup (115 g) black-eyed peas, often
    called cowpeas
1 lb (450 g) smoked pork butt cut into
    ¾-inch (2 cm) slices
3 cups (7.5 dl) chicken bouillon (see page
    35, or use canned)
⅓ cup (75 g) white rice
1 medium yellow onion, peeled and
    finely chopped
Salt, to your taste
Freshly ground black pepper, to your
    taste

This is the fine, satisfying specialty which I have always found at its simple best in the country hotels and restaurants of Georgia. Now, I suppose, they are also serving it in the White House. We are sure that when the French ambassador comes to dinner, he will enjoy it as much as we do.

You will need a pressure cooker of at least 3-quart capacity. Wash and carefully pick over the black-eyed peas, discarding any that are broken. Put the pork slices into the pressure cooker without its base rack. Add the bouillon, plus, if necessary, extra cold water to cover the meat. Heat up just to boiling, put on the lid, bring the pressure up to 15 pounds and cook for exactly 30 minutes.

When the timer rings, turn off the heat, reduce the pressure immediately and drain the hot liquor from the pot into a storage bowl. Dribble the black-eyed peas into the pressure cooker so that they surround and more or less cover the pork. Measure 2 cups of the hot liquor and pour it back into the pot over the black-eyed peas. Put on the lid, bring the pressure back up to 15 pounds and cook for another 15 minutes.

As soon as the timer rings again, turn off the heat and let the pressure reduce gradually, of its own accord. Next, lift out the pork slices, cut them into coarse dice and put them back into the pot with the rice, onions, 1 cup more of the pot liquor, plus salt and pepper to taste. Stir everything gently with a wooden spoon to mix thoroughly without mashing the black-eyed peas. Put back the lid, bring the pressure again to 15 pounds and cook the rice for exactly 4 minutes.

When the timer rings, turn off the heat and let the pressure reduce gradually, of its own accord. Almost all the liquid should have been finally absorbed by the rice, which will be perfectly soft, though nicely chewy. If there is any liquid left on the bottom, boil it off in the open cooker. Again using a wooden spoon, lift rather than stir the Hopping John to lighten and loosen it as you serve it.

A Good and Healthful Menu

A loin of roast pork with crispy crackling and pickled peaches
Authentic Georgia Hopping John
A salad of chunked artichoke bottoms and sprigs of watercress
    without dressing
Fresh fruit pie
Coffee or tea

The Ideal Wines

Moderately Priced

An Italian dry white Soave from the Venice region
    or
A New York State "Lake Country White" from the Finger
Lakes

Italian Chick-Peas with Macaroni Peanuts and Parmesan Cheese

For 2

Cook under pressure at 15 lb for 65 minutes
(or 10 lb for 88 minutes)

¾ cup (170 g) chick-peas, washed and
    picked over
1 clove garlic, peeled and minced
1 medium yellow onion, peeled and
    chopped
Enough fresh dill, minced, to fill 1 Tbs, or
    1 tsp dried
½ tsp dried oregano
½ tsp dried sage
7 cups (1.75 liters) clear beef or chicken
    bouillon (see page 35, or use canned,
    cubed or dehydrated)
1 cup (2.5 dl) dry white wine
⅓ cup (75 g) medium-small macaroni
    shells (see opposite)
⅓ cup (75 g) macaroni peanuts (see
    opposite)
1 cup (2.5 dl) coarsely grated Parmesan
    cheese, plus more for serving
Salt, to your taste
Freshly ground black pepper, to your
    taste
4 Tbs (60 g) butter

This is a famous Italian country dish in which various shapes of pasta are mixed with the little round balls which we know as chick-peas, the Italians as ceci, and the Spanish as garbanzos. We use a mixture of small macaroni shells (maruzzelle) and macaroni peanuts (cavatelli) and, when children come to dinner or lunch, they have a lot of fun picking out and identifying the shapes on their plates. Chick-peas are strong in protein elements (which are magnified, here, by the added cheese), also in vitamin C, calcium, iron and the highest content of almost any dried beans in nutritionally valuable fibers.

You will need a pressure cooker of minimum 4-quart capacity. Remove the base rack and put into the pot the chick-peas, garlic, onions, dill, oregano and sage. Pour in the bouillon and dry white wine. Heat up to the boil, put on the lid, bring up to 15 pounds pressure and cook for 65 minutes.

While the chick-peas are cooking, mix the two types of pasta and cook them in the standard way according to the printed instructions, usually in about 12 to 15 minutes. Drain the macaroni and reserve it, warm.

As soon as the timer rings, turn off the heat and let the pressure reduce gradually of its own accord. Drain the chick-peas and toss them, with the pasta and half the grated Parmesan, plus salt and pepper to taste, in a warm mixing bowl. Serve at once, on very hot plates, with 2 pats of butter nestling and melting on top of each serving. Sprinkle the remaining Parmesan over the top.

A Good and Healthful Menu

Chinese Pork-Stuffed Mushrooms (see page 48)
Italian Chick-Peas with Macaroni Peanuts and Parmesan
    Cheese
Tossed greens with small bits of anchovies with oil and
    vinegar
Sicilian cannoli pastries
Caffè espresso or tea

The Ideal Wines

Luxurious

An Italian red Barolo from the Piedmont region
    or
A California red Zinfandel from the Napa Valley

Everyday

An Italian red Barbaresco from the Piedmont region
    or
A California red Barbera from Sonoma

Sweet-and-Sour Lima Beans

For 2
Cook under pressure at 15 lb for 40 minutes
*   (or at 10 lb for 53 minutes)*
Oven baking for 25 minutes

1 cup (225 g) dried limas, large
1 cup (2.5 dl) dry white wine
8 cups (2 liters) clear beef or chicken
    bouillon (see page 35, or use canned,
    cubed or dehydrated)
1 Tbs good olive oil
3 Tbs tarragon white wine vinegar
3 Tbs pure maple syrup
¼ cup (60 ml) chutney, preferably top-
    quality Indian mango, coarsely
    chopped

We think that the flavors and textures of this pot are so excellently satisfying that no meat is needed. But the dish goes wonderfully with a barbecued chicken or a grilled ham steak. Limas are particularly rich in vitamin C, calcium, iron and the essential fibers.

You will need a pressure cooker of minimum 4-quart capacity and a bean pot to go into the oven. Wash and pick over the limas, then put them into the pot, without its base rack, and add the white wine and bouillon. Float the olive oil on the surface to prevent frothing. Heat it all up to the boil, put on the lid, bring up the pressure to 15 pounds and cook for exactly 40 minutes.

Meanwhile, mix together in a bowl the vinegar, maple syrup and chutney. Preheat your oven to 350° F (175° C) and put in the bean pot to warm up.

When the timer rings, turn off the heat and let the pressure reduce gradually of its own accord. Then drain the cooking liquid into a storage jar for future use in soups. Put the limas into the bean pot and, with a wooden spoon, gently blend the sweet-sour mixture into them. Set the bean pot, covered, in the center of the oven and bake for another 25 minutes. Then serve immediately on very hot plates.

A Good and Healthful Menu

Barbecued chicken
Sweet-and-Sour Lima Beans
    with corn bread
Romaine lettuce with purple onion and green pepper rings
    tossed with oil and vinegar
Eclairs
Coffee or Indian Assam tea

The Ideal Wines

Luxurious

A French white Montrachet from Burgundy
    or
A California white Pinot Chardonnay from Monterey

Everyday

A French white Mâcon Pinot Chardonnay from Burgundy
    or
A California white Blanc de Blancs from the Livermore Valley

Cranberry Beans with Lamb Chops and Scallions

For 2
Cook under pressure at 15 lb for 60 minutes
*   (or at 10 lb for 80 minutes)*
Plus an extra 10 minutes of open steaming

About 5 Tbs (75 g) sweet butter

4 rib lamb chops, most of their fat
    trimmed off

½ cup (115 g) dried cranberry beans,
    washed and sorted

1 cup (2.5 dl) dry white wine

8 cups (2 liters) clear beef or chicken
    bouillon (see page 35, or use canned,
    cubed or dehydrated)

8 scallions, bulbs and tops cut into ½-
    inch (1.2 cm) pieces

Salt, to your taste

Freshly ground black pepper, to your
    taste

Enough fresh parsley, chopped, to fill 2
    Tbs

To their high nutritional value, cranberry beans add a beautiful appearance. They are speckled and streaked with deep cranberry red. This wonderful combination with lamb and onions would be a spring Sunday-night supper *par excellence*.

You will need a pressure cooker of at least 3-quart capacity. Set it, without its base rack, on medium-high frying heat, melt in it 2 tablespoons of the butter and, as soon as it is thoroughly hot, sauté the 4 lamb chops until they are nicely gilded—usually in about 3 to 4 minutes. Add more butter if necessary. When the chops are done, take them out and set them aside. Discard the fat from the cooker. Now put the cranberry beans into the pot and pour over them the wine and 7½ cups of the bouillon. Heat to the boil, put on the lid, bring up the pressure to 15 pounds and cook for exactly 60 minutes.

When the timer rings, turn off the heat and let the pressure reduce gradually of its own accord, usually in about 4 minutes. Then open up the cooker and drain off any excess liquid into the reserved bouillon. Using a wooden spoon, gently stir into the beans the scallions, 2 more tablespoons of the butter, with salt and pepper to taste. Carefully and gently, bury the 4 lamb chops in the middle of the beans. Add a final measured ½ cup of the bouillon. Set the pot on fairly gentle, simmering heat, uncovered, and let it all cook, with minimum bubbling, for an extra 10 or 15 minutes. Do not stir it during this operation. Then serve at once on very hot plates. Decorate each serving with sprinklings of the bright green parsley.

A Good and Healthful Menu

Grilled cheese canapés
Cranberry Beans with Lamb Chops and Scallions
Green salad vinaigrette
Pear halves marinated in red wine
Coffee or tea

The Ideal Wines

Luxurious

A French red Romanée from Burgundy
    or
A California red Pinot Noir from the Valley of the Moon in Sonoma

Everyday

A French red Volnay from Burgundy
    or
A California red Pinot Noir from the Santa Clara Valley

Yankee Bean Stew with Mixed Sausages and Vegetables

For 4
Cook under pressure at 15 lb for 40 minutes
*   (or at 10 lb for 53 minutes)*

2 meaty ham hocks
1 lb (450 g) smoked pork butt
1 cup (225 g) dried Yankee beans, or navy
    beans, or pea beans, washed and
    picked over
2 bay leaves, crumbled
½ tsp saffron filaments
Salt, to your taste
Up to 4½ quarts (4½ liters) beef bouillon
    (see page 35, or use canned)
3 medium yellow onions, peeled and
    chunked
1 medium green pepper, deseeded and
    chunked
2 cloves garlic, peeled and minced
2 Milwaukee-style smoked beef sausages,
    cut into 1-inch (2.5 cm) chunks
2 Portuguese-style linguica, or Polish-
    style kielbasa sausages, cut into 1-
    inch (2.5 cm) lengths
2 Spanish hot chorizo sausages, or Italian
    peperoni, cut into 1-inch (2.5 cm)
    chunks
2 medium potatoes, peeled and chunked
Freshly ground black pepper, to your
    taste
Half a small head of cabbage, finely
    shredded

This rich, rib-sticking soup is a true product of the Yankee melting pot—with influential overtones from several of our ethnic cultures. The Yankee bean (also called the navy bean, or the pea bean) is a variant of a strain that came originally from the Mediterranean and was called the Greek Salonika. I learned to include the Spanish hot chorizo sausage from Cuban and Spanish friends in Florida. I incorporated a Portuguese recipe from Tampa. And the overall method of assembling and cooking the soup is clearly the technique of the New England boiled dinner.

You will need a large pressure cooker of at least 8-quart capacity. Put into it the ham hocks, pork butt, beans, bay leaves, saffron and a little salt, but go easy at this early stage. Pour in 4 quarts of the bouillon, heat it to the boil, put on the lid, bring the pressure up to 15 pounds and cook for exactly 40 minutes.

When the timer rings, turn off the heat, and let the pressure reduce gradually of its own accord, usually in 4 to 5 minutes. Then take off the lid, set the pot back on simmering heat and add the onions, green pepper, garlic, sausages, potatoes, plus more salt and pepper to taste. Judge the thickness at this stage. It should be rich with solid ingredients, but still a reasonably liquid soup. If necessary, thin it with dashes of the remaining beef bouillon. Continue the simmering, uncovered, until the potatoes are soft and the sausages are heated through. Add more bouillon, if needed. Finally, a couple of minutes before the soup is due to be served, gently stir in the shredded cabbage. It should remain crispily undercooked. Cut the ham hock and pork butt meat into bite-sized cubes and discard the bones. Serve this marvelous stew in deep, large, very hot soup bowls with crusty bread to dip, messily but gloriously, into the juices.

A Good and Healthful Menu

Clam-Stuffed Cherry Tomatoes (see page 51)
Yankee Bean Stew with Mixed Sausages and Vegetables
    A long, crusty French loaf
Salad of Belgian endive with crisp bits of Canadian bacon
    tossed with olive oil
Raspberry sherbet
Coffee or winey Keemun tea

The Ideal Wines

Luxurious

A French red Château Corton from Burgundy
    or
A California red Cabernet Sauvignon from the Napa Valley

Everyday

A French red Mercurey from Burgundy
    or
A California red Cabernet Sauvignon from Monterey

Chapter 8

ONE-DISH MEALS WITH RICE

From New Orleans Jambalaya to
Valencia Paella

Rice is another of the great, universal foods—probably the mainstay of more millions of families everywhere than any other single ingredient. It can be served with total simplicity—just boiled in water and fluffed with a spoonful or two of any kind of fat that is locally available. Or it can be made into a luxurious dish—decorated, filled and garnished with a multiplicity of meats, fish, shellfish and vegetables—all the ingredients of a magnificent and memorable meal. The trouble has always been that these supreme rice dishes took a great deal of time and trouble to prepare. Now, simplified versions of the great *jambalaya* of New Orleans or the *paella* of Valencia can be speeded up in the pressure cooker. Besides these party dishes, this chapter also includes some everyday, family presentations of classic rice dishes.

Remember, always, that all these rice recipes are completely flexible. Once you have learned the basic principles of preparing them, you can substitute other ingredients, invent your own new dishes almost without limitation.

Quick New Orleans Creole Jambalaya
For 6
Cook under pressure at 10 lb for 6 minutes
   (or at 15 lb for 5 minutes)

About 3 Tbs bacon, ham or other pork fat
¾ lb (340 g) lean boiled ham, cut into
   large dice
¾ lb (340 g) slightly peppery sausages
   (see opposite), cut into ½-inch
   (1.2 cm) rounds
3 medium yellow onions, peeled and
   chopped

This is one of the greatest of authentic American regional dishes—a blending of three gastronomic cultures: the French and Spanish rulers of New Orleans and the Choctaw Indians who were there in Louisiana long before the coming of the European settlers. Jambalaya is a worthy brother to the other great rice dishes: the *paella* of Spain, the *pilau* of India, the *pilaf* of the Arab world and the *risotto* of Italy. It keeps perfectly for several days, reheats without loss of quality and is excellent even cold. In Louisiana, you can get a small, hot sausage, called *chaurices*, but in other parts of the country we

1-lb (450 g) can imported Italian peeled
plum tomatoes

2 green peppers, cored and chopped

2 stalks celery, including leaves, chopped

6-oz (170 g) can imported Italian tomato
paste

1½ cups (340 g) long-grain rice

2 cloves garlic, finely minced

Enough fresh leaves parsley, chopped, to
fill ⅓ cup (80 ml)

Enough fresh leaves thyme, chopped, to
fill 3 Tbs, or 1 tsp dried

3 whole bay leaves

Salt, to your taste

Freshly ground black pepper, to your
taste

Red cayenne pepper, to your taste

3 cups (7.5 dl) clear chicken bouillon (see
page 35, or use canned)

¾ lb (340 g) sea scallops, in bite-size
pieces

¾ lb (340 g) boiled, shelled shrimp

use either the slightly peppery Spanish *chorizos* or the Italian *peperoni.*

Incidentally, after preparing this a couple of times, you will be able to substitute many other ingredients, such as clams, oysters, leftover meats, chicken, duck, or goose. . . . The balance of ingredients is almost entirely flexible. The making of this *jambalaya* used to involve more than 4 hours of slow simmering. Now, we can complete it in about half an hour from the moment we walk into the kitchen to the serving of it at table.

You will need a large pressure cooker of a minimum 6-quart capacity, so that the rice will have plenty of room to expand. Set pot, without its base rack, on medium-frying heat, melt in it the fat and, as soon as it is hot, quickly sauté the dice of ham and the rounds of sausage until they are lightly browned, usually in about 3 to 4 minutes. Add the chopped onions and continue sautéing until they are just transparent and wilted. Now hiss in the tomatoes, green peppers, celery and the tomato paste, letting it all bubble hard to boil off some of the excess water. When the sauce shows the first signs of thickening, mix in the rice, garlic, parsley, thyme, bay leaves, with salt, pepper and cayenne to taste. Then stir in 2½ cups of the chicken bouillon. Put on the lid, bring the pressure up to 10 pounds and cook the rice for precisely 6 minutes.

When the timer rings, turn off the heat and reduce the pressure immediately. When you open up the lid, most of the liquid should have been absorbed by the rice, which should now be edibly soft. (If not, add the remaining ½ cup of bouillon and continue the cooking for a few minutes longer, covered, but not necessarily under pressure.) Using a wooden spoon and working gently, with lifting rather than stirring strokes, fold into the rice the scallops and shrimp, evenly distributed. Heat them up for 4 or 5 minutes by letting the remaining bouillon gently simmer, open, over low heat. Then serve at once in hot bowls.

A Good and Healthful Menu

Small mushrooms vinaigrette

Quick New Orleans Creole Jambalaya

Salad of escarole, avocado slices and grapefruit sections, tossed with oil and vinegar

A Southern pecan pie

Café brûlot or tea

The Ideal Wines

Luxurious

A French white Gewürztraminer from Alsace
or
A California white Gewürztraminer from Alexander Valley

Everyday

A French white blended Cordon d'Alsace
or
A California white Chenin Blanc from Monterey

Quick Italian Risotto of Chicken Livers with Vegetables

For 2
Cook under pressure at 10 lb for 7 minutes
(or at 15 lb for 5 minutes)

4 Tbs (60 g) sweet butter
¼ lb (115 g) green beans, topped and
tailed, then chunked
1 small zucchini, coarsely diced
¼ lb (115 g) fresh mushrooms, trimmed
and sliced
1 medium tomato, peeled and chopped
12 Tbs red pimento, chopped
Salt, to your taste
Freshly ground black pepper, to your
taste
1 clove garlic, peeled and finely minced
½ lb (225 g) fresh chicken livers, cut into
bite-sized pieces
½ cup (115 g) raw rice (see note opposite)
1 cup (2.5 dl) clear chicken bouillon (see
page 35, or use canned, cubed or
dehydrated)
Grated Parmesan cheese, to sprinkle on at
serving

Risotto, the world-famous rice specialty of the Italian city of Milan, is just about the equivalent of the jambalaya of New Orleans (preceding recipe). But in the Italian version, the rice grains are not supposed to be separated. They are cooked until soft and creamy, so that they gently stick together to form a marvelously aromatic main dish, a savory rice pudding filled and garnished with all kinds of meats, fish or shellfish, birds or vegetables. For this reason, you should use what is called "short-grain soft rice," or "risotto rice," generally available in Italian groceries. If not, use the standard long-grain rice you can find in the supermarket. Once you have made this recipe a couple of times, you will quickly know how to replace these ingredients with many other kinds of meats and vegetables.

You will need a pressure cooker of minimum 3-quart capacity. Set it, without its base rack, over medium-frying heat, melt in it the butter and, as soon as it is hot, quickly sauté the green beans, zucchini, mushrooms, tomatoes and red pimentos, until they are rid of most of their water and are lightly brown. Add salt and pepper to taste. Then add the garlic and chicken livers, stirring them around gently and turning them over until they stiffen and are coated with butter. Next, stir in the rice and chicken bouillon. Blend everything thoroughly, put on the lid, bring the pressure up to 10 pounds and cook for precisely 7 minutes.

When the timer rings, turn off the heat, reduce the pressure immediately and, the moment the lid is off, stir everything again. Almost all the bouillon should have been absorbed, and the rice should be nicely soft but still pleasantly chewy. If there is too much bouillon left on the bottom, boil it hard to evaporate it off, while continuously and gently stirring the rice back and forth to prevent it from sticking. Finally, taste and adjust the seasonings, then serve at once on very hot plates, with the grated Parmesan sprinkled on top.

A Good and Healthful Menu

Italian antipasto
Quick Italian Risotto of Chicken Livers with Vegetables
Italian green salad with arugula
Spumoni
Caffè espresso or tea

The Ideal Wines

Luxurious

An Italian red Gattinara from the Piedmont region
or
A California red Barbera from the Napa Valley

Everyday

An Italian red Valpolicella from the Venice region
or
A California red Barbera from Sonoma

North African Pilaf of Rice à la Parisienne

For 2
Cook under pressure at 10 lb for 6 minutes
(or at 15 lb for 4 minutes)

4 Tbs (60 g) butter
¼ lb (115 g) fresh button mushrooms, whole, or larger ones, quartered
¼ cup (60 g) blanched, slivered almonds
¼ cup (60 g) golden, seedless raisins
1 medium onion, peeled and chopped
Salt, to your taste
Freshly ground black pepper, to your taste
½ cup (115 g) short-grain soft rice or use long-grain rice if you can't find the special variety
1 bay leaf, crumbled
1 clove garlic, peeled and finely minced
¼ tsp saffron filaments
Enough fresh leaves thyme, chopped, to fill 2 Tbs, or ½ tsp dried
1 cup (2.5 dl) clear chicken bouillon (see page 35, or use canned)
2 eggs, hard-boiled and sliced
¼ lb (115 g) pitted black olives
Grated Gruyère cheese, to sprinkle on top at serving

Since France once had a North African empire, the Arab rice pilaf is still strong in the French cuisine, and this is a recipe given us by a young North African chef in Paris. It is one of the simplest rice dishes to prepare—an excellent main dish for lunch or supper. We often serve it with one or more of our own sauces, prepared in advance: either the tomato (page 38), the garlic (page 41), or the hot pili pili (page 42). Take your pick, or forget the sauce, which is not essential.

You will need a pressure cooker of at least 3-quart capacity. Set it, without its base rack, on medium-high frying heat, melt in it the butter and, as soon as it is hot, lightly sauté the mushrooms, almonds, raisins and onions, then add salt and pepper to taste. As soon as everything has lightly gilded, usually in about 3 or 4 minutes, work in the rice, bay leaf, garlic, saffron, thyme and more salt and pepper if needed. Pour in the chicken bouillon and stir everything around to mix thoroughly. Put on the lid, bring the pressure up to 10 pounds and cook for precisely 6 minutes.

When the timer rings, turn off the heat and reduce the pressure immediately, open up the lid and stir the pilaf gently with a wooden spoon, lifting it to fluff it. Almost all the bouillon should have been absorbed, and the rice should be nicely soft but still pleasantly chewy. If there is too much bouillon left on the bottom, boil it hard to evaporate it off, while continuously and gently stirring the rice back and forth to prevent it from sticking. Pile the pilaf in a mound on a hot serving platter, and decorate it with slices of the hard-boiled eggs and black olives. If you are using one of the sauces, dribble it over the top now. Sprinkle the pilaf lavishly with grated Gruyère cheese. Serve at once on very hot plates.

A Good and Healthful Menu

Veal Terrine (see page 50)
North African Pilaf of Rice à la Parisienne
Green salad vinaigrette
Chocolate mousse
Coffee or tea

The Ideal Wines

Luxurious

A French château white from the Graves district of Bordeaux
or
A California white Pinot Chardonnay from Monterey

Everyday

A French white dry Sauvignon from Bordeaux
or
A California white Pinot Blanc from the Napa Valley

Paella as They Do It in Valencia
For 6
Cook at 10 lb first for 10 minutes, and then 6 minutes more
   (or at 15 lb for 8 minutes, and then 4 minutes more)

Up to ½ cup (1.25 dl) top-quality olive oil

3 lb (1.4 kg) frying-roasting chicken, cut into serving pieces

3 garlicky, peppery sausages, either Spanish chorizos or Italian peperoni, cut into chunks

½ lb (225 g) boneless lean pork, cut into bite-sized pieces

3 medium yellow onions, peeled and chopped

4 cups (1 liter) clam juice

Salt, to your taste

Freshly ground black pepper, to your taste

12 mussels in their shells, washed and scrubbed

Up to 2 cups (5 dl) dry white wine

12 hard-shell clams, washed and scrubbed

½ lb (225 g) sea scallops, cut into bite-sized pieces

½ lb (225 g) fresh raw shrimp, shelled and deveined

1 green pepper, seeded and chopped

4 medium tomatoes, peeled and quartered

2 cloves garlic, finely minced

½ tsp saffron filaments

Enough fresh leaves marjoram, chopped, to fill 2 Tbs, or 2 tsp dried

2 cups (450 g) raw rice

1 pkg frozen French-cut green beans, for decoration

⅓ cup (80 ml) red pimentos, neatly trimmed for decoration

The paella of Spain is almost certainly the most famous and the grandest of all the rice dishes of the world. In Valencia, they prepare it in its most luxurious form. Done in the traditional way, on its large, flat, steel platter on top of the stove and in the oven, it takes almost a day of preparation. In our pressure cooker, we do it in under an hour.

You will need a large pressure cooker of at least 6-quart capacity. Set it, without its base rack, over medium-high frying temperature and heat up in it 4 tablespoons of the oil. Then quickly sauté the chicken pieces until they are lightly gilded. Take them out and reserve them. In batches, lightly sauté and brown the other meat and vegetable ingredients: sausages, pork and onions. If necessary, add more oil, tablespoon by tablespoon. When the sautéing is done, stack all the meats neatly back into the cooker and pour over them 1 cup of the clam juice, adding salt and pepper to taste. Put on the lid, bring the pressure up to 10 pounds and cook for exactly 10 minutes.

Meanwhile, in a tightly lidded soup kettle, steam open the mussels by boiling them hard with ¾ cup of the wine, until the shells have opened, usually in about 2 to 3 minutes. Take out the mussels with tongs and reserve them in their shells in a covered dish in a 160° F (70° C) oven. Repeat this steaming operation with the clams, again boiling them hard until their shells are open, usually in about 4 to 5 minutes. Take them out with tongs and set them aside with the mussels.

When the timer rings, turn off the heat and reduce the pressure immediately, open up the pot and add to it the scallops, shrimp, green pepper, tomatoes, garlic, saffron, marjoram, rice, the remaining 3 cups of clam juice, plus more salt and pepper if needed. Mix everything, quite gently, using a wooden spoon. Again, put on the lid, bring the pressure back up to 10 pounds and cook for exactly 6 minutes.

Meanwhile, in two separate small saucepans, each containing ½ cup of the wine, heat up, simmering for a couple of minutes, the green beans and red pimento. Then hold them, warm, ready for the decoration. Also have ready, warmed, a large flat serving platter.

The moment the timer rings, turn off the heat and reduce the pressure immediately. Check the rice for doneness; it should be soft but still slightly chewy, and most of the liquid should have been absorbed. If not, boil it hard for a few minutes to evaporate most of it off. Now begin the final construction job. Spread the rice in a thickish layer on the serving platter. Imbed in it, here and there and all around, the various pieces of meat, scallops and shrimp, so that the whole platter looks like a cornucopia of good things. Decorate, in a planned pattern, with bright green beans and bits of red pimento. Garnish the platter, on top and around the rice, with the clams and mussels in their shells. Any remaining juice from the pot should be sprinkled over the top. A well-made paella is indeed a handsome dish!

A Good and Healthful Menu	An ice-cold gazpacho Paella as They Do It in Valencia A green salad with anchovies and black olives tossed with oil and vinegar Cream cheese with guava jelly Coffee or tea

The Ideal Wines

Luxurious

A Spanish red from the Rioja region
or
A California red Cabernet Sauvignon from the Napa Valley

Everyday

A Spanish red from the Panades region of Barcelona
or
A California "Mountain Red Burgundy"

Chapter 9

ONE-DISH MEALS WITH BEEF

Including Speed Meals Prepared in One Hour or Less from Kitchen Start to Serving at Table

---

With this chapter, we begin the principal, main-dish meat and poultry recipes which are always the solid core of our everyday and party meals. Beef takes wonderfully to pressure cooking. When the steam is precisely and properly controlled (as in the following recipes), the beef comes out juicy and soft, full of flavor and nutrition, velvety on the tongue.

On the following pages, we offer the best steam-pressured, one-dish beef menus we know. They have been demanded by our family, over and over again, for the best part of thirty years. Hundreds of other recipes have been tried, have, after a time, worn out their welcome and been forgotten. These have stayed with us mainly because they are perfectly adaptable to the brilliant speed techniques of the pressure cooker. There is a solid pot roast, delicately touched with the flavor of fruits and olives, cooked in 45 minutes instead of the usual 4 or 5 hours. We marry beef to a sweet-sour sauce based on the red wine of Burgundy, or to a delicately sweet white wine, each dish completed in 15 minutes. There is an authentic Hungarian goulash for a party (15 minutes), the simplicity of short ribs uplifted by the aromatic interest of brandy (45 minutes), beef under the Spanish influence (17 minutes), chili for a party, under the influence of Texas (1½ hours), sauerbraten under the influence of the German Rhineland (45 minutes), beef sirloin on a string as they do it in France (1 hour), or in a *bollito misto* from the Alps of northern Italy (40 minutes).

There is also a trick recipe, a complete steak dinner for two, with an array of accompanying seasonal vegetables and a steam-baked dessert, all prepared in a single pressure cooker in under 15 minutes. You can hardly do better than that on a chaotically frenzied night!

Sweet-Sour Beefsteak in Burgundy

For 4

Cook under pressure at 10 lb for 15 minutes
(or at 15 lb for 11 minutes)

4 Tbs (60 g) butter
½ lb (225 g) fresh small mushrooms,
wiped clean, trimmed and sliced
¼ lb (115 g) salt pork, washed and diced
2 lb (1 kg) boneless, entirely lean beef,
either bottom or top round, rump or
sirloin, cut into squares of about 1½
inches (3.5 cm)
2 medium yellow onions, peeled and
chopped
12 small white boiler onions, peeled, left
whole
1 green pepper, cored and cut into ⅜-
inch (1 cm) strips
2 Tbs flour
About 2 cups (5 dl) red wine, preferably
an inexpensive Burgundy
Enough fresh leaves basil, chopped, to fill
1 Tbs, or 1 tsp dried
The same amount tarragon
The same amount thyme
1 clove garlic, peeled and finely minced
Salt, to your taste
Freshly ground black pepper, to your
taste
Up to ½ cup (1.25 dl) light soy sauce
Up to 4 Tbs (60 g) brown sugar
1½ tsp ground ginger
Up to ⅓ cup (80 ml) freshly squeezed
lemon juice
Enough fresh leaves parsley, chopped, to
fill 3 Tbs

Burgundy purists will scream, but we thrive on variety and we cannot see why the Burgundy should not once in a while be influenced by the Chinese. Let us call this the Peking Mandarin variation of Beef in Burgundy!

You will need a pressure cooker of at least 6-quart capacity. Set it, without its base rack, over medium-high frying heat, melt in it the butter and, as soon as it is hot, quickly sauté the sliced mushrooms. Keep moving them around with a wooden spoon until the hissing dies down to show that they have given up their water and absorbed some of the butter. Take them out with a slotted spoon and set aside. Add the diced salt pork to the pot and stir it around until the dice have given up their fat and are quite crisp. Lift them out with a slotted spoon and drain them on absorbent paper. In the hot fat remaining in the pot quickly brown the squares of beef, adding both the chopped and whole onions, and the green pepper strips. When the meat is brown, sprinkle on and work in the flour. Now hiss in enough of the red wine just to cover the beef. Add the basil, tarragon, thyme and garlic, with salt and pepper to taste. Put on the lid, bring the pressure up to 10 pounds and cook for exactly 15 minutes.

When the timer rings, turn off the heat, reduce the pressure immediately and stir in the mushrooms, ⅓ cup of the soy sauce, 3 tablespoons of the brown sugar, the ginger and ¼ cup of the lemon juice. Taste and adjust both the flavors and seasonings as needed. You can add saltiness with a few more drops of soy, sweetness with a teaspoon more brown sugar, or sourness with a drop or two more lemon juice. Serve in hot bowls with the crisp dice of salt pork and chopped parsley sprinkled on top.

A Good and Healthful Menu

An assortment of thinly sliced raw vegetables
Sweet-Sour Beefsteak in Burgundy
Boiled rice
Tomato slices with basil and watercress
Baked apples
Coffee or tea

The Ideal Wines

Luxurious

A French red Beaujolais from the district of Moulin-à-Vent
or
A California red Gamay Beaujolais from Sonoma

Everyday

A French red Côte Rotie from the Valley of the River Rhone
or
A California red Zinfandel from Sonoma

Superspeed Dinner for Two—All Together in a Single Cooker: Small Sirloin Steaks with Vegetables and Steam-Baked Cinnamon Peach Dessert

For 2
Cook under pressure at 15 lb for 3 minutes
     (or 10 lb for 4 minutes)

½ cup (115 g) coarse, natural, raw bran flakes––now generally available in supermarkets––or bread crumbs (optional)

1 whole egg, lightly beaten

2 Tbs milk

4 Tbs (60 g) butter

Salt, to your taste

Freshly ground black pepper, to your taste

2 single-portion sirloin steaks, each about ¾ inch (2 cm) thick

2 to 4 potatoes, according to size, peeled and sliced about ¾ inch (2 cm) thick

2 portions each of any 3 or 4 of the following vegetables, chosen according to season and availability: Brussels sprouts; medium carrots, scraped and halved lengthwise; green beans, topped and tailed; white or yellow turnips, peeled and cut into 1-inch (2.5 cm) cubes; yellow squash or zucchini, halved lengthwise; small yellow onions, peeled and left whole; 1-inch (2.5 cm) chunks of fresh fennel or white leeks

4 peach halves, stone removed, fresh if possible

1 tsp ground cinnamon

1 tsp ground ginger

4 tsp brown sugar

¾ cup (1.85 dl) red wine

8 tsp pure maple syrup

About 4 tsp filbert nutmeats, chopped

The way you arrange the various ingredients inside the pressure cooker is extremely important. The steaks can be coated with high-fiber bran for health and to seal in the juices. (Bran for cooking, distributed under a nationally known label, is now available in almost all supermarkets, or if you cannot find it, you can use bread crumbs.) You may vary the vegetables according to the season or your taste, but they must be capable of being cooked within the 3-minute time allowance. (See chart on page 190.) The peach halves must be tightly wrapped in foil to avoid any cross absorption of flavors. Finally, do not build up any of the ingredients of the upper level in such a way that they might block the vent in the lid. The top level of the food must be at least a couple of inches below the inside of the lid. An excellent natural sauce develops automatically in the bottom of the cooker. You may thicken it if you wish, but we think that would be a crime. Once you have prepared this dinner-for-two a couple of times, you will understand the principles involved and will be able to adapt it to any of your own combinations of alternative ingredients.

As to the size of the cooker, if you have reasonable appetites and can hold down on the amount of vegetables, you can prepare this in a 3-quart cooker. But if you have large appetites, it is safer to use a 6-quart. Never try to squeeze too much food into too small a cooker. You might cause a blockage of the vent pipe.

You will need a pressure cooker of either 2-quart or 6-quart capacity (see note, above). Spread out the bran flakes evenly across a dinner plate. Lightly beat together, with a fork, the egg and milk, then spread the egg mixture across a second dinner plate. Set the pressure cooker, without its base rack, onto medium-high frying heat and quickly melt the butter in it. Lightly salt and pepper each steak on both sides, then press each side and the edges down onto the bran flakes, then into the egg and milk, then back onto the bran flakes so as to crust each steak all around. The moment the butter is hot, nicely brown the steaks, then take them out and reserve. Next, sauté the potato slices until they too are browned. Turn off the heat. Spread out the potatoes into a neat, even layer and rest the 2 steaks on top. Place the base rack of the casserole on top of the steaks. Arrange the assorted vegetables on the rack, leaving space for the dessert packages.

Sprinkle the hollow of each of the 4 peach halves with a ¼ teaspoon each of the cinnamon and ginger, plus 1 teaspoon of the brown sugar. Keeping them cut side up, tightly wrap them, in pairs, in aluminum foil, so that you will have two flattish packages. Place these on the rack with the vegetables. Now carefully dribble the wine into the casserole—preferably pouring it down the side, so as not to disturb or wash away anything. Put on the lid, bring the pressure up to 15 pounds and cook for exactly 3 minutes.

The moment the timer rings, turn off the heat, reduce the pressure immediately and serve the meal. There will be an excellent natural gravy on the bottom. While you eat the first course, keep the peach packages warm in an oven at 165° F (75° C). Finally, open up the peach packages and dribble into each half 2 teaspoons of maple syrup and 1 teaspoon of the high-fiber, chopped filbert nutmeats.

A Good and Healthful Menu	Small Sirloin Steaks with Vegetables Steam-Baked Cinnamon Peach Dessert Coffee or gunpowder tea
The Ideal Wines	*Moderately Priced* A French red Beaujolais-Villages or A California red "Burgundy"

Beef Pot Roast with Mixed Fruits and Olives

For 4
Cook under pressure at 10 lb for 45 minutes
(or at 15 lb for 34 minutes)

3 lb (1.4 kg) pot roast, either eye roast, bottom or top round, rump or sirloin
2 dozen cocktail green olives stuffed with red pimento
3 oz (85 g) salt pork, washed and cubed
4 Tbs very good quality olive oil
⅓ cup (about 60 g) each of as many as possible of the following dried fruits: apple rings or slices, apricot halves, dates, figs, muscat grapes, peach halves, pear slices, softened prunes, or white seedless raisins
2 medium yellow onions, peeled and sliced
1 lemon, peeled, seeded and thinly sliced
2 cloves garlic, peeled and finely minced
Salt, to your taste
Freshly ground black pepper, to your taste
1 cup (2.5 dl) clear beef bouillon (see page 35, or use canned, cubed or dehydrated)
1 cup (2.5 dl) good red wine
4 or 5 glacéed orange slices (optional) for decoration

Dried fruits do much more than add their attractive and refreshing flavors to a beef pot roast; they also bring their above-average share of health-giving vitamins, minerals and high content of fibers. Some foolish people say that fruit and meat do not make a good marriage. What about the classic orange with duck, applesauce with goose, gooseberry jelly with lamb, cranberries with turkey, or red currants with venison?

You will need a minimum 6-quart pressure cooker. Wipe your pot roast clean and dry. Then, with a sharp knife, make small incisions all around the meat. Into each of them, push a stuffed olive and a cube of salt pork. Set the pressure cooker, without its base rack, on medium-high frying heat, pour in the oil and, when it is thoroughly hot, sear and brown the pot roast on all sides. Turn off the heat, lift out the beef, put the base rack into the pot, set the beef back on top of it and pack in around the meat all the dried fruits, onions, lemon slices, garlic, with salt and pepper to taste. Then pour the bouillon and red wine over the beef. Put on the lid, bring the pressure up to 10 pounds and cook for exactly 45 minutes.

When the timer rings, turn off the heat and let the pressure fall gradually of its own accord, usually in about 5 minutes. Lift out the beef and set it in the center of a warm serving platter. Decorate it with the glacéed orange slices, using, if necessary, tiny toothpicks. Take out the base rack and vigorously stir the sauce in the bottom of the pressure cooker, then taste it and adjust the seasoning, if necessary. We prefer to serve this lovely sauce as it is, with some of the fruits still lumpy. But certainly, if you prefer, you can run it all for a second or two through an electric blender or one of the chopping-churning machines to smooth the sauce.

A Good and Healthful Menu

Clear Asparagus Bouillon (see page 36)
Beef Pot Roast with Mixed Fruits and Olives
    Corn bread
Salad of green beans with raw mushrooms tossed with oil and
    vinegar
Ice cream
Coffee or Darjeeling tea

The Ideal Wines

Luxurious

A French red Beaujolais from the Village of Brouilly
    or
A California red Cabernet Sauvignon from the Alexander
    Valley

Everyday

A French red Beaujolais from the Village of Fleurie
    or
A California red Cabernet Sauvignon from Paicines in San
    Benito

Beef Stew in Soft White Wine with Celery-Ginger Dumplings

For 4
Cook under pressure at 10 lb for 15 minutes
*   (or at 15 lb for 12 minutes)*
Plus an extra 15 minutes for steaming dumplings

Up to ⅓ cup (80 ml) very good olive oil
2 lb (1 kg) boneless, entirely lean
    beefsteak, either bottom or top
    round, rump or sirloin, cut into 1½-
    inch (3.5 cm) squares
1 lb (450 g) boneless, entirely lean lamb,
    preferably from the leg, cut into 1¾-
    inch (4.5 cm) squares
2 medium yellow onions, peeled and
    fairly thickly sliced
2 cloves garlic, peeled and finely minced
½ tsp ground cinnamon
2 bay leaves, crumbled
Enough fresh leaves thyme, chopped, to
    fill 1 Tbs, or 1 tsp dried

There is no unbreakable rule that red beef must be cooked in red wine. Here, we use a soft, gently sweet white wine, with its small content of sugar firmly counterbalanced by the careful choice of aromatic herbs and spices and by the absorbent flavors of the vegetables and dumplings. The result, we think, is dramatic and memorable, with no hint of oversweetness. But you must be careful to maintain the balance of this recipe. Do not substitute other ingredients, or vary the amounts.

You will need a pressure cooker of at least 6-quart capacity. Set it, without its base rack, on medium-high frying heat, lubricate its bottom with 4 tablespoons of the oil and, as soon as it is thoroughly hot, quickly sauté the pieces of beef and lamb in batches, until they are nicely browned. Then lift them out with a slotted spoon and set aside.

Salt, to your taste
Freshly ground black pepper, to your
     taste
1 cup (2.5 dl) clear chicken bouillon (see
     page 35, or use canned)
1 cup (2.5 dl) softly sweet white wine
1 cup (225 g) trimmed and chunked green
     beans
1 cup (225 g) green peas
3 medium carrots, scraped and cut into
     ⅜-inch (1 cm) chunks

For the Dumplings

2 cups (450 g) sifted flour
2 tsp double-acting baking powder
¾ tsp salt
¼ tsp ground ginger
1 Tbs finely chopped parsley
1 Tbs finely grated onion
1 tsp celery seeds
1 Tbs butter
1 whole egg, lightly beaten
½ cup (1.25 dl) milk

Add more oil, if needed, and sauté the onions until they are lightly gilded. Turn off the heat and neatly pack all the meat in the bottom of the pressure cooker. Add the garlic, cinnamon, bay leaves, thyme, plus salt and pepper to taste. Pour in the bouillon and wine, put on the lid, bring up the pressure to 10 pounds and cook for exactly 15 minutes.

Meanwhile, mix the dough for the dumplings. Sift together the flour, baking powder, salt and ginger. Blend in the parsley, grated onion, celery seeds, and cut in the butter until the blend is crumbly. In a separate small mixing bowl quickly beat together the egg and milk. Now lightly and quickly work this liquid mix into the flour blend, just until the dry ingredients are moistened, no more. There should be minimum stirring and the dough should remain quite stiff.

When the timer rings, turn off the heat, reduce the pressure immediately and add to the pot the green beans, peas and carrots. Set the pressure cooker back on medium heat and bring the wine sauce up to a merry bubbling to provide a supply of steam. Use a long-handled metal spoon to drop the dumplings onto the surface of the bubbling stew. Dip the spoon for a second into the hot liquid, then immediately scoop up a neat spoonful of the dough and easily slide it off the spoon onto the top of the stew. Do not put in too many dumplings at once. Leave room between them for expansion. Put on the pressure cooker cover, but do not lock it into position. Do not put on the pressure control weight. Leave the steam vent open. In this enclosed space, steam the dumplings for 12 to 15 minutes (see testing instructions on page 55). As soon as the dumplings are done, serve them, with the stew, in very hot soup bowls.

A Good and Healthful Menu

Black and green olives
Beef Stew in Soft White Wine with Celery-Ginger Dumplings
Tossed green salad
Fresh fruit
Coffee or Earl Grey tea

The Ideal Wines

Luxurious

A French white Meursault from Burgundy
     or
A California white Pinot Chardonnay from the Napa Valley

Everyday

A French white Mâcon-Lugny from Burgundy
     or
A California white Pinot Chardonnay from Monterey

An Authentic Hungarian Goulash

For 4
Cook under pressure at 10 lb for 15 minutes
(or at 15 lb for 11 minutes)

Up to 4 Tbs (60 g) butter
¼ lb (115 g) salt pork, washed and diced
2 lb (1 kg) boneless, entirely lean
    beefsteak, either bottom or top
    round, rump or sirloin, cut into 1½-
    inch (3.5 cm) squares
6 to 8 medium yellow onions, according
    to size, peeled and sliced
Salt, to your taste
Up to 3 Tbs paprika, preferably imported,
    medium-sweet Hungarian
12 smallish potatoes, peeled, then stored
    underwater
2 medium green peppers, seeded and
    coarsely chopped
Up to 1½ cups (3.75 dl) dry white wine
Up to 3 Tbs tomato paste
1 cup (2.5 dl) sour cream
2 tsp whole caraway seeds

Goulash (or, more correctly, *gulyas*) is the Hungarian word for stew. This is a recipe from the Debrecen region, where it is made with beef. In the old city of Szeged, they do it with pork. In other parts of the country, they do it with lamb or veal. We spent our honeymoon, years ago, hiking across Hungary, and, at a farmhouse near Lake Balaton where we stayed overnight, an old woman who was a marvelous cook prepared this for us. Then, in the morning, with considerable language difficulty, she gave us her recipe. . . .

You will need a pressure cooker of at least 6 quarts. Set it, without its base rack, over medium-high frying heat, quickly melt in it 3 tablespoons of butter and add the dice of salt pork. When plenty of hot fat has been released, sauté the beef squares until they are lightly browned. As the operation proceeds, add all the sliced onions and work them in among the meat squares. Add the final tablespoon of butter, if necessary. Near the end of the sautéing, sprinkle with salt to taste, and 1 tablespoon of paprika. Depending on your taste for peppery spiciness, add more paprika, teaspoon by teaspoon. Put into the pot the potatoes and green pepper. In a small bowl, beat together ¾ cup of the wine and 2 tablespoons of the tomato paste. Then hiss this mixture into the pressure cooker. Check the liquid at the bottom. A good goulash should be almost dry, but not entirely so. Add more wine and tomato paste, if necessary, to make sure that there is at least ¼ inch of liquid across the bottom of the cooker. Put on the lid, bring the pressure up to 10 pounds and cook for exactly 15 minutes. Meanwhile, mix together ½ cup of the sour cream with the caraway seeds.

When the timer rings, turn off the heat, reduce the pressure immediately and gently work the sour cream–caraway mix into the goulash. Keep it on simmering heat for 2 or 3 minutes longer to warm the cream, then serve it at once in very hot bowls. There can be an extra dollop of sour cream on top, nicely colored with more sprinkled paprika.

A Good and Healthful Menu

A cold fruit soup
An Authentic Hungarian Goulash
    A crusty long loaf
Salad
Fresh apricot halves marinated in Hungarian apricot brandy
Coffee or tea

The Ideal Wines

Moderately Priced

A Hungarian red Villanyi "Burgundy"
    followed by
A white Tokaji Aszu (with the dessert)

Short Ribs Poached in Aromatic Brandy

For 4
Marinate the meat overnight
Cook under pressure at 10 lb for 30 minutes, plus 15 more
    (or at 15 lb for 22 minutes, plus 11 more)

4 lb (2 kg) lean, meaty beef short ribs, cut up by your butcher into practical serving pieces
1 medium yellow onion, peeled and chopped
1 bay leaf, crumbled
2 cloves garlic, peeled and finely minced
Enough fresh leaves parsley, chopped, to fill 2 Tbs
Enough fresh leaves thyme, chopped, to fill 1 Tbs, or 1 tsp dried
4 Tbs good olive oil
Freshly ground black pepper, to your taste
1 cup (2.5 dl) good California brandy
½ cup (1.25 dl) dry white wine
Salt, to your taste
4 medium carrots, scraped
4 medium potatoes, peeled and quartered and held in water
4 medium white turnips, peeled

The quality of the ribs you buy is a matter of importance to the success of this dish. Some ribs are very fatty. Some have comparatively little meat in relation to the size of the bone. Be warned. Tell your butcher that you want exceptional ribs— then make sure that you get them. Beef ribs are much the same as pork spareribs. When they are good, they are very, very good, especially when marinated in brandy and softened by the pressure casserole.

You will need at least a 6-quart pressure cooker and a largish, covered refrigerator storage bowl in which to marinate the beef overnight. Neatly arrange the rib pieces in this bowl and interleave them with the onion, bay leaf, garlic, parsley, thyme, 2 tablespoons of the oil, with pepper to taste. Wet it all down with the brandy, cover and set in the refrigerator overnight. First thing in the morning, turn the beef pieces around, so as to keep them moist on all sides.

When you are ready to start preparing the dish, lift out the rib pieces and pat them dry. Hold the marinade. Set the pressure cooker, without its base rack, on fairly high frying heat and lubricate its bottom with the remaining 2 tablespoons of olive oil. When the oil is good and hot, sauté the rib pieces until they are well browned on all sides. Then hiss in the marinade, with all its solid ingredients, plus the wine and salt to taste. The moment it all comes to the boil, put on the lid, bring the pressure up to 10 pounds and cook for exactly 30 minutes.

When the timer rings, turn off the heat, reduce the pressure immediately and put into the cooker the carrots, potatoes and turnips. Bring the pressure back up to 10 pounds and cook for a final 15 minutes.

As soon as the timer rings again, reduce the pressure immediately. Take the ribs and vegetables out of the cooker and skim any excess fat from the surface of the sauce. Serve at once in very hot bowls.

A Good and Healthful Menu

Tiny Cocktail Marinated Mushrooms (see page 50)
Short Ribs Poached in Aromatic Brandy
    with carrots, turnips and potatoes
Green salad vinaigrette
Vanilla ice cream
Coffee or tea

The Ideal Wines

Moderately Priced

A French red Hermitage from the Valley of the River Rhone
    or
A California red Zinfandel from the Napa Valley

Beef as They Do It in Barcelona

For 4
Marinate the beef overnight
Cook under pressure at 15 lb for 17 minutes
    (or at 10 lb for 23 minutes)

In the narrow streets of Barcelona around the great food market, the Mercado de San José, in small restaurants with marble-topped tables, sawdust on the floor and the scent of garlic in the air, this is what a food merchant is likely to order for his lunch.

3 lb (1.4 kg) boneless, entirely lean beefsteak, either bottom or top round, rump or sirloin, cut by your butcher into 1½-inch (3.5 cm) squares
2 medium yellow onions, peeled and sliced
2 cloves garlic, peeled and finely minced
½ fresh lemon, peeled, seeded and thinly sliced
2 whole bay leaves, crumbled
Enough fresh leaves basil, chopped, to fill 1 Tbs, or 1 tsp dried
The same amount thyme
Up to 2 cups (5 dl) clear beef bouillon (see page 35, or use canned)
2 cups (5 dl) good red wine, preferably a Spanish Rioja
6 medium potatoes, peeled and reserved underwater
4-oz (110 g) jar Spanish roasted red pimento, chunked
12 pitted Spanish black olives
12 Spanish pitted green olives
12 pitted, softened prunes
Salt, to your taste
Freshly ground black pepper, to your taste

You will need a pressure cooker of at least a 6-quart capacity, and a covered refrigerator storage bowl in which to marinate the beef overnight. Neatly pack the pieces into the bowl, interleaving between them the onions, garlic, lemon slices, bay leaves, basil and thyme. Wet it all down with 1 cup of the bouillon and the red wine. Refrigerate overnight. First thing in the morning, turn over the pieces of beef to keep them moist on all sides.

When you are ready to start preparing the dish, turn the entire contents of the marination bowl into the pressure cooker, without its base rack. Heat up, not too quickly, to the boil, put on the lid, bring the pressure up to 15 pounds and cook for exactly 17 minutes. Meanwhile, boil the potatoes in slightly salted water until they are just soft through, then hold them until the main dish is ready.

When the timer rings, turn off the heat and reduce the pressure immediately. Then add to the cooker the pimento, black olives, green olives, prunes, potatoes, plus salt and pepper to taste. Heat it up, uncovered, to simmering on top of the stove, stirring with a wooden spoon gently, so as not to break up anything. It will usually take 10 minutes to heat completely through. If the sauce is too much reduced, add a bit more of the remaining bouillon. Serve in very hot bowls, preferably pottery.

A Good and Healthful Menu

Cold Boiled Shrimp with Garlic Sauce (see page 41)
Beef as They Do It in Barcelona
Green salad with small cubes of Spanish Manchego cheese
Spanish flan custard
Coffee or tea

The Ideal Wines

Moderately Priced

A Spanish red "Sangre de Toro" from the Panades district of Catalonia
    or
A California red Pinot Noir from Monterey

Beef Flank Steak Stewed with Pork Sausages
For 2
Cook under pressure at 10 lb for 35 minutes
   (or at 15 lb for 26 minutes)

2 Tbs olive oil, or alternative
1 lb (450 g) approx. beef flank steak, all
   fat trimmed off, then cut into 1½-
   inch (3.5 cm) squares
4 full-sized (or 8 small) pork sausages
1 medium yellow onion, peeled and
   sliced
1 frozen package lima beans
2 fairly tart cooking apples, peeled, cored
   and sliced
1 clove garlic, finely minced
1 tsp Worcestershire sauce
Salt, to your taste
Freshly ground black pepper, to your
   taste
1 cup (2.5 dl) red wine

During the inflationary years, flank steak became, for a while, one of the most popular of the "inexpensive cuts." It has been served to us in at least twenty different ways—usually rolled and stuffed. We have almost always found the meat tasteless and tough. But *not* in this way. The superheated steam makes the beef as soft as lamb, while the spicy pork sausages, the creamy lima beans and the aromatic sauce add their complementary and complimentary flavors to the meat.

You will need a pressure cooker of at least 3-quart capacity. Heat it up, without its base rack, to medium-high frying temperature, lubricate the bottom with the oil and, when it is good and hot, quickly brown the squares of beef on all sides. When they are done, lift out the meat squares with a slotted spoon and set them on absorbent paper. Quickly brown the pork sausages, then lift them out, cut them into 1-inch-long (2.5-cm-long) chunks and set them on the absorbent paper. Pour off all the fat from the pressure cooker except about 1 tablespoon. In this, quickly sauté the onion slices until they are just limp and transparent. Turn off the heat. Neatly pack into the pressure cooker the beef squares and sausage chunks. Add the lima beans, apples, garlic, Worcestershire sauce, plus salt and pepper to taste. Finally, pour in the red wine, put on the lid, bring the steam pressure up to 10 pounds and cook for exactly 35 minutes.

When the timer rings, turn off the heat and let the steam pressure reduce gradually of its own accord. Serve the dish in hot, wide bowls.

A Good and Healthful Menu

Tiny Cocktail Marinated Mushrooms (see page 50)
Beef Flank Steak Stewed with Pork Sausages
Corn bread
Salad of romaine lettuce, sliced avocado, diced onion and green pepper, bits of anchovy, all dressed with oil and vinegar
Fresh fruit of the season
Coffee or tea

The Ideal Wines

Moderately Priced

A French red Côtes du Rhone
   or
A California red Cabernet Sauvignon from Santa Clara

The Greatest and Most Authentic Texas Chili con Carne

For 4
Cook under pressure at 10 lb for 65 minutes
(or at 15 lb for 49 minutes)
Plus oven baking for 30 minutes longer

2 cups (450 g) dried red chili beans, or
    red kidney beans
5½ quarts (5½ liters) clear beef bouillon
    (see page 35, or use canned)
3 cups (7.5 dl) dry white wine
2 tsp ground cumin*
1 tsp ground allspice*
2 tsp dried, crumbled oregano*
4 to 6 Tbs chili powder, preferably the
    best Mexican style, the precise
    amount to your taste
2 Tbs paprika, preferably medium-sweet
    imported Hungarian
½ cup (1.25 dl) rendered, nicely browned
    bacon grease, or beef suet, or other
    alternative fat
6 medium yellow onions, peeled and
    sliced
3 lb (1.4 kg) boneless, entirely lean,
    bottom or top round steak, cut into
    ½-inch (1.2 cm) cubes
2 medium green peppers, deseeded and
    chopped
3 cloves garlic, peeled and finely minced
Salt, to your taste
3 to 6 Tbs masa harina, a form of corn
    flour, generally available in Mexican
    or Spanish groceries, or a flour and
    wine mix (see opposite)
2 Tbs red wine vinegar
2 or more dried red hot chilis, soaked in
    boiling water for about 15 minutes,
    strictly optional, according to your
    taste

* If you prefer to grind your own spices, put 3 tsp of
cumin seeds, 2 tsp allspice berries, and 2 tsp dried
crumbled oregano into your electric spice mill or
hand mortar and powder them.

This is our pressure cooker adaptation of the most luxurious chili we have ever known—a private and secret recipe given us, years ago, by President Eisenhower. If you cannot find the masa harina (which all true Texans use to thicken the sauce), make a creamy mixture of about 6 tablespoons flour and about ½ cup white wine, then stir it in, tablespoon by tablespoon, until the chili achieves a good solid body. You may not, of course, need to use the full amount of the thickener. Stop as soon as the chili is as you like it.

You will need a minimum 8-quart pressure cooker, a large fry or sauté pan and a 5-quart lidded pot to go into the oven. Wash and pick over the beans, then put them into the pressure cooker without the base rack, cover them with 4½ quarts of the bouillon and 2 cups of the wine, put on the lid, bring the pressure up to 10 pounds and cook for precisely 65 minutes. Meanwhile, quickly blend the aromatic chili mix by mixing together completely the cumin, allspice, oregano, 4 tablespoons of the chili powder and the paprika. At this point, start preheating your oven to 350° F (175° C) and set the lidded pot in it to warm up.

Next, prepare the beef. Place your large fry or sauté pan on medium-high frying heat, melt in it the fat and, as soon as it is reasonably hot, put in the onions and fry them until they are just translucent, but not browned. Now add the beef, separating the pieces and lightly browning them on all sides. The moment the beef is browned, work into it the chili powder mix, the green peppers, and the garlic, with salt to taste. Then begin working in, tablespoon by tablespoon, the masa harina (or alternative flour and wine mix), sprinkling it evenly over the top of the beef, then working it down with a wooden spoon, until it absorbs and combines with the fat to form a thickish paste. This may require anything from 3 to 6 tablespoons of the masa. Now begin wetting down the beef with equal parts of the remaining bouillon and wine, ¼ cup by ¼ cup, working it evenly into the masa paste, so as to dilute it. Add enough liquid so that the whole thing is gloppy. Also add the red wine vinegar. Keep it all gently simmering, uncovered, for about 10 minutes, to develop the flavors. This is the time to adjust the peppery heat of the chili to your liking. Work in, if you wish, more chili powder. If you want it really hot, pick one or more of the red hot chilis out of their soaking water. Skin, seed and mash them, then begin working this fiery paste into the meat mixture, adding as much heat as you can stand. When the 10 minutes of simmering is completed, turn off the heat, take the pot out of the oven and turn the entire contents of the sauté pan into it. Cover and put it back into the oven until the beans are ready.

When the timer rings for the beans, turn off the heat and let the pressure reduce gradually, of its own accord, usually in about 5 minutes. Drain the beans and put them into the chili pot as the top layer. Put the pot, again covered, back in the oven and continue the baking for at least 30 minutes—the longer the better. Check after 15 minutes by opening up a hole down the center of the beans, with a wooden spoon, to make sure that the chili beef at the bottom has not dried out. It should continue to be gloppy. If not, quickly bring to the boil some of the remaining bouillon and/or wine and add it to the pot. When the baking is complete, the chili should still be a bit runny. If the sauce is too thin, you can always work in some extra masa harina. If you wish, skim off any excess fat from the top surface. Serve the chili, preferably in hot pottery bowls, now with beans and beef mixed evenly together. Always remember that chili is even better when reheated the next day.

A Good and Healthful Menu

Guacamole salad
Chili con Carne
   with tortillas
Guavas in syrup
Coffee or tea

The Ideal Drink

A light Mexican beer

Real Rhineland Sauerbraten

For 4
Marinate overnight
Cook under pressure at 10 lb for 45 minutes
   (or at 15 lb for 34 minutes)

A solid chunk of about 3 lb (1.4 kg)
   boneless lean beef, either eye roast,
   top round, rump or sirloin
2 cups (5 dl) beef bouillon (see page 35, or
   use canned)
1 cup (2.5 dl) red wine vinegar
3 whole bay leaves
8 whole cloves
1 clove garlic, peeled and minced
2 Tbs dry mustard
Enough parsley, chopped, to fill 3 Tbs
2 fresh sage leaves, chopped, or ½ tsp
   dried
Enough fresh leaves thyme, chopped, to
   fill 1 Tbs, or 1 tsp dried

Around the sweeping bends of the great River Rhine, there are, on both banks, small restaurants with terraces that seem to hang out over the water. On their menus, sauerbraten is always the favorite festive dish—the tanginess of the vinegar balanced by the smooth richness of the gingered sour cream sauce.

Any remaining meat may be gently reheated the next day and will probably taste even better. Or you can slice it thinly for cold cuts or a picnic—the slices laid on crisp lettuce leaves, with dabs of the almost-jellied sauce, a garnish of small dill pickles and German mustard on the side.

You will need a pressure cooker of at least a 6-quart capacity. Wipe the beef and put it into a lidded refrigerator storage bowl. Mix together in a saucepan the bouillon, vinegar, bay leaves, cloves, garlic, dry mustard, parsley, sage, thyme, plus pepper to taste. Bring to the boil and at once pour over the

Freshly ground black pepper, to your
    taste
6 Tbs all-purpose flour
6 Tbs (90 g) sweet butter
4 medium yellow onions, peeled
8 whole carrots, scraped
½ calf's foot, cut up by your butcher
½ cup (1.25 dl) dry white wine
¼ cup (60 ml) good brandy
Salt, to your taste
2 tsp ground ginger, or 1 Tbs fresh ginger
    root, minced
1 cup (2.5 dl) sour cream
12 good gingersnaps, crumbled

beef, turning it so as to soak it on all sides. Let it marinate, covered, in the refrigerator overnight, turning it and basting it in the morning.

When you are ready to start cooking, take out the beef and dry it, holding the marinade. Place the pressure cooker, without its base rack, on medium-high frying heat, melt in it the butter and, when it is hot, quickly sear the beef on all sides until it is walnut brown. Take out the beef and work the flour into the butter and juices until it is all quite smooth. Now, stirring continuously, gradually add the marinade and let it come just to the boiling point. Put back the beef and place around it the onions, carrots and the pieces of calf's foot. Pour the wine and brandy over the beef, plus salt to taste. Put on the lid, bring up the pressure to 10 pounds and cook for 45 minutes. Meanwhile, blend the ginger into the sour cream and set aside.

When the timer rings, turn off the heat, and let the pressure reduce gradually of its own accord, lift the beef out of the pot and keep it warm, covered, with the carrots and onions in an oven at 175° F (80° C). Remove the pieces of calf's foot from the pressure cooker, discard the bones, dice the gelatinous meat and put it back into the sauce. (If you want to be fussy, also pick out and discard the whole cloves. We do not bother.) Now stir into the sauce the crumbled gingersnaps and gingered sour cream. Heat it all up to just below boiling. Do not let it boil. Pour the hot sauce over the beef and serve it at once.

A Good and Healthful Menu

A bacon and Swiss cheese quiche
Real Rhineland Sauerbraten
    with macaroni shells, potato dumplings or saffron rice
Salty rye bread
A salad of young spinach leaves,
    with chopped walnuts, diced
    hard-boiled eggs and a light
    vinaigrette
German pfeffernuss
Coffee or tea and brandy

The Ideal Wines

Luxurious

A German white Bernkasteler from the Moselle Valley
    or
A California white Pinot Chardonnay from the Napa Valley

Everyday

A German white Bernkasteler Riesling from the Moselle Valley
    or
A California white Pinot Chardonnay from the Paicines in San Benito

Beef Sirloin on a String

For 4

Prepare the broth the day before

Cook under pressure at 10 lb for 45 minutes, plus 15, plus 10 more

(or at 15 lb for 33 minutes, plus 11, plus 8 more)

2 lb (1 kg) quite-inexpensive, lean soup beef

2 lb (1 kg) beef soup bones, cut into pieces by the butcher

3 medium carrots, scraped, left whole

3 white leeks, carefully desanded, left whole

1 stalk celery, chunked, with its leaves chopped

1 largish yellow onion, peeled, with 4 whole cloves stuck in it

1 medium white turnip, peeled, left whole

2 cloves garlic, peeled and sliced

2 whole bay leaves

Enough fresh leaves of basil, chopped, to fill 1 Tbs, or 1 tsp dried

The same amount tarragon

The same amount thyme

Salt, to your taste

Freshly ground black pepper, to your taste

3 lb (1.4 kg) piece of top-quality roasting beef, well shaped, squarish, boneless, entirely lean, top round, rump or sirloin, etc., firmly tied with string and with a loop as a handle for lifting or lowering it

2½ lb (1.1 kg) good boiling potatoes, peeled and reserved underwater

Additional vegetables, 2 or 3 of the following, as available: 8 white boiling onions, peeled; 2 medium parsnips, scraped; a small head of cabbage, quartered; a fennel bulb, quartered

Enough fresh parsley, chopped, to fill 2 Tbs

2 bunches fresh watercress, for sprigs with which to garnish the beef

Dill pickles for garnish

Horseradish, to serve with the beef

Coarse crystal salt, to serve with the beef

This is one of the great, classic country dishes of France and it is superb in any language. The timing is all important. You must know the exact weight of your piece of beef and pressure-cook it at 10 pounds for precisely 5 minutes per pound. Then, when you carve the thin slices, it will be beautifully rare inside and will release a gorgeous, natural juice. Why is the string so important? Easy. If you were to lift it out by sticking a fork into it, you would release the juices too soon and they would be lost into the soup. The string is the essential handle to the meat. Remember that you must prepare the broth the day before.

You will need a large pressure cooker of a minimum 6-quart capacity. Put into it, without its base rack, the soup beef and bones and cover them with 3 quarts of cold water. Heat it up to boiling, skimming off any scum. Then add the carrots, leeks, celery, onion with cloves, turnip, garlic, bay leaves, basil, tarragon, thyme, with salt and pepper to taste. Put on the lid, bring the pressure up to 10 pounds and cook for exactly 45 minutes.

When the timer rings, turn off the heat and let the pressure reduce gradually, of its own accord, usually in 4 to 5 minutes. This completes the making of the bouillon. Let it cool, uncovered, then store it, with all its solid ingredients, in the refrigerator. After a few hours, it will have a layer of hardened fat across its top surface. Lift it off and get rid of this fat.

When you are ready to cook, take the bouillon out of the refrigerator, remove every scrap of fat and strain it. (The meat and vegetables will be pretty well washed out, but parts of them can often be used later to add, say, some texture to a salad.) Pour the liquid back into the pressure cooker and heat it up to simmering. You must now know the precise weight of your main piece of beef. It is to be pressure-cooked in the bouillon for exactly 5 minutes per pound. Even 5 minutes too long may make the beef tough. Lift your chunk of beef by its string loop and lower it gently into the boiling bouillon. Put on the lid, bring up the pressure to 10 pounds and, if the piece of beef is exactly 3 pounds, cook it for exactly 15 minutes. Warm up a large serving platter to receive it.

When the timer rings, turn off the heat and let the pressure reduce gradually, of its own accord. Lift out the piece of beef by its string and keep it warm on its serving platter, covered by a piece of aluminum foil, in an oven at 170° F (75° C). At once put the potatoes and your eating vegetables into the still-bubbling bouillon in the pressure cooker. Put on the lid, again bring the pressure up to 10 pounds and cook everything for exactly 10 minutes.

When the timer again rings, turn off the heat and reduce the pressure immediately. Lift out all the vegetables with a slotted spoon and arrange them around the beef on the serving platter. Remove the string before bringing the platter to the dining table. Carve the beef in thinnish slices. You will be surprised how beautifully juicy and tender the beef is inside. You can begin the meal with bowls or cups of the gorgeously perfumed bouillon. Then serve the sliced beef and its vegetables, sprinkled with chopped fresh parsley, plus sprigs of bright green watercress, dill pickles, coarse crystal salt and horseradish. A meal to remember in your dreams!

A Good and Healthful Menu

The clear beef bouillon from the boiling
Beef Sirloin on a String
   with assorted vegetables, dill pickles, grated horseradish
   and coarse crystal salt
A long crusty loaf of French bread
A platter of cheeses with fresh fruits
Café filtre or tea

The Ideal Wines

Luxurious

A French red Châteauneuf-du-Pape from the Valley of the River Rhone
   or
A California red Pinot Noir from Monterey

Everyday

A French pink Tavel from the Rhone
   or
A California pink Grignolino Rosé from the Napa Valley

Italian Boiled Dinner of Mixed Meats

For 4
Cook under pressure at 10 lb for 22 minutes, plus 18 more
   (or at 15 lb for 16 minutes, plus 13 more)

You will need about 4 lb (2 kg) of roughly ¾ lb (340 g) each of any 4 or 5 of the following meats: a piece of well-smoked raw ham, a similar piece of lean beef, the same of veal, a couple of calves' feet, Italian cotechino sausage (from Italian butchers), some chicken and/or turkey breasts, a calf's tongue, some corned beef . . . your choice is very wide

Up to 4 quarts (4 liters) clear beef or chicken bouillon (see page 35, or use canned)

Salt, to your taste

What the New England boiled dinner is to America and the *pot-au-feu* is to France, the *bollito misto* (mixed boil) is to the Alpine region of northern Italy. Some visitors to that lovely area pass over the *bollito* in local restaurants, jumping to the conclusion that boiled meats must be dull. They are foolish and quite wrong. The variety of mixed meats, the range of various vegetables, the several different sauces, even the choice of different mustards, all make the Italian mixed boil one of the greatest of party dishes. The huge serving platter, with its many different colors and shapes of good things to eat, is a sight to behold and remember. Traditionally, it is a long, slow dish to prepare. This is our speeded-up pressure cooker version.

You will need a large pressure cooker to hold at least 8 quarts. Trim the various pieces of meat, cutting off any excess

Freshly ground black pepper, to your
  taste
An assortment of vegetables, any 3 or 4 of
  the following, as available: 6 smallish
  potatoes, peeled and halved; 4
  smallish onions, peeled; a medium
  turnip, peeled; 4 medium carrots,
  scraped; a small head of cabbage,
  quartered

Optional garnishing accompaniments:

A batch of our garlic sauce (see page 41)
A batch of our pili pili hot sauce (see
  page 42)
A batch of our tomato sauce (see page 38)
At least 2 kinds of imported mustard,
  say, a French blend from Dijon and a
  German from Düsseldorf
Coarse crystal salt

fat and then neatly packing them into the pressure cooker, without its base rack. Cover the meats with enough of the bouillon to rise about 1 inch (2.5 cm) above the top surface of the packed meats, but the liquid must remain at least 2 inches (5 cm) below the inside of the lid. Taste the bouillon, adding salt and pepper, if needed. Put on the lid, bring the pressure up to 10 pounds and cook for exactly 22 minutes.

When the timer rings, turn off the heat, reduce the pressure immediately and lift out the various pieces of meat with a slotted spoon. Set them on a large, heated serving platter and keep them warm, lightly covered with aluminum foil, in an oven at 170° F (75° C). Put the assorted vegetables into the still-bubbling bouillon, put on the lid, bring the pressure up to 10 pounds and cook the vegetables for precisely 18 minutes.

As soon as the timer again rings, turn off the heat, lower the pressure immediately and lift out the vegetables with a slotted spoon, placing them handsomely around the meats on the serving platter.

A Good and Healthful Menu

Small bowls or cups of the beautiful boiling bouillon
Italian Boiled Dinner of Mixed Meats
  with assorted vegetables and various sauces, imported mustards and coarse crystal salt
A Pot of Sweet-and-Sour Lima Beans (page 67)
Granita di limone—Italian lemon sherbet
Caffè espresso or tea

The Ideal Wines

Luxurious

An Italian red Gattinara from the Piedmont
  or
A California red Cabernet Sauvignon from the Napa Valley

Everyday

An Italian red Valpolicella from the Venice region
  or
A red "California Burgundy"

French Daube of Beef from Provence

For 4
Marinate the meat overnight
Cook under pressure at 10 lb for 22 minutes
  (or at 15 lb for 17 minutes)

About 2 lb (1 kg) boneless, entirely lean
  beef, either bottom or top round,
  rump or sirloin, cut into 1½-inch (3.5
  cm) squares

This is the way the farmers' wives prepare beef for Sunday dinner all across southern France. It is so simple, so good, that we are foolish if we do not adopt it for ourselves. You do have to marinate the meat in wine overnight, but that takes only a couple of minutes of active work to prepare it. Also, you do need to get from your butcher a piece of bacon rind large

3 medium yellow onions, peeled, 1 stuck
    with 2 whole cloves, the other 2
    sliced
1 clove garlic, finely minced
2 bay leaves
Enough fresh leaves thyme, chopped, to
    fill 1 Tbs, or 1 tsp dried
Freshly ground black pepper, to your
    taste
¼ cup (60 ml) good olive oil
¼ cup (60 ml) good brandy
2 cups (5 dl) good dry white wine
1 square bacon rind (see opposite)
½ lb (225 g) smoky, raw ham, cut into ½-
    inch (1.2 cm) cubes
Enough fresh leaves parsley, chopped, to
    fill ⅓ cup (80 ml)
Enough fresh leaves basil, chopped, to fill
    1 Tbs, or 1 tsp dried
The same amount tarragon
2 medium carrots, scraped and sliced
2 medium tomatoes, chunked
½ cup (115 g) pitted black olives
Salt, to your taste

enough to cover the bottom of your pressure cooker. If you cannot get it, then either cover the bottom of your cooker with rashers of streaky bacon, or dot it with dice of salt pork. In France, in the old days, the pot used to simmer on the back of the stove for 12 hours. Our pressure cooker version is done in less than half an hour.

You will need a pressure cooker of at least 6-quart capacity and, also, a fairly large, covered refrigerator storage bowl in which to marinate the meat overnight. Neatly pack the squares of beef into it and interleave them with the sliced onions, the garlic, bay leaves, crumbled, the thyme, plus pepper to taste. Dribble over the meat 3 tablespoons of the oil, the brandy and wine. Store in the refrigerator, covered, overnight. First thing in the morning, turn the squares of beef around, so as to keep them moist on all sides.

The following day, when you are ready to start preparing the dish, remove the base rack from your pressure cooker and lay flat on its bottom the piece of bacon rind or its alternative. On top of the rind, turn into the pot the entire contents of the marinating bowl, including the beef, wine and all the other aromatic ingredients. Add the ham, the onion stuck with cloves, the remaining tablespoon of oil, parsley, basil, tarragon, carrots, tomatoes, olives, with salt to taste. Put on the lid, bring the pressure up to 10 pounds and cook for exactly 22 minutes.

When the timer rings, turn off the heat and reduce the pressure immediately. Remove and discard the bacon rind and the 2 whole cloves. Then serve at once on very hot plates with the remaining parsley sprinkled over the top.

A Good and Healthful Menu

Tiny Cocktail Marinated Mushrooms (see page 50)
Daube of Beef Provençale
    A crusty loaf of French bread
Salad of thinly sliced purple onions with watercress, tossed
    with oil and vinegar
A platter of French cheeses with fruit
Coffee or tea

The Ideal Wines

Luxurious

A French red Cahors from the Southwest
    or
A California red Cabernet Sauvignon from the Napa Valley

Everyday

A French red Beaujolais-Villages from Burgundy
    or
A California red Gamay-Beaujolais from Sonoma

Pressure-Fried Marinated Medallions of Round Steak

For 4
Marinate 8–12 hours or overnight
Pressure-fry at 5 lb for 4 minutes

1½ lb (675 g) lean round steak, cut by butcher into uniform rounds, 2 inches (5 cm) across, ½ inch (1.2 cm) thick

½ batch of the Aromatic Marinade recipe on page 43

5 cups (1.25 liters) vegetable oil

Salt, to your taste

Freshly ground black pepper, to your taste

Warning: This recipe can only be prepared in the specially designed pressure fryer-cooker described on page 21. Pressure frying should never be attempted in a standard pressure cooker, which does not have the proper lid closure for this kind of superspeed frying.

Since the browning and frying of the meat goes forward so quickly, it is most important that all the little rounds of beef should be the right (and the same) size and thickness. You must make sure that your butcher does his cutting accurately, and then you must do your pounding evenly and steadily on each piece. For the preliminary, very brief browning, the oil must be at exactly 350° F (175° C), so you should use an accurate deep-frying thermometer.

After you get to know this recipe, you can experiment with different cuts of beef at different price levels: bottom round, chuck, flank steak, etc. The forceful combination of the pounding of the fibers of the meat and the very quick application of heat will tenderize even the toughest cuts.

Always use the exact amount of oil indicated. If you try to run the pressure fryer half empty (or overfull), the timing will be different. After the experience of preparing this recipe once or twice, you will learn how to adjust for the variations. The whole operation is very flexible. When the timer rings at the end of the pressure frying, you can depressurize quickly by at once turning off the heat and then inserting the tines of a two-pronged fork into the hole in the pressure regulator weight and tilting it slightly, so that the steam will hiss out quickly. No need to remove the regulator. As soon as the steam stops hissing, take off the lid of the cooker.

You will need a 4-quart, specially designed pressure fryer of the type described on page 21. (Do not, under any circumstances, attempt this recipe in a standard pressure cooker, which does not have the proper lid closure for pressure frying.) Place the medallion steaks, between several thicknesses of wax paper, on a heavy wooden board and pound them on both sides with a meat hammer, using even, steady strokes, until they have nicely softened and have expanded to about 2½ inches (6.5 cm) diameter. Put them into a covered refrigerator storage bowl, pour over them the aromatic marinade and leave them to marinate in the refrigerator for 8 to 12 hours, or overnight. When convenient to do so, turn the steaks over, so that both sides are equally soaked.

When you are ready to start cooking the beef, put exactly the 5 cups of oil into the pressure fryer, set it over high heat and, with the help of a deep-frying thermometer, bring it up to 350° F (175° C). Watch it carefully. The oil heats up very fast and can easily overheat. Meanwhile, remove the steaks from the marinade and dry them thoroughly. Also, turn on your oven to "keep warm" 170° F (75° C) and set in it a serving platter to heat up. When the oil is at the right temperature, gently lower into it, using a slotted spoon or tongs, the first 4 steaks. Let them brown and seal for exactly 1 minute. Then put on the lid, with the pressure regulator already in place. The working pressure of 5 pounds will be reached in less than 1 minute and the regulator will begin to hiss and/or jiggle. Set the timer for 4 minutes. Turn down the heat to medium and adjust it to keep the hissing and/or jiggling going gently.

The moment the timer rings, turn off the heat, use the tines of a fork to tilt the pressure regulator to an angle, so that the steam hisses out fast. (There is no need to remove the regulator.) As soon as the hissing stops and the pressure is down, take off the lid, lift out the steaks, drain and dry them on absorbent paper, salt and pepper them to your taste, then keep them warm on the serving platter in the oven. Pressure-fry the remaining steaks in exactly the same way. When they are all done, serve them at once.

A Good and Healthful Menu   A chicken liver pâté with dry Melba toast
Medallions of Round Steak
    with spinach puree and baked potatoes
Beet and celery salad
Baba au rhum
Indian Assam tea

The Ideal Wines   *Luxurious*

A rich red French Beaune from Burgundy
    or
A rich California Petite Sirah from the Livermore Valley

Everyday

A red French St. Joseph from the Rhone Valley
    or
A red California Zinfandel from the Alexander Valley

Chapter 10

ONE-DISH MEALS WITH
LAMB

*Including Speed Meals Prepared in One Hour
or Less from Kitchen Start to Serving at Table*

We think that lamb is not prepared in the United States with as much variety as it should be—as it is, in fact, in Europe. For this reason, we offer, below, a modernized, speeded-up version of a French-style *blanquette d'agneau*, chunks of poached lamb in a richly creamy sauce, but, in the low-high cuisine method, without cream. There is, also, a fast version of the famous, classic French *navarin* of spring lamb, an irresistibly good, steamed stew of meat and fresh garden vegetables. Lamb seems to take exceptionally well to the pressure cooker. The texture remains light, yet firmly chewy and, with proper trimming, there need be virtually no fat. Of all the standard meats, lamb is among the easiest to handle in the pressure cooker. As a starter, try the first recipe, following, a complete lamb chop dinner for two, including seasonal vegetables and a steam-baked banana custard dessert—all prepared, cooked and served within 15 minutes.

Superspeed Dinner for Two All Together in a Single Cooker: Glazed Lamb Chops with Grapes and Seasonal Vegetables—with Dessert of Steam-Baked Banana-Brandy Custard
For 2
*Cook under pressure at 15 lb for 3 minutes
(or at 10 lb for 4 minutes)*

For the Banana-Brandy Custard Dessert

1 egg
¾ cup (1.85 dl) light cream, warmed until
    it feels hot to the tip of your finger,
    but not scalding

How you assemble the various parts in the pressure cooker is very important, to avoid any crossover of flavors between the meat, the vegetables and the delicate custard dessert. Wrap the custard cups completely and tightly in aluminum foil (see basic notes on custards on page 174). Also, use a large enough pressure cooker so that the ingredients on the upper level do not come up too close to the inside of the lid. Always leave

95

1 Tbs sugar
Pinch salt
¾ oz (22 ml) brandy
½ banana
1 tsp butter

Two ½-inch-thick (1.2 cm) large loin or
    shoulder lamb chops, or four ½-
    inch-thick (1.2 cm) smaller rib chops,
    with almost all fat trimmed off and
    the edges slashed every inch, to
    avoid curling
6 Tbs (90 g) butter
1 medium yellow onion, peeled and
    chopped
Salt, to your taste
Freshly ground black pepper, to your
    taste
½ cup (1.25 dl) orange juice
½ cup (1.25 dl) pineapple juice
¼ tsp ground cinnamon
2 cloves garlic, peeled and finely minced
For the vegetables, choose any 3 or 4 of
    the following, according to the
    season, making sure to cut each
    precisely to the indicated size:
  4 beets, peeled and sliced ¼ inch (7
      mm) thick
  2 to 4 (according to size) broccoli stems,
      the tough parts cut off and the
      stems deeply slashed into quarters
  6 heads of Brussels sprouts, coarse
      outer leaves and tough stalks
      trimmed, the heads left whole
  4 medium young carrots, scraped and
      trimmed, halved lengthwise
  4 medium potatoes, peeled and cut into
      ⅜-inch (1 cm) slices
  2 yellow squash, halved lengthwise
  2 zucchini, halved lengthwise
  6 oz (170 g) fresh mushrooms, wiped
      clean, trimmed and sliced
⅔ cup (150 g) seedless grapes, washed
½ cup (1.25 dl) sour cream

A Good and Healthful Menu

about 2 inches (5 cm) of space between the topmost ingredients and the inside of the lid.

As to the size of the cooker, if you have reasonable appetites
and can hold down on the amount of vegetables, you can prepare this in a 3-quart cooker. But if you have large appetites, it
is safer to use a 6-quart. Never try to squeeze too much food
into too small a cooker. You might cause a blockage of the vent
pipe.

To prepare the dessert, mix all ingredients together according to the Banana-Brandy Custard recipe opposite. Divide
mixture between 2 individual custard cups, wrap them completely and tightly in aluminum foil and hold them aside. Precisely prepare and cut your chosen vegetables and hold them
aside.

Now fry and glaze the lamb chops. You will need a 3-quart
or a 6-quart pressure cooker (see note, above). Heat it, without
its base rack, to medium-high frying temperature, melt in it 5
tablespoons of the butter and, when it is quite hot, quickly
brown the lamb chops on both sides. As they begin to color,
add the chopped onion and work it around the lamb until it is
limp and transparent. Add salt and pepper to taste, hiss in the
orange and pineapple juices, then sprinkle on the ground cinnamon and garlic. Arrange the lamb chops slightly overlapping each other, so that, when you rest the base rack on top of
them, as little as possible of the liquid will be above the rack.

Now place the two wrapped custard cups on the rack and
assemble all the vegetables except mushrooms beside them.
As noted above, keep everything well below the inside of the
lid as you put it on. Bring the pressure up to 15 pounds and
cook for exactly 3 minutes.

When the timer rings, turn off the heat and reduce the pressure immediately. Take out the custard cups, vegetables and
lamb chops. Then keep the lamb and vegetables warm, covered, in an oven at 170° F (75° C). Quickly boil down the liquid in the pressure cooker at high heat. While this is in progress, melt the remaining tablespoon of butter in a frying pan,
lightly and quickly sauté the sliced mushrooms, then work in
the grapes and the sour cream. Stirring it often, let it heat up
almost to boiling, but do not let it actually bubble. As soon as
the fruit juices in the pressure cooker show signs of becoming
sticky and thick, turn off the heat and work in the sour cream
mixture from the sauté pan. Pour this sauce over the lamb
chops as you serve them with the vegetables. Leave the two
dessert custards to cool until you are ready to serve them.

Mixed black and green olives
Glazed Lamb Chops and Grapes with Seasonal Vegetables
    served on a bed of rice
Green salad
Steam-Baked Banana-Brandy Custard
Darjeeling tea or coffee

The Ideal Wines

Luxurious

A French white Chablis from Burgundy
or
A California white Pinot Chardonnay from the Napa Valley

Everyday

A French white Mâcon Pinot Chardonnay from Burgundy
or
A California white Riesling from the Napa Valley

French Blanquette of Lamb

For 4
Cook under pressure at 10 lb for 14 minutes, plus 9 more
(or at 15 lb for 10 minutes, plus 6 more)

1 cup (2.5 dl) dry white wine
1 medium yellow onion, peeled, left
　whole, with 2 cloves stuck in it
2 medium carrots, scraped and sliced
4 small or 2 large leeks, white parts only,
　washed and desanded, then sliced
½ cup (1.25 dl) peeled and chopped
　celery root
Enough whole fresh leaves basil,
　chopped, to fill 1 Tbs, or 1 tsp dried
The same amount tarragon
The same amount thyme
Salt, to your taste
Freshly ground black pepper, to your
　taste
2 lb (1 kg) boneless, entirely lean lamb,
　preferably from the leg, ribs, or
　shoulder, cut into 1-inch (2.5 cm)
　cubes
6 Tbs (90 g) butter
3 Tbs flour
2 lb (1 kg) medium potatoes, peeled, left
　whole, reserved under water which
　has been acidulated with a few
　spritzes of lemon juice to prevent the
　potatoes from darkening
12 small white boiling onions, peeled, left
　whole
Enough fresh watercress leaves, coarsely
　chopped, to fill ½ cup (1.25 dl)
2 cloves garlic, peeled and finely minced
12 fresh mushrooms, wiped clean and
　trimmed, then sliced
Up to 3 egg yolks
Juice of ½ fresh lemon

The French word *blanquette* comes from *blanc*, white—meat colored white by being served enveloped in a cream sauce. Ours is a modernized, lightened version—without the cream. But our sauce is still luxuriously rich and velvety on the tongue. The French usually make this classic dish with veal. We prefer the flavor and texture of lamb. This recipe is adapted from our previous book, *Revolutionizing French Cooking*.

You will need a large pressure cooker of at least 8-quart capacity. Put into it, without its base rack, the wine and 2½ cups of cold water, then bring it up quickly to the boil. While it is heating up, add the whole onion stuck with cloves, carrots, leeks, celery root, basil, tarragon, thyme, with salt and pepper to taste. The moment the liquid begins to bubble, drop in the 2 pounds of cubed lamb, put on the lid, bring the pressure up to 10 pounds and cook for exactly 14 minutes.

When the timer rings, turn off the heat, reduce the pressure immediately and separate the solids from the liquid by straining through a sieve, reserving each in a separate bowl. Wipe out and dry the inside of the pressure cooker. Heat it to medium-high frying temperature, melt in it 4 tablespoons of the butter and, when it is reasonably hot, pick out the cubes of meat from among the vegetables and quickly brown them in the hot butter. After the cubes are browned, sprinkle on the flour and work it into the butter. Now begin gradually hissing in and amalgamating, ¼ cup by ¼ cup, the reserved liquid broth. After the first cup has been blended in and thickened with the butter-flour mixture, you can add the rest of the broth more quickly. Dry the potatoes and add them to the pot with the 12 small onions, watercress and garlic. Taste again and adjust the seasonings. Put on the lid, again bring up the pressure to 10 pounds and cook for exactly 9 minutes. Meanwhile, melt the remaining 2 tablespoons of butter in a frying pan and quickly sauté the mushrooms until the hissing subsides to indicate that they have given up their water. Turn off the heat and hold them in the pan. Now turn your attention to the vegetables from the first boiling. Find the whole onion, pull out and discard its cloves, then chunk it. Puree it and all the vegetables by passing them either through a Cuisinart chopper-churner (or one of the similar machines), an electric blender, a food mill or a hand sieve. Reserve this puree to use instead of cream as a natural thickener for the sauce.

When the timer rings, turn off the heat and reduce the pressure immediately. Have ready a warm, lidded serving bowl and, using a slotted spoon, transfer into it from the pressure cooker the meat, onions, potatoes and any other solid pieces. Keep them warm, covered, in an oven at 165° F (75° C). Now begin thickening the sauce in the bottom of the pressure cooker. Blend into it a tablespoon or two of the vegetable puree. In a small bowl, beat the first egg yolk with ¼ cup of the hot broth. Blend this into the sauce. Then add, alternately, as much more of the vegetable puree and as many yolks as may be needed to produce a sauce with the consistency of heavy cream. At the last moment add a few spritzes of lemon juice. Serve the lamb with its mushrooms, onions and potatoes, glisteningly covered by this sauce. Both the food and the serving plates must be very hot. Eat it with fork and spoon— the lamb will be so tender that you will not need a knife.

A Good and Healthful Menu

Green Asparagus Bouillon (see page 36)
French Blanquette of Lamb
   with French bread
Salad of watercress with sliced avocado, lightly salted, without
   dressing
Lemon sherbet splashed with rum
Coffee or tea

The Ideal Wines

Luxurious

A light French red from the Saint-Emilion district of Bordeaux
   or
A light California red Cabernet Sauvignon from San Benito

Everyday

A light French red Bandol from Provence
   or
A light California red Gamay from the Napa Valley

A French Navarin of Spring Lamb

For 4
Cook under pressure at 10 lb for 8 minutes, plus 17 minutes
(or at 15 lb for 6 minutes, plus 13 minutes)

4 Tbs (60 g) butter
2 lb (1 kg) boneless, entirely lean spring lamb, preferably from the leg or shoulder, cut into 1-inch (2.5 cm) cubes
12 small white boiling onions, peeled, left whole
3 Tbs flour
1 cup (2.5 dl) dry white wine
Salt, to your taste
Freshly ground black pepper, to your taste
6 small carrots, scraped, trimmed, left whole
2 medium parsnips, peeled and cut into ½-inch (1.2 cm) chunks
6 medium white turnips, peeled and sliced ⅛ inch (3 mm) thick
1 Tbs chopped fresh basil leaves, or 1 tsp dried
The same amount marjoram
The same amount summer savory

This is one of the simplest of all French country dishes. Spring lamb used to be available only in the spring, but now, thanks to the marvels of sex education among sheep, it is available all the year round.

You will need a pressure cooker of at least 6-quart capacity. Heat it, without its base rack, to medium-high frying temperature, and melt in it the butter. As soon as it is fairly hot, quickly brown the cubes of lamb. Using a slotted spoon, take them out and set aside for a couple of minutes while you brown the onions, stirring them around until they are speckled on all sides. Put back the meat and sprinkle over it the flour, thoroughly working it into the butter until it forms a slight paste. Now hiss in the wine, slowly at first, blending it into the butter-flour paste, then more quickly. Add an extra ½ cup (1.25 dl) of water, plus salt and pepper to taste. Put on the lid, bring the pressure up to 10 pounds and cook for exactly 8 minutes.

When the timer rings, turn off the heat, reduce the pressure immediately and add at once the carrots, parsnips, turnips, basil, marjoram, summer savory, with more salt and pepper if needed. Put back the lid, again bring the pressure up to 10 pounds and cook for exactly another 17 minutes.

When the timer rings again, turn off the heat, reduce the pressure immediately and serve the navarin in hot, wide bowls—the lamb surrounded by the vegetables, with some of the aromatic broth poured over. Eat this with fork and spoon.

A Good and Healthful Menu

Tiny Cocktail Marinated Mushrooms (see page 50)
French Navarin of Spring Lamb
   Whole wheat farmhouse bread
Salad of mixed greens vinaigrette
Lime-Fluff Custard with Walnuts (see page 216)
Coffee or tea

The Ideal Wines

Luxurious

An Italian red Barolo from the Piedmont region
   or
A light California red Cabernet Sauvignon from the Napa Valley

Everyday

An Italian red Barbera from the Piedmont region
   or
A light California red Cabernet Sauvignon from Santa Clara

Quick Lamb Stew with Leeks and Potato Dumplings

For 4
Cook under pressure at 10 lb for 20 minutes, plus 10 more
(or at 15 lb for 15 minutes, plus 7 more)

4 Tbs olive oil
2 lb (1 kg) boneless, entirely lean lamb, preferably from leg, ribs or shoulder, cut into 1-inch (2.5 cm) cubes
3 Tbs flour
1 cup (2.5 dl) dry white wine
1 cup (2.5 dl) chicken bouillon (see page 35, or use canned)
6 medium carrots, scraped and cut into 1-inch (2.5 cm) pieces
2 cups (450 g) of the white parts of leeks, carefully washed and desanded, then cut into 1-inch (2.5 cm) lengths
2 medium yellow onions, peeled and quartered
3 medium white turnips, peeled and sliced ¼ inch (7 mm) thick
1 Tbs Worcestershire sauce
1 bay leaf
Salt, to your taste
Freshly ground black pepper, to your taste
1 cup (225 g) green beans, broken into 1-inch (2.5 cm) lengths
2 stalks celery, cut into 2-inch (5 cm) pieces
1 clove garlic, peeled and finely minced
Enough fresh leaves basil, chopped, to fill 1 Tbs, or 1 tsp dried
The same amount rosemary
The same amount thyme

For the Potato Dumplings

6 medium starchy potatoes, boiled ahead, uncovered, in their jackets, then peeled and riced
2 whole eggs
1½ tsp salt
½ cup (60 g) all-purpose white flour
About 18 to 24 walnut or pecan halves, or whole hazelnuts
½ cup (1.25 dl) melted butter
⅓ cup (80 ml) dry bread crumbs

This is our favorite among all the dozens of lamb stews we have tried over many years. It is aromatic with the delicate onion flavor of leeks. It is rich and solid with the buttery dumplings that German cooks call *kartoffelklosse*, made, not from a standard ready-made mix, but from riced boiled potatoes. You should boil them a few hours in advance and let them cool in the refrigerator to develop a good flavor and texture.

You will need a pressure cooker of at least 6-quart capacity. Heat it, without its base rack, to medium-high frying temperature, lubricate its bottom with 2 tablespoons of the oil and, when it is quite hot, quickly brown the lamb cubes on all sides. Add more oil as necessary. When the lamb is nicely colored, sprinkle in the flour and work it thoroughly into the oil. Then hiss in, tablespoon by tablespoon at first, the wine and blend it with the flour-oil paste until it thickens slightly. When all the wine is in, add the cup of bouillon, preheated almost to boiling. The moment the combined liquids in the pot start bubbling, add the carrots, leeks, onions, turnips, Worcestershire sauce, the crumbled bay leaf, plus salt and pepper to taste. Put on the lid, bring the pressure up to 10 pounds and cook for exactly 20 minutes.

Meanwhile, in a mixing bowl, blend the dough for the potato dumplings. Put in the riced potatoes, eggs, salt and flour. Beat it all together with a wooden fork until it is fluffy. With your wetted fingers, pull off a small piece of dough and roll it around a nut until you have a ball about 1 inch (2.5 cm) in diameter. You should finish up with 18 to 24 balls. Set them aside on a tray without touching each other.

When the timer rings, turn off the heat, reduce the pressure immediately and add at once the green beans, celery, garlic, basil, rosemary, thyme, plus more salt and pepper if needed. Put on the lid, bring the pressure back up to 10 pounds and continue cooking for another 10 minutes.

When the timer rings again, turn off the heat and reduce the pressure immediately. Open the cooker, turn the heat back on and adjust it so that the liquid inside is just gently simmering. Drop in as many of the potato balls as will fit on the surface with about a ¼-inch (7 mm) space between the balls, to allow for their expansion. Put back the pot lid, but do not lock it into the pressure position and do not put the pressure control weight onto the vent. Leave it open, so that steam can escape. Let the potato balls steam in this enclosed space until they are done through, usually in just about 12 minutes. (Test them for doneness as explained on page 55.) While this is in progress, blend together the melted butter and the bread crumbs. Serve the lamb, with its variety of vegetables and its aromatic broth, in wide, hot soup bowls, with dumplings resting on top.

Spoon the buttered bread crumbs onto each dumpling. For seconds, steam the remaining dumplings in the rest of the lamb stew in the pot. Or you can steam extra dumplings in a separate, covered saucepan with about ½ inch (1.2 cm) boiling, salted water.

A Good and Healthful Menu

Clam-Stuffed Cherry Tomatoes (see page 51)
Quick Lamb Stew with Leeks and Potato Dumplings
Salad of cucumber slices marinated in garlic vinegar, dressed
   with sour cream
Cheese and fruit
Coffee or tea

The Ideal Wines

Luxurious

An Italian Gattinara from the Piedmont region
   or
A California red Cabernet Sauvignon from the Alexander Valley

Everyday

An Italian Valpolicella from the Venice region
   or
A California Rosé of Cabernet from the Alexander Valley

Poached Leg of Lamb with Persian Sauce of Mixed Fruits

For 4
Cook under pressure at 10 lb for 12 minutes, plus 7 minutes more
   (or at 15 lb for 9 minutes, plus 5 minutes more)

4 Tbs (60 g) butter
About 3 lb (1.4 kg) leg of lamb, boned
   and rolled, either a small whole leg,
   or half a larger one, trimmed of all fat
4 medium carrots, scraped and sliced
3 medium yellow onions, peeled and
   chopped
2 medium white turnips, peeled and
   coarsely diced
Salt, to your taste
Black pepper, to your taste
2 tsp whole cumin seeds
2 cloves garlic, peeled and finely minced
1 cup (2.5 dl) clear beef bouillon (see page
   35, or use canned)
Juice of 1 whole fresh lemon
¼ lb (115 g) dried apple slices or rings
¼ lb (115 g) dried apricot halves
¼ lb (115 g) dried whole figs, preferably
   Smyrna
¼ lb (115 g) dried peach halves

This is a modern adaptation of an ancient Persian dish called *bareh miveh*. You can use fresh fruits, in season, or the healthy, vitamin-rich dried fruits at any time of the year. The refreshing tang of the poached fruit is an excellent foil to the velvety softness of the lamb.

You will need a pressure cooker of minimum 6-quart capacity. Make sure that the leg of lamb fits easily into it, with room to spare for the fruit all around. Heat the pressure cooker, empty and without its base rack, to medium-high frying temperature, melt in it 2 tablespoons of the butter and, when it is good and hot, quickly and lightly brown the lamb on all sides. Add more butter as needed. Then lift out the lamb and set it aside. Add to the pot the carrots, onions and turnips and sauté them until they are lightly gilded. While this is in progress, lightly sprinkle and pat the lamb all around with salt and pepper, to taste. Lay it back in the pot on its bed of vegetables, sprinkle over it the cumin seeds and garlic, then hiss in, down the side of the pot, the bouillon. Put on the lid, bring the pressure up to 10 pounds and cook for exactly 4 minutes per pound of meat—in this case, 12 minutes.

Meanwhile, prepare the dried fruits. In a separate 3-quart saucepan, bring 2 quarts of water up to the boil and squeeze

¼ lb (115 g) dried pear slices
¼ lb (115 g) soft, stoned prunes
½ tsp saffron filaments
1 whole fresh tangerine, in season
   (optional)
½ cup (1.25 dl) dry white wine

in the juice of the lemon. The moment the water starts bubbling, drop in, all at once, the apples, apricots, figs, peaches, pears and prunes. As soon as the water returns to the boil, drain the fruits and leave them in the sieve to continue dribbling until they go into the pressure cooker.

When the timer rings, turn off the heat, reduce the pressure immediately and carefully place the fruits in a neat circle all around the lamb. Sprinkle the fruits with the saffron filaments for color and flavor, then gently pour in the wine, at the side. Replace the lid, bring the pressure back up to 10 pounds and cook for exactly another 7 minutes. While this is in progress, grate the outer rind of the tangerine and set aside in a small, covered jar. Peel the tangerine, discarding the rest of the skin, divide it into its segments, pit them and set aside.

When the timer rings again, turn off the heat, reduce the pressure immediately, add the tangerine segments to the fruit already in the pot and sprinkle the grated tangerine rind over everything. Now check to make sure that there is not too much liquid in the bottom of the pot. The fruits should be moistly soggy, but they should not be swimming in liquid. If there is too much, turn up the heat, so that there is a merry bubbling and let it continue, the pot uncovered, until the excess liquid is boiled away. As soon as you achieve the right degree of thickness of the fruity sauce, serve everything at once on very hot plates. You will hardly need to "carve" the lamb—it will be meltingly soft and with memorable flavor.

A Good and Healthful Menu

Smoked salmon with lemon wedges and slices of pumpernickel
Poached Leg of Lamb with Persian Sauce of Mixed Fruits
   with mashed potatoes
Salad of watercress with sliced avocado sprinkled with unsweetened lime juice and olive oil
Chocolate cake
Coffee or tea

The Ideal Wines

Luxurious

A fruity white Corton-Charlemagne from Burgundy
   or
A fruity white California Johannisberg Riesling from the Napa Valley

Everyday

A fruity French regional white Burgundy from the city of Beaune in Burgundy
   or
A fruity white California Sauvignon Blanc from Santa Clara

Chapter 11

ONE-DISH MEALS WITH PORK

Including Speed Meals Prepared in One Hour or Less from Kitchen Start to Serving at Table

We love pork, not only crackling-crispy-crusty—as roast loins or grilled chops—but also soft, melt-in-the-mouth, luxuriously velvety, braised or poached in the pressure cooker. The speed of preparation is extraordinary. Here, first, is a full pork chop dinner for two—complete with glazed figs, browned potatoes, cheesed vegetables and stuffed baked apples—all prepared in a single cooker from the start of the work to the serving at table in 15 minutes. Then, there follows a variety of other recipes, including pork liver, an Alsatian sauerkraut with pork and sausages, pork loin and pork pot roast.

Superspeed Dinner for Two All Together in One Cooker: Pork Chops with Browned Potatoes, Glazed Figs, Cheesed Vegetable and Nut-Filled, Steam-Baked Apples

For 2
Cook under pressure at 15 lb for 5 minutes
(or at 10 lb for 7 minutes)

For the Dessert Apples

2 good-sized baking apples, cored about
    ¾ way down, but not right through,
    with only the top ⅓ peeled around
    the hole
2 Tbs (30 g) butter
2 Tbs brown sugar, preferably natural, if
    available
2 Tbs bitter orange marmalade
2 Tbs toasted slivered almonds

⅓ cup (80 ml) natural, raw bran flakes
    (from health food store), or bread
    crumbs
1 whole egg, lightly beaten
2 Tbs milk

Assembling the various parts correctly in the pressure cooker is most important. Never allow the upper ingredients to get too close to the inside of the lid. Keep them at least an inch or two below the steam vent.

For the apples, during fall and winter we use, of course, the supreme baking apple, the Rome Beauty. At other times of the year there are the excellent Northern Spy and Winesap. You can vary the marmalade with almost any other kind of jam or jelly, but it should be fruity and tart to balance the sweetness of the apples. You can also stuff them with chopped dates, figs, prunes or all kinds of glacéed fruits and almost every variety of nuts.

As to the size of the cooker, if you have reasonable appetites and can hold down on the amount of vegetables, you can prepare this in a 3-quart cooker. But if you have large appetites, it is safer to use a 6-quart. Never try to squeeze too much food into too small a cooker. You might cause a blockage of the vent pipe.

Salt, to taste

Freshly ground black pepper, to taste

2 center-cut loin or rib pork chops, each about ¾ inch (2 cm) thick, most fat trimmed off

4 Tbs (60 g) butter

2 medium potatoes, peeled and sliced ⅜ inch (1 cm) thick

2 medium carrots, scraped and halved lengthwise

½ cup (1.25 dl) white wine

About 6 cauliflowerets

½ cup (1.25 dl) grated Swiss Gruyère cheese

4 whole Kadota figs (usually available canned)

2 Tbs maple syrup

First, prepare the apples. Set them each on a square of aluminum foil large enough to enclose the fruit completely. Quickly cream together the butter and brown sugar. Put 1 tablespoon of this into each apple and push it down lightly. Above this, put into each apple 1 tablespoon of the marmalade, then 1 tablespoon of the almonds, finally another tablespoon of the butter-sugar mix. Completely and tightly wrap each apple with the foil and set aside.

For the assembly of this dish, you will need a pressure cooker of either 3-quart or 6-quart capacity (see note, above). Spread the bran flakes or bread crumbs evenly on a dinner plate. Lightly beat the egg with 1½ tablespoons of the milk and spread this on a second dinner plate. Pat salt and pepper, to taste, all around the pork chops. Press them firmly into the bran flakes to coat both sides and the edges. Press them, similarly, into the egg-milk mixture. Then, again, into the bran flakes until you have a thickish crust. If the egg becomes too thick, add the remaining milk. Heat the pressure cooker, without its base rack, to medium-high frying temperature, melt in it 3 tablespoons of the butter and, when it is good and hot, quickly sauté both pork chops until you have a nicely brown crust. Carefully lift out the pork chops and reserve. Add the fourth tablespoon of butter to the pot and lightly brown the potato slices and carrots, with a little more salt and pepper, to taste. When they are done, turn off the heat, spread these vegetables as a single, even layer, and pour the wine over them. Place the pork chops neatly on top. Rest the base rack on the pork. Put the cauliflowerets into a small, open dish (or a small saucer), salt and pepper them lightly, then sprinkle them with half the grated cheese and place the dish in the cooker. Place the 4 figs directly on the base rack. Put the apples, right side up, on the rack. Put on the lid, bring the pressure up to 15 pounds and cook for exactly 5 minutes.

When the timer rings, turn off the heat and reduce the pressure immediately. Unwrap the apples and glaze them by dribbling a tablespoon of the maple syrup over each. Let them cool until you are ready to bring them to table. Serve the pork chops with the potatoes, carrots, figs and cheesed cauliflower. Scrape the bottom of the casserole to incorporate the brown glaze into the natural wine sauce. Spoon it over the pork. Sprinkle the rest of the grated cheese over everything.

A Good and Healthful Menu

Carrot sticks lightly dribbled with salted olive oil

Pork Chops with Browned Potatoes, Glazed Figs, Cheesed Vegetable

Nut-Filled Baked Apples

Coffee or black oolong tea

The Ideal Wines

Moderately Priced

A French "Pinot Rosé d'Alsace"

or

A California "Grignolino Rosé" from the Napa Valley

Corn-Stuffed Pork Chops with Pickled Peaches

For 4
Cook under pressure at 10 lb for 20 minutes
(or at 15 lb for 15 minutes)

5 Tbs (75 g) butter

Four 1-inch-thick (2.5 cm) center-cut, loin or rib pork chops, most fat trimmed off and a deep pocket cut into the lean meat from the outer edge

¾ cup (170 g) chopped celery

3 medium onions, 2 thinly sliced, 1 chopped

1 cup (225 g) natural, raw bran flakes or bread crumbs

¾ cup (170 g) whole-kernel corn

½ tsp dried sage

Salt, to your taste

Freshly ground black pepper, to your taste

8 pickled peach halves

½ cup (1.25 dl) vinegary juice from the peaches

Jars of peaches pickled in a light wine vinegar are now widely available in the specialty departments of supermarkets. If you cannot find them, you can soak some fresh, canned or frozen peach halves overnight in a light tarragon wine vinegar with a teaspoon or two, to your taste, of sugar. Bran flakes make this a high-fiber dish.

You will need a pressure cooker of at least 6-quart capacity. Heat it, without its base rack, to medium-high frying temperature, melt in it 3 tablespoons of the butter and, when it is nicely hot, quickly and lightly brown the pork chops on both sides. Lift them out and set aside. Melt in the remaining 2 tablespoons of the butter and quickly sauté in it the chopped celery and chopped onion. Then, add the bran flakes, corn, sage, plus salt and pepper to taste. This is the stuffing for the pork chops. Turn off the heat. Spoon out the stuffing and press it, most easily with your clean fingers, into the pockets in the pork chops. This job completed, put the base rack into the pressure cooker, neatly stack the pork chops on top of it, lightly salt and pepper them and cover them with the sliced onion. Place the peach halves in the corners, around and on top of the chops, then pour in the peach juice. Put on the lid, bring the pressure up to 10 pounds and cook for exactly 20 minutes.

When the timer rings, turn off the heat and bring the pressure down immediately. Serve on very hot plates. Take out the base rack from the pressure cooker, scrape the glaze from its bottom, amalgamate it with the natural juices and spoon this fine sauce over the chops.

A Good and Healthful Menu

Clams on the half shell with lemon wedges
Corn-Stuffed Pork Chops with Pickled Peaches
   with baked potatoes
   Swedish crisp bread
Salad of cucumber slices marinated in tarragon vinegar and
   lightly dressed with sour cream
Raspberry sherbet
Coffee or tea

The Ideal Wines

Luxurious

An Italian red Amarone from the Venice region
   or
A California red Cabernet Sauvignon from the Napa Valley

Everyday

An Italian Valpolicella from the Venice region
   or
A California red Cabernet Sauvignon from Sonoma

Creamed Pork Chops Poached with Apples in Tomato Sauce

For 4
Cook under pressure at 10 lb for 10 minutes
    (or at 15 lb for 8 minutes)

6 oz (170 g) salt pork, washed and diced
Four ¾-inch-thick (2 cm) center-cut loin
    or rib pork chops, most fat trimmed
    off
1 lb (½ kg) cooking apples, preferably
    Greenings, in season, peeled, cored
    and sliced ¼ inch (7 mm) thick
Salt, to your taste
Freshly ground black pepper, to your
    taste
2 medium yellow onions, peeled and
    chopped
1 clove garlic, peeled and finely minced
1 Tbs fresh basil leaves, or 1 tsp dried
The same amount tarragon
The same amount thyme
8-oz (225 g) can of tomato sauce
¼ cup (60 ml) dry white wine
½ cup (1.25 dl) heavy cream

Here are pork chops married to not one, but two of the slightly tart fruits that are the most excellent partners of the creamy-rich meat.

You will need a pressure cooker of at least 3-quart capacity. Heat it, without its base rack, to medium-high frying temperature and put in the diced salt pork. Stir it around until it has given up most of its fat and the dice are crackly-crisp. Take them out with a slotted spoon and drain them on absorbent paper. In the remaining hot fat, quickly brown the pork chops on both sides, then turn off the heat. Lift out the pork chops and set aside. Leaving the small amount of remaining fat in the bottom of the pressure cooker, cover it with neat layers of overlapping apple slices. Put back the chops on top of the apples. Lightly salt and pepper the meat to taste. Sprinkle over the top the onion, garlic, basil, tarragon and thyme. Blend together the tomato sauce and wine, then pour this gently over the ingredients in the pressure cooker. Put on the lid, bring the pressure up to 10 pounds and cook for exactly 10 minutes.

When the timer rings, turn off the heat and bring down the pressure immediately. Lift out the chops (scraping them, so as to leave all other ingredients in the pot) and set them on a warm serving platter. Set the pot back on medium heat and work into it, carefully and gradually, the ½ cup cream. Stirring continuously, heat everything almost to the boiling point, but not quite. Taste and adjust seasonings, as needed, pour this sauce over the chops and serve at once on very hot plates.

A Good and Healthful Menu

Clam-Stuffed Cherry Tomatoes (see page 51)
Creamed Pork Chops Poached with Apples in Tomato Sauce
    with buttered spaghetti
Watercress salad
Muenster cheese with guava paste
Coffee or tea

The Ideal Wines

Luxurious

A Spanish red Cabernet Sauvignon from the Panades district
    of Barcelona
    or
A California red Zinfandel made in Santa Clara

Everyday

A Spanish red Sangre de Toro from the Panades district of Bar-
    celona
    or
A California red Barbera from the Livermore Valley

Stuffed Juicy Pork Spareribs with Rice and Pineapple Sauerkraut

For 4
Cook under pressure at 10 lb for 25 minutes
*   (or at 15 lb for 19 minutes)*

4 lb (2 kg) meaty pork spareribs, uncut
8-oz (225 g) package dry stuffing mix
2 stalks celery, chopped
2 medium yellow onions, peeled and
    chopped
Up to ½ cup (1.25 dl) milk
Salt, to your taste
Freshly ground black pepper, to your
    taste
1 cup (2.5 dl) good red wine
1 cup (2.5 dl) beef bouillon (see page 35,
    or use canned)
1 Tbs light soy sauce
1 Tbs brown sugar, preferably natural
    cane (usually available at health food
    stores)
1 cup (225 g) brown rice
1 cup (225 g) crushed pineapple, with its
    juice
1 cup (225 g) preprepared sauerkraut,
    with most of its vinegar soaked out
Enough fresh parsley, chopped, to fill ⅓
    cup (80 ml) fairly loosely

Sometimes we long for our spareribs to be as crispy as a cracker. Then, we broil or grill them. But, when we want them succulently juicy and aromatic with herbs, we prepare them in this way in the pressure cooker in about half the time of the standard method.

You will need a pressure cooker of at least 6-quart capacity. First deal with the spareribs. Preheat your broiler nearly to its highest temperature (about 450 to 500° F—230 to 260° C). Cut the sheets of ribs into pieces which will fit easily into the pressure cooker. Now put each separate sheet on a cutting board and, with a pointed, sharp knife, score the flesh and skin between each rib bone, so that they are partially separated but still hang together. Set them out in a single layer on the broiler pan and broil them, fairly close to the heat, until they have given up some of their fat and are nicely browned, usually in about 4 to 5 minutes on one side and 3 to 4 minutes on the other. Turn off the broiler.

Next, in a bowl, blend the stuffing mix, celery, onions and just enough of the milk to make a moist, thickish paste. When the ribs are browned, make a three- or four-decker sandwich of them (with the thick ends on alternating sides), with equal layers of the stuffing in between. Salt and pepper each layer to taste. Tie this construction firmly with string. Remove the base rack from the pot and sprinkle, or pour into it, in turn: the red wine, beef bouillon, soy sauce, brown sugar, brown rice and a little more salt and pepper to taste. In a separate mixing bowl, lightly blend together the pineapple and sauerkraut. Put the ribs on top of the layer of rice, then cover them with the pineapple and sauerkraut. Put on the lid, bring the pressure up to 10 pounds and cook for exactly 25 minutes.

When the timer rings, turn off the heat and reduce the pressure immediately. Pull out the spareribs, cut away the string and divide the meat into single ribs. On each hot serving plate, spread a bed of the rice mixture and lay the single ribs on top. Serve the pineapple sauerkraut at the side of each plate and decorate with a sprinkling of bright green parsley.

A Good and Healthful Menu

Celery sticks with salted olive oil
Pork Spareribs with Rice and Pineapple Sauerkraut
Green salad vinaigrette
Orange sherbet
Coffee or tea

The Ideal Wines

Moderately Priced

A French red Corbières from the Southwest
    or
A California red Ruby Cabernet

Southern Barbecued Spareribs—Speed Method

For 4
Sauce: cook under pressure at 15 lb for 10 minutes
  (or at 10 lb for 13 minutes)
Ribs: cook under pressure at 10 lb for 20 minutes
  (or at 15 lb for 15 minutes)

For the Barbecue Sauce

16 Tbs (240 g) butter
2 medium yellow onions, peeled and
  chopped
8-oz (225 g) can Italian plum tomatoes
½ cup (1.25 dl) chili sauce
1 Tbs freshly squeezed lemon juice
1 Tbs tarragon or Spanish sherry wine
  vinegar
2 Tbs Worcestershire sauce
1½ Tbs honey
1 Tbs chili powder
2 cloves garlic, peeled and minced
1 tsp allspice
1 tsp dried oregano
Salt, to your taste
Freshly ground black pepper, to your
  taste
Tabasco, to your taste

For the Rubbing Mixture

1½ Tbs chili powder
1½ Tbs dry mustard
¾ tsp red cayenne pepper

4 lb (2 kg) meaty pork spareribs, cut into
  single ribs
3 Tbs olive oil
½ cup (1.25 dl) dry white wine

This is the nearest thing we know to turning spareribs all day over a charcoal pit, while basting them with the barbecue sauce. But, when we only have an hour to prepare the meal, we do them this way.

You will need a pressure cooker of at least 6-quart capacity. First, mix the barbecue sauce. Heat the pressure cooker, without its base rack, to medium-high frying temperature and melt in it the butter. Then sauté the onions until they are nicely golden, usually in 4 to 5 minutes. Add to the pot and stir in, ingredient by ingredient, the tomatoes, chili sauce, lemon juice, vinegar, Worcestershire sauce, honey, chili powder, garlic, allspice, oregano, plus salt, pepper and Tabasco to taste. Put on the lid, bring the pressure up to 15 pounds and cook for exactly 10 minutes.

Meanwhile, in a mixing bowl, blend the chili powder, dry mustard and cayenne to make the rubbing mix. Cut away the obviously excess fat from the ribs. Then firmly rub each rib all over with the mix, working it with your fingers into all the cracks and crevices.

When the timer rings for the sauce, turn off the heat, reduce the pressure immediately and pour the sauce into a storage bowl. Wipe out the pressure cooker, reheat it to frying temperature, lubricate its bottom with the oil and, when it is thoroughly hot, brown the ribs, in batches, until they are a light mahogany. As they are done, set them on a board or platter. Turn off the heat. Put the base rack into the pressure cooker and pour in the wine. Thickly coat each rib with the barbecue sauce and arrange them neatly in the pressure cooker. Put on the lid, bring the pressure up to 10 pounds and cook for exactly 20 minutes.

When the timer rings, turn off the heat and reduce the pressure immediately. If you want to add a final extra crispness to your ribs, preheat your broiler to high temperature and set the ribs under it, basting them with extra barbecue sauce and turning them, until they are crisply glazed—usually in 2 to 4 minutes. Serve the ribs on very hot plates.

A Good and Healthful Menu

Tiny Cocktail Marinated Mushrooms (see page 50)
Southern Barbecued Spareribs
  with boiled potatoes and green beans
Lemon meringue pie
Coffee or tea

The Ideal Wines

Moderately Priced

A French red Cahors from the Southwest
    or
A California red Pinot Noir from Santa Clara

Amazingly Quick Alsatian Sauerkraut with Pork Chops

For 4
Cook under pressure at 10 lb for 20 minutes
(or at 15 lb for 15 minutes)

2 Tbs olive oil
4 pork loin chops, each about ½ inch (1.2 cm) thick, most fat trimmed off
3 medium yellow onions, peeled and sliced
2 lb (900 g) good sauerkraut (see opposite)
1 clove garlic, peeled and finely minced
1 bay leaf, crumbled
8 whole black peppercorns
¼ tsp ground mace
Salt, to your taste
6 medium boiling potatoes, each about 2 to 2½ inches (5 to 6.5 cm) across, peeled
1½ cups (3.75 dl) dry white wine
4 smoked beef sausages, or garlic frankfurters, or smoky pork sausages, whatever is available, cooked in advance

In the "old way," an Alsatian sauerkraut required 3 days of simmering and soaking. In this new way, with a few of the frills cut off, the time involved is about 40 minutes. It still tastes most excellently good. Much depends on the quality of the sauerkraut. Get the best you can find. If it is strong with vinegar, soak it for several hours in several changes of water. It must finally be crisp in texture, gently refreshing in flavor.

You will need a pressure cooker of at least 6-quart capacity. Heat it, without its base rack, to medium-high frying temperature, lubricate its bottom with the oil and, when it is thoroughly hot, quickly brown the pork chops on both sides. Take them out and sauté the sliced onions until they are just limp and transparent. Turn off the heat. Set the pork chops neatly on top of the onions, then cover them with the sauerkraut. Sprinkle on the garlic, bay leaf, peppercorns, mace, plus salt to taste. Half bury the potatoes in the sauerkraut. Now gently pour in the wine, put on the lid, bring the pressure up to 10 pounds and cook for exactly 20 minutes.

When the timer rings, turn off the heat, reduce the pressure immediately and dig the sausages into the sauerkraut. Keep the sauerkraut simmering very gently, uncovered, until the sausages are heated through, usually in 3 to 4 minutes. Then serve at once on very hot plates.

A Good and Healthful Menu

Alsatian snails in garlic butter
Alsatian Sauerkraut with Pork Chops
   with a long French loaf
Fruit tart
Coffee or tea

The Ideal Wines

Luxurious

An Alsatian white Riesling from the Upper Rhine
   or
A California white Riesling from the Napa Valley

Everyday

An Alsatian white Riesling from the Lower Rhine
   or
A California white Riesling from Monterey

Quick Pork Liver with Macaroni and Mixed Vegetables in Tomato Sauce

For 4
Cook under pressure at 10 lb for 3 minutes
  (or at 15 lb for 2 minutes)

½ lb (225 g) elbow macaroni
1½ lb (675 g) pork liver, sliced by your
  butcher ½ inch (1.2 cm) thick, then
  cut into 1-inch (2.5 cm) squares
½ cup (115 g) natural, raw bran flakes or
  bread crumbs
Salt, to your taste
Freshly ground black pepper, to your
  taste
4 Tbs (60 g) butter
6 slices Canadian bacon
2 medium yellow onions, peeled and
  chopped
2 medium carrots, scraped and cut into
  large dice
6 oz (170 g) button mushrooms, wiped
  clean, trimmed, caps left whole,
  stalks diced
2 medium green peppers, cored, seeded
  and cut into large dice
2 medium white turnips, peeled and cut
  into large dice
20-oz (560 g) can peeled plum tomatoes
1 clove garlic, peeled and finely minced
1 tsp whole cumin seeds
1 tsp dried oregano
Grated Parmesan cheese, to sprinkle on at
  serving

Pork liver seems to be dreadfully good for you—positively bursting with iron, phosphorus, other healthful minerals and huge amounts of all the important vitamins.

You will need a pressure cooker of at least 6-quart capacity, plus a largish soup kettle of boiling salted water in which to cook the macaroni. Start the water going first, since the macaroni will take about 7 to 12 minutes of actual boiling, and then it can be kept warm for a couple of minutes and drained when the liver is ready to serve.

With the macaroni on the way, spread the bran flakes on a dinner plate and lightly sprinkle them with salt and pepper to taste. Dredge the liver squares in the seasoned flakes and hold them on a board or platter. Heat the pressure cooker, without its base rack, to medium-high frying temperature, melt in it 2 tablespoons of the butter and, when it is nicely hot, sauté the Canadian bacon slices until they are quite crisp. Lift them out, coarsely crumble them and reserve. Next, sauté the onions in the remaining 2 tablespoons of the butter until they are just transparent, then very quickly sauté the liver squares. Minimum sautéing is essential to avoid the liver toughening into leather. Each square should be in contact with the heat for hardly more than 15 seconds on each side. Keep moving them and turning them. Lift out each square the instant it is done. Never mind if it is still quite limp. It will stiffen up and cook through under pressure. As soon as all the liver squares are out, put into the pot the carrots, mushrooms, green peppers and turnips, then sauté them around for 2 or 3 minutes. Add the tomatoes, garlic, cumin, oregano, plus extra salt and pepper if needed. Stir everything around thoroughly and put back the pork liver squares. Close the lid, bring the pressure up to 10 pounds and cook for exactly 3 minutes.

The instant the timer rings, cut off the heat and reduce the pressure immediately. Serve at once on a bed of hot macaroni, all well sprinkled with the crumbled bacon and the grated Parmesan cheese. We prefer the elbow macaroni to spaghetti because the tomato sauce fills the hollows of the elbows, so that each mouthful is a juicy and tangy pleasure.

A Good and Healthful Menu

Green bean and raw mushroom salad
Pork Liver with Macaroni and Mixed Vegetables in Tomato
  Sauce
Hot Southern biscuits
Fresh fruit
Coffee or Darjeeling tea

The Ideal Wines   *Luxurious*

A Spanish estate red from the Rioja region
or
A California red Cabernet Sauvignon from Monterey

Everyday

A Spanish red regional Rioja
or
A California red Gamay from the Napa Valley

Poached Pork Loin with Herb Butter and Garden Vegetables

For 4
Cook under pressure at 10 lb for 36 minutes, plus 3 minutes more
(or at 15 lb for 11 minutes, plus 2 minutes more)

3 lb (1.4 kg) pork loin roast, bones in,
    most fat trimmed off
Salt, to your taste
Freshly ground black pepper, to your
    taste
Up to 4 Tbs (60 g) butter
1 cup (2.5 dl) dry white wine

For the Herb Butter

8 Tbs (115 g) salt butter, slightly softened
3 Tbs chopped leaves of parsley
2 Tbs chopped fresh chives
2 tsp chopped fresh mint leaves

For the garden vegetables, choose any 3
    of the following:
    Beets, cut into ¼-inch (7 mm) slices
    Whole stalks of broccoli, with tough
        ends cut off and remaining stalks
        deeply slashed
    Brussels sprouts, whole, with tough
        outer leaves removed
    Carrots, cut in halves, lengthwise
    Fennel, cut in halves, lengthwise
    Leeks, desanded, left whole
    Medium yellow onions, cut in 1-inch
        (2.5 cm) slices or quartered
    Potatoes, cut into ¼-inch (7 mm) slices

Sometimes we like to have some crispness on our pork. Then, we use the pressure cooker to speed the internal cooking and a short, final spell in a fairly hot oven, with steady basting, to develop the crust. At the same time, the pressure cooker crisply cooks the vegetables. You must know the weight of your pork loin. You should pressure it at 10 pounds for exactly 12 minutes per pound.

You will need a pressure cooker of at least 6-quart capacity, depending on the size of your pork roast. Rub the meat all over with salt and pepper to taste.

Then heat the pressure cooker, without its base rack, to medium-high frying temperature and melt in it 3 tablespoons of the butter. When it is nicely hot, quickly and lightly brown the pork on all sides. Hiss in ½ cup of the wine, immediately put on the lid, bring the pressure up to 10 pounds and cook the 3-pound loin for exactly 36 minutes.

Meanwhile, in a mixing bowl, cream the 8 tablespoons butter with the parsley, chives and mint. Blend lightly but thoroughly, then set aside, covered. Preheat your broiler to its high temperature and have an open baking pan ready to receive the pork.

When the timer rings, turn off the heat and reduce the pressure immediately. Stand the pork in the roasting pan with the curved backside upward, bones down. Pour over it the juices from the pressure cooker. Smear its top with about half of the herb butter. Set the pork under the broiler so that its curved back skin is about 2 inches from the heat to develop its crisp crust, usually in about 10 to 15 minutes.

About every 5 minutes, baste the pork, using the rest of the herb butter and the juices from the bottom of the roasting pan. A bulb baster is best for this. The more steadily and thoroughly you baste, the better and faster the crust will develop. Meanwhile, without rinsing out the pressure cooker, use it to cook the garden vegetables. Place its base rack in position. As soon as the boiling is under way, put your selection of vegetables into the pot. Pour the remaining ½ cup wine over them, put on the lid, bring the pressure back to 10 pounds and cook for exactly 3 minutes.

When the timer rings, turn off the heat and reduce the pressure immediately. Serve the pork with the marvelous juices from the roasting pan as the natural sauce, surrounded by the bright and colorful vegetables. The contrasts of flavors and textures make for a memorable meal.

A Good and Healthful Menu

Chinese Cucumber Submarines (see page 47)
Poached Pork Loin with Herb Butter and Garden Vegetables
    with apples baked in their skins (in the same oven with the
    pork)
Crackling corn bread
Salad of Bibb lettuce leaves without dressing
Cheese and fresh fruit
Coffee or Indian Darjeeling tea

The Ideal Wines

Luxurious

A rich French château red from the Pomerol district of
    Bordeaux
or
A rich California red Pinot Noir from Monterey

Everyday

A French regional red from the Saint-Emilion district of
    Bordeaux
or
A California red Pinot Noir from Sonoma

Pineapple-Glazed Pork Pot Roast Poached in Light Cream or Milk

For 4
Cook under pressure at 10 lb for 25 minutes, plus 20 minutes more
    (or at 15 lb for 18 minutes, plus 15 minutes more)

8-oz (225 g) jar baby cocktail onions
Up to 5 Tbs olive oil
½ cup (115 g) diced boiled ham
3 lb (1.4 kg) boneless pork pot roast, from
    leg or loin, most fat trimmed off,
    then neatly tied
Salt, to your taste
Freshly ground black pepper, to your
    taste
12 whole cloves
1½ cups (3.75 dl) pineapple juice,
    unsweetened
1½ pints (7.5 dl) light cream or milk (see
    opposite)
3 Tbs maple syrup

This is a party dish with a creamy richness and a wonderful balance of different flavors and textures. You should know the exact weight of your piece of pork. Allow ½ pint light cream (or milk, if you are a fanatic about calories) for each pound of meat, and 15 minutes per pound at 10 pounds pressure.

You will need a pressure cooker of at least 6-quart capacity. Drain the baby onions, but save their juice. Heat the pressure cooker, without its base rack, to medium-high frying temperature, lubricate its bottom with 3 tablespoons of the oil and, when it is quite hot, quickly sauté and lightly brown the baby onions and the diced ham. Do not let them get too dark. Lift them out with a slotted spoon and set them aside on absorbent paper. Put in the pork pot roast and lightly gild it on all sides. At the same time, season it with salt and pepper, to taste. If necessary, add more oil. Then, carefully lift out the pork and set it on a board. Pour off excess fat from the cooker. Stud the

2 tsp grated orange peel
½ tsp ground cinnamon
1 bay leaf, crumbled
1 clove garlic, peeled and finely minced
2 tsp whole coriander seeds
1 Tbs chopped fresh basil leaves, or 1 tsp dried
The same amount fennel
The same amount marjoram
3 Tbs cornstarch
3 Tbs (45 g) butter
12-oz (340 g) can pineapple cubes in syrup

pork all around with the cloves. In a mixing bowl beat together the pineapple juice, ½ cup of the cream, the maple syrup, grated orange peel, cinnamon and the crumbled bay leaf. Put the onions and ham back in the pressure cooker and set the pork on this layer. Pour the pineapple juice–cream mixture over it. Put on the lid, bring the pressure up to 10 pounds and cook for exactly 25 minutes.

Meanwhile, in a saucepan combine the remaining 2½ cups of cream with the garlic, coriander seeds, basil, fennel and marjoram, and gently heat them up but do not let them boil. In a small mixing bowl, cream together the cornstarch and butter, then set aside.

When the timer rings, turn off the heat, reduce the pressure immediately and pour in, around the meat, the aromatic cream mixture. Put back the lid at once, bring the pressure back up to 10 pounds and continue the cooking for exactly 20 minutes more.

When the timer rings again, turn off the heat and reduce the pressure immediately. Then carefully lift out the pork, place it on a warm serving platter and keep it hot, covered with foil, in an oven at 175° F (80° C). Add to the cream in the cooker just enough of the juice from the baby onions to give the sauce a delicately faint onion flavor. Add enough of the syrup from the pineapple chunks to give it a very slight sweetness. Add all the pineapple cubes, drained. Now heat up the sauce to the gentlest simmering, stirring fairly continuously. When it shows the first faintest signs of bubbling, work in the butter-cornstarch mixture, teaspoon by teaspoon, until you have added just enough to give the sauce the consistency of heavy cream. Taste it and adjust the seasonings, as needed. With a slotted spoon, lift out the pineapple cubes and other solids, placing them decoratively on and around the pork. Ladle about a cup or so of the sauce, with all its aromatic and grainy little bits, over the meat and bring the rest of the sauce to the table in a warm sauceboat. Next day, this pork will be equally good, if not better, cold.

A Good and Healthful Menu

Black and green olives with salted celery sticks
Pineapple-Glazed Pork Pot Roast in Cream
  with boiled saffron rice
Green salad vinaigrette
Fresh fruit
Coffee or tea

The Ideal Wines

Luxurious

A rich French red Latricières-Chambertin from Burgundy
  or
A rich California red Cabernet Sauvignon from the Napa Valley

Everyday

A French red Côte de Beaune-Villages from Burgundy
  or
A California red Zinfandel from Sonoma

Pressure-Fried, Fruit-Stuffed Pork Chops

For 4
Pressure-fry at 5 lb for 22 minutes

½ cup (115 g) finely minced onion
2 Tbs (30 g) butter, melted
⅓ cup (80 ml) soft white bread crumbs
¼ cup (60 g) seedless raisins
4 tsp finely grated orange peel
¼ cup (60 g) finely grated tart apple,
　　cored, but with skin left on
¼ cup (60 g) finely minced dried apricot
　　halves
½ tsp dried, crumbled sage
Fresh leaves of thyme, finely chopped,
　　enough to fill 1 Tbs, or 1 tsp dried
Up to 3 Tbs dry white wine
½ tsp salt, more or less, to your taste
Freshly ground black pepper, to your
　　taste
4 lean loin, or rib, pork chops, each about
　　¾ inch (2 cm) thick, a deep pocket
　　cut into the lean meat from the outer
　　edge toward the bone
1 whole egg, lightly beaten
1 cup (2.5 dl) milk
1 cup (2.5 dl) dry bread crumbs
6 cups (1.5 liters) vegetable oil

Warning: This recipe can only be prepared in the specially designed pressure fryer-cooker described on page 21. Pressure frying must never be attempted in a standard cooker, which does not have the proper lid closure for this kind of superfast frying.

See the preliminary instructions on pressure frying in the introduction to the beef recipe on page 93. The stuffed chops are covered with an egg-milk wash and rolled in bread crumbs before frying. Do not try to cover them with a batter, which would become too thick and would considerably overcook in the oil long before the meat was done.

You will need a 6-quart specially designed pressure fryer as described on page 21. (Do not, under any circumstances, attempt this recipe in a standard pressure cooker, which does not have the proper lid closure for pressure frying.) In a mixing bowl, combine the ingredients for the stuffing: onions, melted butter, soft bread crumbs, raisins, orange peel, apple, apricot, sage, thyme, with just enough of the wine, added dash by dash, to moisten them all into a workable mass, plus ½ teaspoon salt and pepper, to taste. Spoon up this stuffing and press it (most easily with your clean fingers) into the pockets in the pork chops. Get as much stuffing in as possible, but not so much that the chops bulge. Close the openings of the pockets, either with small trussing pins or by sewing them up with string. Set them aside.

In a mixing bowl, beat together the egg and milk. Spread the dry bread crumbs evenly across a dinner plate. Put the 6 cups of oil into the pressure fryer, set it over high heat and, using a deep-frying thermometer, bring up the oil to 350° F (175° C). Watch it carefully. The oil heats up very quickly and can easily overheat. Dip each pork chop into the egg-milk, then press into the bread crumbs on all sides to make a firm, not-too-thick covering. As soon as the oil is at the correct temperature, gently put in the chops, one at a time, using a slotted spoon or tongs. Work quickly, putting in all 4 chops. Brown and seal them in the open cooker for precisely 1 minute. Then put on the lid, with the pressure regulator already in position. The working pressure will come up to 5 pounds in less than 1 minute, and the regulator will start gently hissing and/or jiggling. Set your timer for 22 minutes. Turn the heat down to medium and then adjust it so that the gentle hissing and/or jiggling continues.

The moment the timer rings, turn off the heat, reduce the pressure immediately by tipping the pressure regulator to an angle with the tines of a two-pronged fork (no need to remove the regulator). As soon as the steam stops hissing and there is no more pressure inside the cooker, take off the lid. Carefully lift out the chops and drain and dry them on absorbent paper. Then serve them at once while they are still very hot.

A Good and Healthful Menu   Sprigs of watercress with walnuts and salted olive oil dressing
Fruit-Stuffed Pork Chops
    with broccoli flowerets and mashed potatoes
A cheese board with crusty French bread
Coffee

The Ideal Wines   *Luxurious*

A light red French Graves from Bordeaux
    or
A light red California Cabernet Sauvignon from Sonoma

Everyday

A pink French Tavel from the Rhone
    or
A pink California Grenache Rosé from Santa Clara

Chapter 12

ONE-DISH MEALS
WITH VEAL

*Including Speed Meals Prepared in One Hour
or Less from Kitchen Start to Serving at Table*

When veal is poached in superheated steam in the pressure cooker it takes on a marvelously glutinous quality, a luxurious richness of texture, satisfying essence of taste—so that a relatively small quantity makes a full meal. Here are a few of our favorite veal recipes, beginning with veal steaks for two with pickled peaches and assorted vegetables, plus a lime-nut custard—all prepared together in one casserole in 20 minutes from start to table. Also, Viennese Veal Paprika, Veal Cubes in Sesame-Seeded Sour Cream, or Stuffed Veal Chops, each in about 30 minutes—and, when you can spare more time, either Pot Roast of Veal in Pinot Chardonnay, or a gorgeous cold buffet platter of Jellied Veal with Lemons and Limes, each in slightly over an hour.

Superspeed Dinner for Two All Together in One Cooker: Veal Steaks with Pickled Peaches and Seasonal Vegetables—with a Steam-Baked Dessert: Lime-Fluff Custard with Walnuts

For 2
*Cook under pressure at 15 lb for 4 minutes
    (or at 10 lb for 5 minutes)*

2 portions of the Lime-Fluff Custard
    (page 216)
  2 eggs, separated
  ¾ cup (1.85 dl) light cream, heated
    until it feels hot to your finger, but
    not scalded

The proper assembly of the various elements of this dinner in the pressure cooker is most important. Never allow the ingredients on the top layer to come up too close to the inside of the lid. Always use a pressure cooker large enough so that the top layer of food will be at least 2 inches (5 cm) below the inside of the lid.

In addition to the protein of the veal, the bran flakes with which the meat is crusted add a healthful, fibrous bulk.

2 Tbs superfine-grind sugar

The grated rind of about 1½ limes, plus up to 1 Tbs of the juice of the lime

Pinch of salt

3 Tbs finely chopped walnut meats

2 tsp butter, for buttering the custard cups

2 glacéed cherries, optional

½ cup (115 g) natural, raw bran flakes, or bread crumbs if you prefer

Salt, to your taste

Freshly ground black pepper, to your taste

1 egg

1 Tbs milk

2 Tbs olive oil (or alternative)

Two ½-inch-thick (1.2 cm) boneless, entirely lean, veal rump steaks, each about ½ lb (225 g)

2 pickled peaches, drained

½ cup (1.25 dl) dry white wine

6 whole Brussels sprouts, washed and trimmed

4 small yellow onions, peeled and cut in half

1 medium-large yam, washed, skin left on, cut in half lengthwise

About 2 Tbs pure maple syrup

As to the size of the cooker, if you have reasonable appetites and can hold down on the amount of vegetables, you can prepare this in a 3-quart cooker. But if you have large appetites, it is safer to use a 6-quart. Never try to squeeze too much food into too small a cooker. You might cause a blockage of the vent pipe.

First, make the dessert by following the recipe for the Lime-Fluff Custard on page 216 and the basic rules for all custards on page 174. Divide between 2 individual custard cups. Cover them completely and tightly with aluminum foil. Set them aside.

Everything will be cooked together in a pressure cooker of either 3-quart or 6-quart capacity (see note, above). Spread the bran flakes or bread crumbs evenly across a dinner plate and sprinkle with salt and pepper, to taste. Lightly beat the egg with the milk and spread across a second dinner plate. Coat each veal steak all around, first with bran flakes, then with the egg-milk mix, then fairly thickly with more bran flakes. Set aside.

Heat the pressure cooker, without its base rack, to medium-high frying temperature, lubricate its bottom with the oil and, when it is quite hot, quickly brown the veal steaks on both sides to a crispy, dark walnut color. Turn off the heat. Arrange the 2 peaches neatly around the veal, pour in the wine and rest the base rack on top of the fruit and meat. Now, on the base rack, organize the custard cups, Brussels sprouts, onions, yam halves, with salt and pepper to taste. Turn the heat back on, put on the lid, bring the pressure up to 15 pounds and cook for precisely 4 minutes.

When the timer rings, turn off the heat and reduce the pressure immediately. As you take out the yam halves, you may, if you wish, skin them—or you can dig them out, at table, as if they were baked potatoes. In either case, dribble some of the maple syrup over them, to your taste. Serve on very hot plates, with the natural juices from the bottom of the pressure cooker poured over the veal. Hold the custard cups at room temperature until their turn to be eaten.

A Good and Healthful Menu

Veal Steaks with Pickled Peaches and Seasonal Vegetables
Cold asparagus salad
Lime-Fluff Custard with Walnuts
Coffee or black oolong tea

The Ideal Wines

Moderately Priced

A French château red from the Médoc district of Bordeaux
or
A California red Cabernet Sauvignon from the Alexander Valley

Viennese Veal Paprika

For 4
Cook under pressure at 10 lb for 10 minutes
*   (or at 15 lb for 8 minutes)*

4 Tbs (60 g) butter
2 lb (1 kg) boneless, lean veal rump steak,
    or best part of shoulder, cut into 1¼-
    inch (3 cm) squares
2 cloves shallots, peeled and minced
2 medium yellow onions, peeled and
    finely chopped
1 Tbs all-purpose white flour
1 Tbs paprika, preferably the best quality
    of medium-hot imported Hungarian
1 cup (2.5 dl) dry white wine
2 bay leaves
2 Tbs chopped fresh parsley
Enough fresh thyme leaves, chopped, to
    fill 1 Tbs, or 1 tsp dried thyme
1 Tbs tomato paste
2 cloves garlic, peeled and minced
Salt, to your taste
1 cup (2.5 dl) sour cream

Centuries ago, when the armies of the Mohammedan Turks conquered and ruled much of Central Europe, they brought with them the strong spices of the Middle East. This is why paprika is still such an important and universal ingredient in Austria and Hungary and why the recipes of that region include some of the best paprika dishes in the world. (See also Paprika Chicken Pot on page 135 and Hungarian Goulash on page 82.)

Heat a pressure cooker of a minimum 4-quart capacity to medium-high frying temperature, put into it the butter and, when it is hot, sauté the veal pieces to a golden brown. While this is in progress, sprinkle in the shallots and onions. When the veal is almost done, lightly sprinkle the flour and the paprika all over the meat. Stir gently but thoroughly with a wooden spoon to incorporate the paprika fully. Complete the browning and then hiss in the wine. Add the bay leaves, crumbled, parsley and thyme, then thoroughly work in the tomato paste. Next, work in the garlic and salt, to your taste. The paprika replaces pepper. Put on the lid, bring up the pressure to 10 pounds and cook for exactly 10 minutes.

When the timer rings, turn off the heat and reduce the pressure immediately. Take out the veal with a slotted spoon and keep it on a warm platter, covered, in an oven at 175° F (80° C). Add sour cream to the juices in the pot and thoroughly work it in. The sour cream will softly counterbalance the stridency of the paprika. Pour this sauce over the veal and it is ready to be served. But this dish can be kept warm for up to an hour and, in fact, it will be improved by keeping.

A Good and Healthful Menu

Paper-thin slices of smoked salmon with buttered oatmeal
    bread
Viennese Veal Paprika
    with creole rice
Salad of Belgian endive with watercress
Praline ice cream
Coffee or tea

The Ideal Wines

Luxurious

A strong French red Le Corton from Burgundy
    or
A California red Cabernet Sauvignon from the Napa Valley

Everyday

A French Côte de Beaune-Villages from Burgundy
    or
A California Cabernet Sauvignon from Monterey

Veal Cubes in Sesame-Seeded Sour Cream

For 4
Cook under pressure at 10 lb for 10 minutes
(or at 15 lb for 8 minutes)

4 Tbs (60 g) butter
2 lb (1 kg) boneless, lean veal rump steak, or from the best part of the shoulder, cut into 1-inch (2.5 cm) cubes
¼ cup (30 g) all-purpose white flour
1 lb (450 g) white boiling onions, peeled, left whole
½ cup (1.25 dl) clear chicken broth (see page 35, or use canned)
½ cup (1.25 dl) dry white wine
1 clove garlic, finely minced
Enough chopped fresh basil leaves to fill 1 Tbs, or 1 tsp dried
The same amount tarragon
The same amount thyme
Salt, to your taste
Freshly ground black pepper, to your taste
1½ cups (3.75 dl) sour cream
¼ cup (60 g) sesame seeds, lightly toasted on an unbuttered pan in a 350° F (175° C) oven for 20 minutes with plenty of stirring
Enough chopped parsley leaves to fill ⅓ cup (80 ml)

This is how veal is cooked along the lovely Loire Valley. Our recipe is adapted from one given us by a famous chef in the city of Tours. This is best served on a bed of egg noodles.

You will need a pressure cooker of at least 4-quart capacity. Heat it, without its base rack, to medium-high frying temperature, melt in it 3 tablespoons of the butter and, when it is good and hot, quickly sauté the veal cubes, each lightly dredged in the flour, until they are nicely browned. If necessary, add the final tablespoon of butter. Take out the veal cubes as they are done and set aside. When all the veal is out, quickly sauté the onions until each is well flecked with brown. Turn off the heat. Put back the veal with the onions, hiss in the chicken bouillon and the wine, and add the garlic, basil, tarragon, thyme, plus salt and pepper to taste. Put on the lid, bring the pressure up to 10 pounds and cook for exactly 10 minutes.

When the timer rings, turn off the heat and reduce the pressure immediately. Stir the 1½ cups of sour cream into the pot and gently heat it up, working carefully so as not to break up the veal. Serve it on very hot plates, over a bed of egg noodles (or rice, if you insist) with the toasted sesame seeds and parsley liberally sprinkled over each portion.

A Good and Healthful Menu

Clam chowder with whole wheat croutons
Veal Cubes in Sesame-Seeded Sour Cream with Brussels sprouts and egg noodles
Fresh fruit
Coffee or Darjeeling tea

The Ideal Wines

Luxurious

A fruity French white from the Graves district of Bordeaux
or
A fruity California white Pinot Chardonnay from the Livermore Valley

Everyday

A French white dry Sauvignon from Bordeaux
or
A California white Orobianco from the Livermore Valley

Stuffed Veal Chops with Canadian Bacon and Gruyère Cheese

For 4
Cook under pressure at 10 lb for 11 minutes
(or at 15 lb for 8 minutes)

4 loin or rib veal chops, ¾ inch (2 cm)
    thick, with most of the fat trimmed
    off
4 thickish slices smoky cooked ham, with
    all fat trimmed off, then diced
¾ cup (170 g) grated Swiss Gruyère
    cheese
Freshly ground black pepper, to your
    taste
About 9 Tbs (130 g) butter
Salt, to your taste
4 slices Canadian bacon
4 medium, good and ripe tomatoes, each
    cut in half horizontally
¼ cup (60 ml) dry white wine
A few spritzes of freshly squeezed lemon
    juice

For this pocket trick, the veal chops must be at least ¾ inch (2 cm) thick. At that thickness, it is hard to cook them evenly all the way through under a broiler or in a fry pan. But the superheated steam of a pressure casserole makes them almost butter-tender inside and out.

You will need a pressure cooker of at least 4-quart capacity. First, cut the pockets in the veal chops, working with a small, very sharp, pointed knife and starting at the edge farthest from the bone. Make each pocket as deep as possible. Divide the diced ham into 4 parts and put 1 part inside each chop, with about 1 tablespoon of the grated Gruyère and 2 or 3 good grinds of pepper. No salt. If you have cut your pockets very neatly, the chops will probably stay together without sewing. If not, put a couple of stitches in the edge with thin string.

Heat up the pressure cooker, without its base rack, to medium-high frying temperature, put in 4 tablespoons of the butter and, when it is nicely hot, quickly brown the chops on both sides. Handle them carefully, so that none of the stuffing falls out. It is usually best to do only 2 chops at a time, to give you the room to move them around and turn them over. Sprinkle them lightly with salt. When all the chops are done and out of the pressure cooker, cover its bottom with the Canadian bacon and let the slices sauté for a couple of minutes to absorb some of the butter. Put back the chops, on the bacon, probably in 2 layers, neatly staggering the chops. Balance ½ tablespoon of the remaining butter on top of each chop. Carefully surround the chops with the tomato halves, the cut sides upward. Balance a teaspoon of butter on top of each tomato. Lightly wet everything with the wine and sprinkle liberally with at least half of the remaining Gruyère cheese. Then put on the lid, bring the pressure up to 10 pounds and steam everything for exactly 11 minutes. Meanwhile, preheat your broiler to a fairly high temperature.

The moment the timer rings, turn off the heat and reduce the pressure immediately. Arrange the chops in a broiling pan, each resting on a slice of Canadian bacon and partnered by 2 tomato halves. Sprinkle the remaining Gruyère cheese on top. Set everything under the broiler until the cheese is brown and crusted, usually in 2 to 3 minutes. Finally, serve each portion on a very hot plate, the veal and tomatoes lightly spritzed with lemon juice.

A Good and Healthful Menu

Mushroom Bouillon (see page 37)
Stuffed Veal Chops with Canadian Bacon and Gruyère Cheese
    with buttered tomatoes and boiled parsley potatoes
Strawberry tarts
Coffee or tea

The Ideal Wines

Luxurious

A fruity French white Condrieu from the Rhone
or
A fruity New York State white Pinot Chardonnay

Everyday

A French white Saint-Joseph from the Rhone
or
A New York State "Lake Country White"

A Decorative Buffet Platter of Cold Jellied Veal with Lemons and Limes

For 8
Cook under pressure at 10 lb for 56 minutes
(or at 15 lb for 42 minutes)

1 lb (450 g) salt pork, washed, reasonably
    desalted and thinly sliced
6 medium yellow onions, peeled and
    sliced
4 medium carrots, scraped and sliced into
    rounds—3 for the bottom of the
    casserole, 1 held for decorating
A 6-lb (2.75 kg), solid, boneless, entirely
    lean, rectangular slab of rump of
    veal, cut by your butcher into a
    shape to fit your largest pressure
    cooker (see opposite)
2 veal knuckles, quartered by your
    butcher
Enough chopped fresh basil leaves to fill
    2 Tbs, or 2 tsp dried
1 tsp dried oregano
The same amount tarragon
The same amount thyme
3 cloves garlic, peeled and finely minced
Salt, to your taste
Freshly ground black pepper, to your
    taste
1 cup (2.5 dl) dry white wine
4 lemons, 2 squeezed for juice, the other
    2 thinly sliced crosswise for
    decoration
4 limes, 2 squeezed for juice, the other 2
    thinly sliced crosswise for decoration
Up to 1½ cups (3.75 dl) chicken bouillon
    (see page 35, or use canned)
½ lb (225 g) well-shaped, light-colored,
    smallish, fresh mushrooms, wiped
    clean, trimmed and cut into hammer
    shapes

If you can give this some imagination, ingenuity and time, you can easily achieve a beautiful display dish for the central place of honor on a party buffet table. The veal will slice beautifully and taste superb with its central stuffing of aromatic vegetables and bright glazing of its natural aspic. It must, of course, be made the day before and completely cooled overnight in the refrigerator. Persuade your butcher to give you a symmetrical, rectangular slab of solid, boneless, entirely lean meat.

For your big party, you will need a larger pressure cooker, a minimum of 8 quarts, or one of the larger, canning types of 12 quarts. Remove its base rack and neatly cover its bottom with a carpet of the salt pork. Spread on it the onions and carrots. Rest the veal, its best-shaped side uppermost, on this aromatic bed, and spread the quartered knuckles around the sides of the casserole. Sprinkle on the basil, oregano, tarragon, thyme, garlic, plus a liberal allowance of salt and pepper. Wet everything with the wine, lemon and lime juices and heat these liquids just to boiling. Stop the bubbling by pouring in 1 cup of the chicken bouillon. Put on the lid, bring the pressure up to 10 pounds and cook for exactly 56 minutes. Meanwhile, lightly sauté the sliced mushrooms and the remaining sliced carrot in 4 tablespoons of the butter and reserve.

When the timer rings, turn off the heat and leave the pressure cooker tightly sealed with its lid and weight in place for at least 7 more minutes. This extra-slow reduction of the pressure helps to make the veal almost butter soft. Finally, open up the lid and, with extreme care to avoid breaking it, lift out the veal piece (using wooden spoons but no forks) and place it on a board or platter. With a long, sharp knife, cut the veal exactly in half horizontally, leaving the bottom and top halves together for the moment. Let it rest while you turn your attention to the remaining contents of the pressure cooker.

Remove the knuckle bones and discard them. Strain out all the remaining aromatic carrot, onion and salt pork mush from the naturally gelatinous liquid, carefully reserving both solids

Up to 6 Tbs (90 g) butter

About a dozen nicely red cherry
    tomatoes, to be cut into various
    shapes for decoration

Enough fresh parsley leaves, chopped, to
    fill ⅓ cup (80 ml)

and liquid. Separate the 2 halves of your piece of veal and spread the aromatic mush across the lower half, making, in effect, a kind of sandwich stuffing when you put back the top half. Now let yourself go in decorating the top and sides of the veal with the yellow rounds of carrot, the gray-white mushroom hammers, the yellow to green lemon and lime slices, red slices or half-rounds of cherry tomato, plus the bright green parsley. You will find that the sides of the veal are just sticky enough so that the slices adhere. On top, of course, you can rest half-rounds of cherry tomatoes. If you run out of room on the veal and still have colorful bits and pieces left, use them at the base of the veal for a decorative frame on the platter.

Finally, taste the liquid and adjust its flavor. It should taste quite definitely, but not overpoweringly, of the lemon-lime. If it is too tart, add a bit more chicken bouillon. Put it back in the pot and boil it down hard until it shows the first sign of thickening, usually in 4 to 7 minutes. Then let it cool until it has the consistency of honey. Now, very gently, spoonful by spoonful, dribble it over the top and sides of the piece of veal. You should aim to coat all the decorations and all the remaining surfaces of the meat with this natural aspic. The moment you have finished, set everything in the refrigerator. After about 24 hours, it will all be shining bright with the aspic glaze. Scrape away anything that has dribbled down onto the platter, and decorate it as pleases you. You will have a beautiful centerpiece for your party buffet table—beautiful, also, in taste and texture.

A Note on a Buffet Menu

Many of the recipes in this book, made in sufficient quantities, can be used within the framework of a fine buffet menu. For example, some of the clear bouillons of Chapter 3 can be served in cups. There could be tureens of some of the soups from Chapter 6; platters of the appetizers from Chapter 5 would make a handsome display. For the rest, there can be salads, cakes, cookies, perhaps hot custards from Chapter 21 and, always, ice creams and sherbets served directly from the kitchen freezer.

The Ideal Wines for a Buffet

The first essential is that the wines be flexible, for they must go with all kinds of foods. This is why rosé wines are so often chosen—but they should be good and true rosés—not artificial mixtures of red and white wines. The best rosés almost always carry the name of a grape on their labels: the Pinot Rosé of Alsace, the Cabernet Rosé of Touraine, the Tavel of the Rhone, the Cabernet, Grenache and Grignolino Rosés of California. They are all fruity, lovely, refreshing—fine accompaniments to memorable food.

Pot Roast of Veal in California Pinot Chardonnay

For 4
Cook under pressure at 10 lb for 45 minutes
(or at 15 lb for 33 minutes)

Up to 4 Tbs olive oil
A 3-lb (1.4 kg), nicely shaped, boneless
    piece of entirely lean rump of veal
4 medium yellow onions, peeled and
    sliced
1 medium green pepper, coarsely
    chunked
Enough chopped fresh leaves parsley to
    fill 1 cup (2.5 dl)
Salt, to your taste
Freshly ground black pepper, to your
    taste
1½ cups (3.75 dl) of a fine-quality
    California Pinot Chardonnay dry
    white wine

When the noble, white grapevine of Europe, the Pinot Chardonnay, was transplanted to California, it took root with such a thriving intensity and vigor that some of the greatest American white wines have been made from this magnificent grape. At its best, the wine is strong, sometimes slightly smoky, with a superb character and personality and a refreshing, fruity quality that goes almost perfectly with veal. Here, we cook the veal in Pinot Chardonnay and, of course, we drink the same wine with the meal when it is served. The timing in this recipe is for a 3-pound roast—for other weights, allow 15 minutes per pound at 10 pounds pressure, or 11 minutes per pound at 15 pounds pressure.

You will need a large pressure casserole of at least a 6-quart capacity. Heat it, without its base rack, to medium-high frying temperature, lubricate its bottom with 3 tablespoons of the oil and, when it is good and hot, quickly and thoroughly brown the roast on all sides. If necessary, add the fourth tablespoon of olive oil. When the job is well done, turn off the heat. Turn the pot roast around so that its best-shaped end is uppermost. Now pack in around it the onions, green pepper, parsley, with salt and pepper to taste. Pour over and around the meat the Pinot Chardonnay. Put on the lid, bring the pressure up to 10 pounds and cook for exactly 45 minutes.

When the timer rings, turn off the heat and allow the pressure to reduce gradually of its own accord. Serve the veal, sliced fairly thinly, with its magnificent natural sauce of pureed onions and white wine, accompanied by three vegetables such as green beans, Brussels sprouts and lima beans.

A Good and Healthful Menu

Beef Consommé (page 35) with chopped fresh fennel
Pot Roast of Veal in Pinot Chardonnay
    with green beans, Brussels sprouts and lima beans
Green apple tart
Coffee or tea

The Ideal Wines

Luxurious

A great California white Pinot Chardonnay from the Napa
    Valley

Everyday

A California white Pinot Chardonnay from Monterey

Chapter 13

ONE-DISH MEALS WITH CHICKEN AND OTHER BIRDS

Including Speed Meals Prepared in One Hour or Less from Kitchen Start to Serving at Table

---

Chicken—in its various forms as fryer, roaster, boiler, etc.—has become one of the most basic of relatively low-cost foods in the United States. We can only wish that fewer of these ubiquitous birds were reared and force-fed in wire battery cages, with no exercise and no contact with Mother Earth. If they could be free to scrabble around in farmyards, scratching for their own choices of bits and pieces of food, they would develop the natural flavor and texture which are now generally missing. You might almost say that our chicken farmers have solved every practical problem of economics and efficiency except one—the problem of producing a good, edible chicken. We might learn from the way they do it in France, where the magnificent "Poularde de Bresse" is protected by a so-called "controlled appellation law" under which no Bresse chicken may be battery-reared or fed a synthetic diet. The difference has to be tasted to be believed.

But the superheated steam of the pressure cooker does help with our bland birds. The poaching in steam gives them a velvety juiciness, and, by carefully managing the herbs and spices, some useful flavor can sometimes be injected into the flesh and the sauce. Also, here are recipes for some other birds—both common and rare—so that you will be armed with the right recipe for any occasion when a hunter friend may bring a feathery gift straight from the woods. It could be duck, goose, partridge, quail, or wild turkey . . . the recipes in this chapter will help to keep you calm and self-assured at moments of gastronomic surprise and stress. We begin, as usual, with one of those superspeed dinners for two in a single pressure casserole—sautéed and poached chicken with assorted seasonal vegetables and a steamed dessert of ripe pears filled with fruits and nuts—all prepared in 15 minutes from start to service at table.

Superspeed Dinner for Two All Together in a Single Cooker:
Sautéed and Poached Chicken with Broccoli and Carrots—with a Dessert of Steamed Fresh Pears Stuffed with Coconut, Dates, Walnuts and Maple Syrup

For 2

Cook under pressure at 15 lb for 5 minutes
(or at 10 lb for 7 minutes)

2 Tbs all-purpose flour
2 tsp paprika, preferably good red
　　Hungarian
2 cut-up servings of frying chicken:
　　breasts, drumsticks or thighs
Salt, to your taste
Freshly ground black pepper, to your
　　taste
Enough trimmed broccoli flowerets for 2
　　people
4 medium carrots, scraped but left whole

For the Dessert Pears

2 good ripe eating pears, according to the
　　season
1 Tbs freshly squeezed lemon juice
3 dates, pitted and chopped
6 halves of walnut meat, coarsely
　　chopped
2 Tbs flaked coconut meat
2 Tbs corn or peanut oil
½ cup (1.25 dl) dry white wine
2 Tbs pure maple syrup

Let us repeat, again, that the precise assemblage of the various parts of the meal into the cooker is most important. Never allow the top layer of ingredients to ride closer than 2 inches (5 cm) from the inside of the lid.

As to the size of the cooker, if you have reasonable appetites and can hold down on the amount of vegetables, you can prepare this in a 3-quart cooker. But if you have large appetites, it is safer to use a 6-quart. Never try to squeeze too much food into too small a cooker. You might cause a blockage of the vent pipe.

You will need a pressure cooker of either 3-quart or 6-quart capacity (see note, above). Thoroughly mix the flour and paprika on a plate and spread the mixture out to receive the chicken. Pat each piece of chicken with salt and pepper to your taste, then roll it lightly in the flour-paprika mixture and set aside. Do not separate the broccoli flowerets. Leave them in whole stalks, trimming only the tough bottom end and slashing the remaining stalk into quarters; set aside. Trim off any tough root ends from the scraped carrots; set aside.

Wipe the pears, remove their stalks, cut them in halves lengthwise and scoop out their cores and strings. Rub the cut surfaces at once with the lemon juice to prevent the flesh from darkening. Combine the chopped dates and walnuts with the coconut, then lightly pack this mixture into the hollows and stem channels of the pear halves. Tightly wrap each of the halves (cut side up, of course) in aluminum foil and set aside.

Heat the pressure cooker to medium-high frying temperature, put in the oil and, when it is hot, quickly sauté the chicken pieces on all sides to a golden brown. Turn off the heat and hiss in the wine. Now place the cooking rack on top of the chicken and carefully set on this rack the broccoli, carrots and the 4 packages of pears. Put on the lid, bring up the pressure to 15 pounds and cook for exactly 5 minutes.

When the timer rings, turn off the heat, reduce the pressure at once and serve the chicken with its two vegetables. Leave the pear packages to cool toward room temperature. When you are ready to serve the dessert, dribble ½ tablespoon of the maple syrup over each pear half.

A Good and Healthful Menu

Black and green olives
Sautéed and Poached Chicken with Broccoli and Carrots
Crusty French bread
Fruit- and Nut-Stuffed Pears
Coffee or tea

The Ideal Wines *Moderately Priced*

A French dry white Meursault from Burgundy
or
A New York State dry Pinot Chardonnay

Chicken with Vegetables and Rice in White Wine

For 4
Cook under pressure at 10 lb for 7 minutes, plus 6 more
    (or at 15 lb for 5 minutes, plus 4 more)

4 Tbs good olive oil
3 to 3½ lb (1.4 to 1.6 kg) frying chicken,
    cut up
8 small white onions, peeled
4 medium tomatoes, whole
2 green peppers, cored, but left whole
2 cloves garlic, peeled and minced
Salt, to your taste
Freshly ground black pepper, to your
    taste
¾ cup (1.85 dl) dry white wine
1 medium yellow onion, peeled and
    finely minced
6 oz (170 g) fresh button mushrooms,
    sliced in hammer shapes
1 cup (225 g) rice
4 Tbs (60 g) butter
1 cup (2.5 dl) chicken bouillon (see page
    35, or use canned)
Enough chopped fresh parsley to fill ⅓
    cup (80 ml)

The chicken stews to a velvety softness, absorbing the flavor juices of the vegetables. The mushroom sauce is made in the casserole for simplicity and to save pot washing.

Heat a pressure cooker of at least 4-quart capacity, without its base rack, to medium-high frying temperature. Put in the oil and, when it is hot, quickly sauté the chicken pieces until golden on all sides. Take out the chicken and lightly brown the white onions. Put back the chicken, with the tomatoes, green peppers, garlic, plus salt and pepper to taste. Pour over everything ½ cup of the wine. Put on the lid, bring the pressure up to 10 pounds and cook for exactly 7 minutes. Have ready a warm serving platter and, when the timer rings, turn off the heat and reduce the pressure immediately. Using a slotted spoon, take out all the solid pieces of chicken and vegetables and keep them warm, covered, in an oven at 160° F (70° C). Add to the juices left in the pressure cooker the yellow onion, mushrooms and the remaining ¼ cup wine. Boil fairly hard for 3 or 4 minutes, until the mushrooms have absorbed some of the flavor juices. Then, with a slotted spoon, spread these remaining solids over the chicken on its platter. You should now have only liquid left in the pot. Heat it up to gentle bubbling, add the rice and stir it around steadily for about 1 minute to mingle with the flavorful juices. Next, dot its top surface with the butter and add salt and pepper to your taste. Gently pour in the chicken bouillon, put on the lid, bring the pressure up to 10 pounds and cook for exactly 6 minutes.

When the timer rings, turn off the heat, reduce the pressure immediately, check the rice for doneness. It should be soft but still chewy; if not, continue cooking under pressure for another 2 or 3 minutes. Finally, most of the liquid should have been absorbed; if not, boil it off quite hard in the open pan. Spoon the rice around the platter, sprinkle the bright green parsley over everything and serve at once.

A Good and Healthful Menu   Boiled small shrimp in their shells (each guest peels his own)
Chicken with Vegetables and Rice in White Wine
    with hot rolls
Green salad vinaigrette
Baba au rhum
Coffee or tea

The Ideal Wines   *Luxurious*

A light French red Beaune from Burgundy
  or
A California Grignolino Rosé from the Napa Valley

Everyday

A light Spanish red Cabernet Sauvignon from the Panades region of Barcelona
  or
A California Cabernet Rosé from the Alexander Valley

English Stewed Chicken with Whole Wheat Dumplings

For 4
Cook under pressure at 10 lb for 20 minutes, plus 10 more
  (or at 15 lb for 15 minutes, plus 7 more)

3½ to 4½ lb (1.5 to 2 kg) roasting or boiling chicken, cut up into serving pieces
1 cup (2.5 dl) clear chicken bouillon (see page 35, or use canned)
1 cup (2.5 dl) dry white wine
2 medium yellow onions, peeled and sliced
1 bay leaf
Salt, to your taste
Freshly ground black pepper, to your taste
12 white boiling onions, peeled, left whole
9 small boiling potatoes, peeled, reserved underwater to avoid darkening
1 lb (450 g) can whole-kernel corn niblets
½ lb (225 g) button mushrooms, trimmed, wiped clean, left whole
Enough chopped fresh parsley to fill ⅓ cup (80 ml)

For the Dumplings

1 cup (115 g) whole wheat flour, sifted
2 tsp double-acting baking powder
1 tsp salt
3 Tbs (45 g) butter, slightly softened
½ cup (1.25 dl) milk

One of the oldest ways of cooking a chicken is still one of the best—now made even more luscious by the "drawing-out power" of the superheated steam in a pressure cooker. It can always be made ahead and reheated. It is equally good cold in its natural jelly.

You will need at least a 6-quart pressure cooker. Pack in the pieces of chicken on the base rack. Pour in the bouillon and wine. Fit the sliced onions into the odd corners. Crumble the bay leaf and sprinkle it on, adding salt and pepper to taste. Put on the lid, bring the pressure up to 10 pounds and cook for exactly 20 minutes.

While this is in progress, mix the dough for the dumplings. Sift together in a bowl the flour, baking powder and salt. With a pastry cutter, work in the softened butter until you achieve the consistency of cornmeal. Work the milk in with your fingers, lifting rather than pressing or stirring. Keep it all fluffy and light. Set this dough aside to dry out and stiffen slightly.

When the timer rings, turn off the heat, reduce the pressure immediately and add to the pot the whole onions and potatoes. Put back the lid, bring the pressure back up to 10 pounds and cook for precisely 10 minutes more. Preheat your oven to keep-warm temperature, 170° F (75° C), and set in it a lidded serving dish for the chicken and its accompanying vegetables.

When the timer again rings, turn off the heat, reduce the pressure immediately and transfer the chicken pieces, plus the whole onions and potatoes, to the serving dish in the oven. Leave all the liquid in the pressure cooker. Adjust the heat so that the liquid is gently simmering. Put in the corn and mushrooms. Dip a metal tablespoon into the hot liquid and use it to scoop the dumplings from the dough and drop them gently onto the bubbling surface. Do not crowd them. Give them room to expand. Put back the lid, but do not snap it into the closed position. Do not put on the pressure control weight. Let steam escape from the vent pipe. The dumplings should be perfectly done in 8 to 10 minutes (see page 55 for testing method).

Finally, using a slotted spoon, place the dumplings around the chicken in the serving dish. Remove the base rack from the pot and, again with the slotted spoon, fish out the corn and mushrooms, adding them to the chicken. Quickly boil down the juices in the pot until they begin just slightly to thicken. Spoon this magnificent natural sauce over the servings on the hot plates. Sprinkle with bright green parsley.

A Good and Healthful Menu

Anchovies on toast
English Stewed Chicken with Corn, Mushrooms, Onions, Potatoes and Whole Wheat Dumplings
Apple and carrot salad
Fruit-stuffed melon
Coffee or Keemun tea

The Ideal Wines

Luxurious

A French dry white Montrachet from Burgundy
or
A California dry white Pinot Chardonnay from the Napa Valley

Everyday

A French white Mâcon-Lugny from Burgundy
or
A New York State white Johannisberg Riesling

Braised Limey Goose with Mixed Vegetables

For 4
Cook under pressure at 10 lb for 20 minutes
 (or at 15 lb for 15 minutes)

Up to 4 Tbs (60 g) goose fat or olive oil
A small young goose about 3 to 3½ lb (about 1.4 to 1.6 kg), cut into serving pieces (or alternative, see opposite)
1 cup (2.5 dl) clear chicken bouillon (see page 35, or use canned)
2 whole fresh limes, the outer rind grated, the flesh thinly sliced
Enough chopped fresh tarragon leaves to fill 1 Tbs, or 1 tsp dried
Salt, to your taste
Choose 2 or 3 of the following:
    4 beets, cut in half
    4 carrots, scraped
    12 chestnuts, peeled
    6 medium white or yellow onions, peeled
    4 medium boiling potatoes, peeled
    4 turnips, scraped

A British sailor used to be called a "limey" because of all the lime juice he consumed on long sea voyages to overcome the lack of vitamin C from feeding on dried, unrefrigerated foods. So if our goose consumes a lot of lime juice during its cooking, we feel we have the perfect right to call it a limey. The refreshing tartness is a fine foil to the richness of the goose flesh. (Incidentally, if goose is not available, you could use, instead, pieces of a large chicken, duck or turkey.)

You will need a pressure cooker of at least 6-quart capacity. Heat it up, without its base rack, to medium-high frying temperature, lubricate its bottom with 2 tablespoons of the fat or oil and, when it is good and hot, quickly sauté and lightly brown the pieces of goose on all sides, taking each piece out as it is done. Add more fat or oil, as needed. Then turn off the heat and neatly pack all the goose pieces into the pot. Pour over them the chicken bouillon. Sprinkle on the grated lime rind, tarragon, with salt to taste. Fit the lime slices into the odd corners between the goose pieces, and then put the various vegetables on top. Put on the lid, bring the pressure up to 10 pounds and cook for exactly 20 minutes.

When the timer rings, turn off the heat and reduce the pressure immediately. Take out all the pieces of goose and the vegetables and keep them warm, covered, while you complete the sauce. Heat up the liquids in the pressure cooker to a rolling boil and keep boiling them down until they show the first signs of thickening, usually in about 5 to 7 minutes. Serve everything on very hot plates, with the natural sauce—slightly tangy and tart—poured over the goose.

A Good and Healthful Menu

Cold asparagus vinaigrette
Braised Limey Goose with Carrots, Chestnuts and Turnips
French bread
Watercress with diced cranberry jelly dressed with sour cream and dry mustard
Grapes and strawberries tossed in kirsch
Coffee or tea

The Ideal Wines

Luxurious

A French château red from the Médoc district of Bordeaux
or
A California red Cabernet Sauvignon from the Alexander Valley

Everyday

A French château red from the Saint-Emilion district of Bordeaux
or
A California red Merlot from the Napa Valley

Goose Ragout with California Brandy and Red Wine

For 4
Cook under pressure at 10 lb for 20 minutes
(or at 15 lb for 15 minutes)

About 4 Tbs (60 g) melted goose fat (or you can substitute butter)
A small young goose about 3 to 3½ lb (about 1.4 to 1.6 kg), cut into serving pieces
2 medium yellow onions, peeled and quartered
2 medium carrots, scraped and diced
2 medium white turnips, peeled and diced
About 3 Tbs all-purpose white flour
¼ cup (60 ml) good California brandy
1 clove garlic, peeled and finely minced
Enough chopped fresh parsley leaves to fill ⅓ cup (80 ml)
Enough chopped fresh basil leaves to fill 1 Tbs, or 1 tsp dried

The success of this recipe depends mainly on your getting rid of most of the fat that is usually layered under the skin of the bird. If the goose is frozen, thaw it slowly in the refrigerator for about 24 hours, then cut it into serving pieces. From each piece, cut off (or pull away with your fingers) all visible fat. Use a little of it for the immediate frying of the goose. The rest can be melted down and stored for future use. For many cooking processes, rendered goose fat is superior to butter. (Incidentally, if goose is not available, you can use, instead, pieces of a large chicken, duck or turkey.)

You will need at least a 6-quart pressure cooker. Heat it, without its base rack, to medium-high frying temperature, lubricate its bottom with 2 tablespoons of the fat (or butter) and, when it is good and hot, quickly and lightly brown the pieces of goose. Add more fat, as needed. When the goose is showing the first signs of beginning to color, add the onions, carrots and turnips, sautéing them also by working them around

The same amount tarragon
The same amount thyme
Salt, to your taste
Freshly ground black pepper, to your
    taste
2 lb (1 kg) small boiling potatoes, peeled
1 cup (2.5 dl) red wine (we use California
    Burgundy)

between the goose pieces. When the job is done, sprinkle on 2 tablespoons of the flour and work it in thoroughly, so that it absorbs the fat. Use a third tablespoon of flour, if necessary, depending on the amount of fat. Wet everything with the brandy, setting it alight and shaking the pot until the flames die down. Sprinkle in the garlic, half the parsley, the basil, tarragon and thyme, with salt and pepper to taste. Place the potatoes on top. Pour in the red wine, put on the lid, bring the pressure up to 10 pounds and cook for exactly 20 minutes.

When the timer rings, turn off the heat and reduce the pressure immediately. Transfer all the solid ingredients to a warmed, lidded serving dish. Quickly spoon off as much fat as possible from the surface of the natural sauce at the bottom of the cooker, scrape the bottom to release the aromatic glaze, then pour this natural sauce over each serving of goose and potatoes.

A Good and Healthful Menu

Salted sticks of carrots, celery and zucchini
Goose Ragout with California Brandy and Red Wine
    with boiled potatoes
Grilled tomatoes
Pumpernickel
Salad of romaine lettuce with walnut halves
Raspberry sherbet
Coffee or tea

The Ideal Wines

Luxurious

A French red Chambertin from Burgundy
    or
A California red Zinfandel made in Monterey

Everyday

A French regional red from Burgundy
    or
A California red Petite Sirah from Santa Clara

Poached Partridge Stuffed with Brandied Raisins and Pecans

For 4
Cook under pressure at 10 lb for 9 minutes
    (or at 15 lb for 7 minutes)

¾ cup (170 g) seedless raisins
¾ cup (1.85 dl) brandy
1 cup (225 g) shelled pecans
About ½ cup (1.25 dl) olive oil
Salt, to your taste
Freshly ground black pepper, to your
    taste
2 mature partridges, plucked and
    eviscerated, dressed and trimmed,
    ready for cooking; giblets removed
    and held separately

If a hunting friend brings you a gift of partridges, this is what to do with them. Remember that a full-grown bird serves 2 people. With the pressure cooker, you don't have to worry about the age of the birds. Whether the flesh is young and soft, or old and tough, the superheated steam will give it the texture of velvet. At the same time, the stuffing will inject into it a memorable balance of flavors. (Incidentally, if you would like to try this recipe sometime when you don't have partridge available, prepare it with Rock Cornish game hens.)

You will need a pressure cooker of at least 6-quart capacity. Put the raisins into a mortar with ¼ cup of the brandy to wet them thoroughly. Pound them with the pestle until they are

1 lemon, cut in half

6 thin slices salt pork, washed under cold running water to get rid of the surface salt

2 medium carrots, scraped and diced

2 medium yellow onions, peeled and finely chopped

Enough chopped fresh basil leaves to fill 1 Tbs, or 1 tsp dried

The same amount fresh tarragon

The same amount fresh thyme

½ cup (1.25 dl) dry white wine

broken up into a fairly coarse mush. Set aside, covered. Put the pecans into a bowl and wet them fairly thoroughly with about ¼ cup of the oil. Also coarsely crush these nuts by pounding them with the pestle, and let them stand, covered. Finely chop the hearts and livers of the partridges and mix them into the brandied raisins. Then, blend them together with the nuts, adding salt and pepper to taste. This is the stuffing.

Wipe the partridges clean and rub them, inside and out, with the cut sides of the lemon halves. Stuff the partridges with the nut-raisin mixture and tie them up or truss them. Firmly tie 3 slices of the salt pork across the breast of each bird. Heat up the pressure cooker, without its base rack, to medium-high frying temperature, lubricate its bottom with 3 tablespoons of the remaining oil and, when it is good and hot, quickly sauté and brown the partridges on all sides. Take them out, then quickly sauté the carrots and onions. Turn off the heat, put the birds back into the pot and sprinkle over them basil, tarragon and thyme, plus more salt and pepper to taste. Pour over the birds ¼ cup of the brandy and the wine. Put on the lid, bring the pressure up to 10 pounds and cook for exactly 9 minutes.

When the timer rings, turn off the heat and reduce the pressure immediately. Remove the salt pork from the breasts of the partridges, quickly chop it up and add it to the natural sauce remaining in the cooker. Skim as much as possible of the fat from the surface of this sauce. Add the remaining brandy and set it on fire, shaking the pot until the flames die down. Using sharp poultry shears, cut each partridge in half, serve on a very hot plate and pour the superb sauce over it. Need one add that you should remove any bits of string or trussing pins?

A Good and Healthful Menu

Quick Terrine of Veal with Mushrooms (see page 50)
Poached Partridge Stuffed with Brandied Raisins and Pecans with green beans and boiled rice
Corn bread
Watercress with orange sections
Crème caramel
Coffee or tea

The Ideal Wines

Luxurious

A French château red from the Graves district of Bordeaux
or
A California red Cabernet Sauvignon from the Napa Valley

Everyday

A French château red from the Saint-Emilion district of Bordeaux
or
A California red Cabernet Sauvignon from the Mendocino region

Belgian Braised Pheasant with White Cabbage

For 4
Cook under pressure at 10 lb for 15 minutes, plus 5 more
  (or at 15 lb for 11 minutes, plus 3 more)

A smallish, young pheasant about 3 to
  3½ lb (1.4 to 1.6 kg) ready for
  cooking and bringing to table
1 lemon, cut in half
4 Tbs (60 g) plus a ¼-lb stick (115 g)
  butter
Salt, to your taste
Freshly ground black pepper, to your
  taste
¾ cup (1.85 dl) dry white wine
1 medium white cabbage of about 2 lb
  (about 1 kg), stalk trimmed, tough
  outer leaves removed, cut into
  quarters

We learned this recipe from the chef of a lovely, small auberge in the heart of the forest of Ardennes in Belgium. He had true, wild pheasant and beautifully white, young local cabbages. The cabbage and the pheasant made an extraordinary marriage, each seeming to magnify and uplift the flavor of the other. Ever since, this has been our favorite way with pheasant. (But, if you absolutely cannot get to Belgium for a pheasant, you could make do with a 3½-pound chicken, a duck of about the same size or one-half a 7-pound turkey.)

Depending on the exact size of the pheasant, you will need a pressure cooker of a minimum 6-quart capacity. Clean and refresh the pheasant by rubbing it all over, inside and out, with the cut sides of the lemon halves. Heat up the pressure cooker, without its base rack, to medium-high frying temperature, melt in it 4 tablespoons of the butter and, when it is nicely hot, sauté and lightly brown the pheasant all over. Turn off the heat, take out the bird and deal with its inside cavity. Salt and pepper it, to taste. Place inside the ¼-pound solid stick of butter. Put the pheasant back into the pot. Pour in the wine, put on the lid, bring the pressure up to 10 pounds and cook for exactly 15 minutes.

When the timer rings, turn off the heat and reduce the pressure immediately. Arrange the cabbage quarters around the pheasant, add more salt and pepper, put back the lid, bring the pressure up to 10 pounds and cook for another 5 minutes.

When the timer rings again, turn off the heat and reduce the pressure immediately. Carve the pheasant and serve it with the cabbage, preferably on a bed of boiled rice. Pour some of the winey juices over each serving.

A Good and Healthful Menu

Small steak of cold boiled salmon with fresh dill, oil and vinegar
Belgian Braised Pheasant with White Cabbage
Boiled rice
Greek salad with black olives and feta cheese
Lemon soufflé
Coffee or tea

The Ideal Wines

Luxurious

A French red Beaujolais from the Village of Morgon
  or
A California red Gamay Beaujolais from Sonoma

Everyday

A French red Beaujolais-Villages
  or
A California red Gamay Beaujolais from the Mendocino region

Braised Squab with Rummy Pineapple
For 4
Cook under pressure at 10 lb for 14 minutes
(or at 15 lb for 10 minutes)

8 rings pineapple
⅓ cup (80 ml) good dark rum
4 young squabs about 1 lb (about 450 g)
    each, dressed ready for cooking and
    the table (or alternative, see
    opposite)
1 whole fresh lemon, cut in half
8 small white boiling onions, peeled, left
    whole
Salt, to your taste
Freshly ground black pepper, to your
    taste
8 thin slices salt pork, washed and
    desalted
½ cup (1.25 dl) slightly sweet white wine

Squab are now widely available at fancy butchers and in some supermarkets. They are a domesticated, farm-bred variation of the wild pouter pigeon. The flesh is darkish, with almost a meaty taste. The average squab weighs about 1 pound and, allowing for the bones, we usually serve 1 to a person. (If you can't get squab, you may use Rock Cornish game hens.)

You will need a pressure cooker of at least 6-quart capacity. Marinate the pineapple rings in the rum. Clean and refresh the squabs by rubbing them, inside and out, with the cut sides of the lemon halves. Then cut the lemon into quarters and put a quarter inside each bird. Complete the stuffing of each bird with 2 whole onions, 1 rummy pineapple ring, plus salt and pepper to taste. Wrap the breasts of each bird with 2 slices of the salt pork, firmly tied on with string. Set the 4 squabs on the base rack in the pressure cooker, breasts upward, and surround them with the remaining pineapple slices. Wet everything with the rum not absorbed by the pineapple, and the wine. Put on the lid, bring the pressure up to 10 pounds and cook for exactly 14 minutes.

When the timer rings, turn off the heat and reduce the pressure immediately. Cut away the strings. If you like, quickly chop the salt pork and use it as an additional garnish—or simply discard it. Remove the lemon quarter from the inside of each squab and squeeze a little of its juice over the bird. Serve each bird on a pineapple ring.

A Good and Healthful Menu

Mushroom Bouillon (see page 37)
Braised Squab with Rummy Pineapple
    with Greek rice
Green salad vinaigrette
Peach halves sprinkled with port wine
Coffee or winey Keemun tea

The Ideal Wines

Luxurious

A French red Côte Rotie from the Rhone Valley
    or
A California red Pinot Noir from Monterey

Everyday

A French red Côte du Rhone
    or
A California red Pinot Noir from San Benito

Small Quail Filled with Grapes

For 4
Best cooked at 10 lb for 10 minutes
(or at 15 lb for 7 minutes)

4 whole quail, dressed for cooking, with their livers intact (or alternative, see opposite)
1 whole fresh lemon, cut in half
Salt, to your taste
Freshly ground black pepper, to your taste
8 Tbs (115 g) butter
8 thin slices salt pork, washed and desalted
A solid bunch of about 1 lb (450 g) nicely sweet white grapes, picked off the stalks and well washed
1 cup (225 g) finely chopped celery
1 cup (225 g) finely chopped yellow onions
½ cup (1.25 dl) slightly sweet white wine
4 tsp whole juniper berries
8 tsp green Chartreuse liqueur
½ cup (1.25 dl) heavy cream

The quail is another game bird which seems normally to involve too much cooking fuss. This is the simplest way to achieve a lovely, aromatic, succulent flesh in about a quarter of the normal time. The quail is such a small bird that it is served one to a person. We think the finest accompaniment is a dish of baked, glazed cinnamon bananas. (Incidentally, if no one has brought you a gift of quail, you can, in a pinch, use Rock Cornish game hens.)

You will need a fairly large pressure cooker of at least 6-quart capacity. Remove the livers from the quail and chop them in a mortar, where they will later be pounded. Set aside, covered. Rub each quail, inside and out, first with the cut sides of the lemon halves, second with salt and pepper, third with a tablespoon each of the butter. Neatly tie 2 slices of salt pork over the breast of each bird. Then stuff them with equal parts of the grapes, celery and onions. Carefully set the 4 quail, side by side, breast up, on the base rack in the pressure cooker. Wet them with the wine. Put on the lid, bring the pressure up to 10 pounds and cook for exactly 10 minutes. The quail should then be perfectly done, tenderly rare. If not, just give them an extra couple of minutes under pressure.

While the cooking is in progress, prepare the sauce. Add the juniper berries to the chopped livers in the mortar and start pounding them to pulp with a pestle. At the same time, work in the remaining 4 tablespoons of butter. The final result should be a fairly stiff paste. Reserve.

When the timer rings, turn off the heat and reduce the pressure immediately. Spoon over each quail 2 teaspoons of the green Chartreuse liqueur and set it on fire, shaking the pot until the flames die down. Lift the quail out of the pot and keep them warm on a serving platter. Skim as much fat as possible from the pot juices. Then, scraping the bottom to release the aromatic glaze, work in the cream and the liver mixture from the mortar. When it is all thoroughly blended and quite hot but not boiling, spoon it over the quail and serve them at once.

A Good and Healthful Menu

Clams or oysters on the half-shell with lemon wedges
Small Quail Filled with Grapes
   with baked and glazed cinnamon bananas
Guava or quince jelly
Boiled curried rice
Salad of watercress and orange sections, lightly dressed with oil and vinegar
Baked stuffed pears
Coffee or tea

The Ideal Wines

Luxurious

A great French château red from the Graves district of Bordeaux

or

A great California red Cabernet Sauvignon from the Napa Valley

Everyday

A fine French regional red from Bordeaux

or

A fine California red Cabernet Sauvignon from Sonoma

Hungarian Paprika Chicken Pot for a Party

For 12 to 16 guests
Best cooked at 10 lb for 20 minutes, plus 15, plus 10 more
(or at 15 lb for 15 minutes, plus 11, plus 7 more)

3½ lb (1.5 kg) chicken backs and necks
2 lb (1 kg) chicken giblets
3½ lb (1.5 kg) chicken wings
4 medium yellow onions, peeled and quartered
6 stalks celery; 3 chopped with some leaves, 3 left whole
Enough chopped parsley leaves to fill ½ cup (1.25 dl)
Salt, to your taste, about 4 tsp
½ cup (115 g) pearl barley
1-lb (450 g) can cooked red kidney beans
6 medium-sized ripe tomatoes, or a 20-oz (560 g) can plum tomatoes
About 6 oz (170 g) raw young spinach leaves, well washed, stalks removed
2 cloves garlic, peeled and finely minced
2 whole bay leaves
10 whole black peppercorns
6 whole cloves
8 whole allspice berries
Enough chopped fresh marjoram leaves to fill 1 Tbs, or 1 tsp dried
Medium-hot paprika, preferably imported Hungarian, to your taste, about 3 or 4 Tbs
12 small white boiling onions, peeled, left whole
12 small boiling potatoes, peeled, left whole
1 lb (450 g) fresh shelled peas, or a frozen package

This is a fair-sized production for the memorable feeding of a fair-sized party. But the work is easy and the ingredients, regardless of inflation, are always below the average in cost. On the other hand, if you positively enjoy spending more money, you can substitute fleshier pieces (say legs, thighs, etc.) for the backs and necks. Do not leave out the giblets, which provide valuable flavor, or the wings, which provide gelatinous body to the broth. For extra simplicity and speed, we do use some canned or frozen ingredients (naturally, no "convenience packages"), but, with a bit of planning and preparation the day before, these packaged foods could easily be switched to fresh products. Incidentally, it is far, far better to prepare this pot the day before. The flavors mingle marvelously overnight and the slow reheating on the day seems to lift and sharpen the balance of a memorable meal.

For this production, you need a really large pressure cooker—preferably about 12 quarts minimum. Or you can cook everything in a smaller pot in batches. Don't overfill a single pressure cooker of any size. Rinse the chicken parts under running cold water, then put them all (backs, necks, giblets, wings) into the pressure cooker, without its base rack. Cover the meats with 3 quarts of cold water and heat it up quickly just to boiling. While it is coming up, add the quartered onions, the whole celery stalks, ¼ cup of the parsley and about 4 teaspoons salt. Put on the lid, bring the pressure up to 10 pounds and cook for exactly 20 minutes to draw out the glutinous richness from the chicken bones.

When the timer rings, turn off the heat and let the pressure reduce gradually of its own accord. Then, empty the pressure cooker completely and strain the pure liquid stock back into it, leaving all the solids in a big bowl. As soon as the chicken is cool enough to handle, arm yourself with a small, sharp knife and perform meticulous surgery. Neatly separate every bit of edible meat, discarding the bones and putting all the bite-sized chunks into a separate bowl. (By "chunks," we mean, of course, not only the white meat of the wings, but also cut up the hearts, kidneys, livers, gizzards, etc.) Finally, discard the remaining large vegetables, which have by now given their all to the stew (onions and celery stalks). You can usefully squeeze out the juices from these vegetables and add it to the aromatic liquid in the cooker. Now add to the pot the barley, the remaining 3 chopped celery stalks with leaves, the kidney beans, tomatoes, spinach leaves, garlic, the bay leaves, crumbled, the peppercorns, cloves, allspice berries, marjoram, and more salt if you like. Put on the lid, bring the pressure again up to 10 pounds and cook for exactly another 15 minutes.

When the timer rings, turn off the heat and let the pressure reduce gradually of its own accord. Lightly sprinkle the chicken chunks with about 3 or 4 tablespoons of paprika, more or less, depending on your taste. The chicken now being nicely red, return it to the pot, with the white onions and potatoes. Put back the lid and give the contents another 10 minutes of cooking at 10 pounds pressure.

When the timer rings for the last time, again reduce the pressure gradually, then put in the peas and the remaining ¼ cup of chopped parsley, continuing the simmering open, until the peas are just done and everything else seems exactly right, usually in another 7 to 12 minutes. This magnificent pot can then go onto "hold" for a few hours, or a few days.

A Good and Healthful Menu

Hot Sausages with French-Style Lyonnaise Potato Salad (page 45)
Hungarian Paprika Chicken Pot
  with big chunks of whole wheat bread
A tossed green salad
Hungarian Dobos torte
Coffee or tea

The Ideal Wines

Moderately Priced

An ice-cold French Tavel rosé from the Rhone
  or
A California Grignolino Rosé from the Napa Valley

Braised Duck with Bing Cherries in Red Wine
For 4 to 6
Cook under pressure at 10 lb for 40 minutes
(or at 15 lb for 30 minutes)

3½- to 4½-lb (1.6 to 2 kg) duck (see
opposite), cut into serving pieces
1 cup (225 g) natural, raw bran flakes
(now available at supermarkets
under a nationally known label)
4 Tbs (60 g) butter
2 medium yellow onions, peeled and
quartered
The white parts of 2 leeks, washed and
desanded, cut into 1-inch (2.5 cm)
chunks
2 stalks celery, leaves chopped, the stalks
chunked
The juice of 1 whole fresh lemon
1 cup (2.5 dl) red wine
Salt, to your taste
Freshly ground black pepper, to your
taste
1 lb (450 g) pitted Bing cherries, during
their short season, or a 1-lb (450 g)
can, out of season (if only sour
cherries are available, use them, but
marinate them first with some sugar)
4 tart cooking apples, cored and
quartered
1-lb (450 g) can cranberry jelly

If you can forget that you ever tasted crackly-crisp, roasted duck skin, this is a magnificent way of preparing a duck. Because the flesh is kept continuously moist and is teamed with the refreshing tartness of fruits, there is a memorably attractive flavor and juiciness to every tender slice. A fresh-killed, farmhouse duck, if you can find one, is, of course, better than the frozen, superfatted, Long Island type.

You will need a large pressure cooker of at least 8-quart capacity. Wash and dry the pieces of duck, then pat and press into them, all around, a coating of bran flakes. Heat up the pressure cooker, without its base rack, to medium-high frying temperature, melt in it 2 tablespoons of the butter and, when it is nicely hot, quickly brown all the duck pieces to a good golden color. Add more butter, as needed. Then pack all the pieces neatly in the pressure cooker and add the onions, leeks, celery with chopped leaves, juice of the lemon, red wine, with salt and pepper to taste. Put on the lid, bring the pressure up to 10 pounds and cook for exactly 40 minutes.

When the timer rings, turn off the heat and let the pressure reduce gradually of its own accord. Then add to the pot the cherries, apples and half the cranberry jelly. Let all this simmer, without pressure, but with the lid just resting on top, until the apples are heated through and crisply edible, with the cranberry jelly melted over the duck pieces. Serve on very hot plates, with the apples, cherries and winey juices spooned over the duck and the rest of the cranberry jelly as a side garnish.

A Good and Healthful Menu

New England clam chowder
Braised Duck with Bing Cherries in Red Wine
with boiled brown rice
Russian salad
Rum baba
Coffee or tea

The Ideal Wines

Luxurious

A French red Corton from Burgundy
or
A California Champagne Blanc de Noir from the Napa Valley

Everyday

An Italian red Valpolicella from the Venice region
or
A California regional champagne

A Decorative Centerpiece for a Party Buffet: Molded Cinnamon Turkey with Vegetables in a Cream Sauce

For 4
Cook under pressure at 10 lb for 15 minutes, plus 26 more
(or at 15 lb for 11 minutes, plus 19 more)

½ lb (225 g) green beans, left whole but all trimmed to the same length

½ lb (225 g) medium carrots, scraped, 1 sliced crosswise, the rest quartered, all trimmed to the same length

Up to 9 Tbs (130 g) butter

½ lb (225 g) small boiling potatoes, peeled and quartered

1 lb (450 g) spinach leaves, well washed, tough stalks cut away

3 cloves shallots

¼ lb (115 g) chicken livers

3 lb (1.4 kg) turkey parts, breasts, legs, thighs, etc.

1 medium yellow onion, peeled and sliced

Up to 1 tsp ground cinnamon

½ bottle good-quality dry white wine

1¼ cups (3.15 dl) sour cream

Salt, to your taste

Freshly ground black pepper, to your taste

4 whole eggs

Up to ¼ cup (60 ml) light cream

2 egg yolks

¼ lemon

We have tried many experiments with the preparation of turkey. Here is one of our most revolutionary and, we think, one of the best of all ways—a kind of turkey pie—fit to be presented to even the fussiest guest. Superheated steam makes sure that it is all creamy, juicy, as tender as a turtledove.

You will need a large pressure cooker of at least 8-quart capacity, and a handsomely shaped mold to fit inside the pressure cooker. First, deal with the vegetables. Cook the green beans and quartered carrots together, lightly and quickly so that they retain their crispness and color, in boiling salted water in which 1½ tablespoons of the butter have been melted, usually about 3 to 5 minutes. Heat 2 more tablespoons of the butter in a sauté pan and quickly brown the quartered potatoes to a light golden color, in about 5 to 6 minutes. The moment the potatoes are browned, lift them out of the sauté pan with a slotted spoon and set them aside on absorbent paper. Melt another 2 tablespoons of butter in a largish covered saucepan, then throw into it the washed spinach leaves, quickly pressing them down and stirring them around with a wooden spoon until they are just limp, usually in about 3 or 4 minutes. As soon as the spinach is cool enough to handle, squeeze out in your hands as much as possible of the juice and coarsely chop the mash of leaves with a chef's knife. In the same sauté pan used for the potatoes, add another tablespoon of butter, shallots and chicken livers. Quickly sauté them just enough to stiffen the livers, usually in about 3 to 4 minutes. Transfer the livers and shallots to a board and chop them. Here endeth the precooking.

Heat up the pressure cooker, without its base rack, to medium-high frying temperature, melt in it 2 more tablespoons of the butter and, when it is quite hot, quickly sauté and gild the pieces of turkey on all sides. As each piece is done, take it out. When all the turkey is out, quickly sauté in the remaining butter (adding a bit more, if necessary), the sliced carrot and the onions, until they are just soft, usually in 2 or 3 minutes. Turn off the heat. Neatly pack the turkey pieces back into the pressure cooker with the carrots and onions, sprinkling the pieces as they go in with as much of the cinnamon as pleases your taste. Empty the ½ bottle of wine into a mixing bowl and thoroughly blend into it a cup of sour cream. Pour this mixture into the pot, dribbling it gently down the side so as not to wash away the cinnamon. Add salt and pepper, to taste. Put on the lid, bring the pressure up to 10 pounds and cook for exactly 15 minutes.

Meanwhile, get to work assembling and filling the mold. Thoroughly butter its inside. Cover its bottom (which will eventually be the top) with several folded thicknesses of aluminum foil, to make it easy to unmold later. Put the chopped spinach into a mixing bowl and thoroughly work into it 1 of the eggs. On top of the foil at the bottom of the mold, spoon in enough of this spinach to make a neat layer just about 1 inch (2.5 cm) deep. Now carefully construct a picket fence all around the inside of the mold, using alternate sticks of green beans and carrots, close together, touching each other to form a solid fence. You make the beans and carrots stand up in their places by pushing them way down into the edge of the spinach. The sticks must all stand up quite straight if they are to look good when unmolded. Set this construction in the refrigerator while you deal with the turkey.

When the timer rings for the turkey, turn off the heat and reduce the pressure immediately. Lift out each piece of turkey with a pair of tongs, scraping it with a spoon to remove any adhering sauce, and set the turkey pieces on a cutting board. Pour the wine sauce from the pot into a storage bowl. Cover and reserve. The moment the turkey pieces are cool enough to handle, remove all the flesh from the bones and cut the edible meat into bite-sized pieces, discarding the skin. When you have them all done, pack them, firmly but not too tightly, into the center space of your mold. Next, pack in the browned potato quarters, taking care not to crush them. Put the chicken liver mixture into a mixing bowl and thoroughly work into it the remaining 3 eggs and enough of the light cream to make a thickish sauce. Taste it and add salt and pepper, as needed. Pour this cream sauce into and around the mold, so that it runs down between the potatoes and fills all the spaces among the turkey pieces. Also spread in, at this point, any remaining green beans and carrot sticks, coarsely chopped, plus any leftover puree of spinach. By now, the mold should be almost completely filled. Cover it with foil and let it set in the refrigerator, while you complete the sauce. (At this point, if you wish, you can simply leave everything for several hours. Start up again about half an hour before you plan to serve the meal.)

For the final cooking of the mold, set it, on the base rack, in the pressure cooker and pour in, down the side, 1 cup of water. The top of the mold must be completely and tightly covered with aluminimum foil. Put on the lid, bring the pressure up to 10 pounds and cook for exactly 26 minutes.

Meanwhile, deal with the wine sauce in the storage bowl. Reheat it in a saucepan, but do not let it boil. Then smooth it out by passing it through a Cuisinart chopper-churner (or one of the slightly similar other machines), an electric blender, a food mill or by hand through a sieve. Put the sauce back into the pan and boil it hard, to reduce it and concentrate its flavors, for just about 5 minutes. Turn off the heat. Bind and thicken the sauce by working in, one by one, the egg yolks— each being first mixed with a spoonful or two of hot liquid and then, at once, vigorously stirred in to avoid lumping, before the next yolk is added in the same way. Also work in the remaining ¼ cup of the sour cream and a spritz or two of lemon juice. Gently reheat this sauce, stirring continuously, until it thickens to the consistency of heavy cream.

When the timer rings for the mold, turn off the heat and reduce the pressure immediately. Unmold the turkey "pie" onto a warmed serving platter. Bring it at once to the table to dazzle your guests. Serve the sauce separately in a warmed sauceboat.

A Good and Healthful Menu

Chilled melon
Consommé Bellevue (equal parts of chicken bouillon and clam juice)
Molded Cinnamon Turkey with Vegetables in a Cream Sauce
Salad of Belgian endive with chopped walnuts
Coffee ice cream
Coffee or Darjeeling tea

The Ideal Wines

Luxurious

A great French Champagne Blanc de Blancs
or
A noble California Champagne Brut from the Napa Valley

Everyday

A French Champagne
or
A New York State Champagne Brut

Pressure-Fried Southern-Style Chicken
Makes 1¾ lb
Pressure-fry at 5 lb for 15 minutes

1¾-lb (800 g) small or large frying chicken, cut up as described opposite
1 whole egg, lightly beaten
1 cup (2.5 dl) milk
1 cup (115 g) flour
1 Tbs salt, more or less, to your taste
1½ tsp freshly ground black pepper, more or less, to your taste
½ tsp celery seed
½ tsp marjoram
½ tsp tarragon—must be dried, fresh would burn—or any alternative herbs or spices from the list opposite
6 cups (1.5 liters) vegetable oil

Warning: This recipe can only be prepared with the specially designed pressure fryer-cooker described on page 21. Pressure frying must not, under any circumstances, be attempted in a standard pressure cooker, which does not have the proper lid closure for the superfast frying operation.

The key to success with this method of pressure frying is to have all the pieces of chicken of exactly the right (and the same) size. It is not quite enough to count on your chicken dealer cutting it up precisely right. One whole side of a breast, for example, is too big. It should be cut in half crosswise. If the leg and thigh have been left joined together, they must be separated. Cut off every bit of visible fat from every piece. Wash and completely dry each piece. Frozen chicken must be completely thawed.

To get the sizes of the pieces right, you should learn to relate the weight of the bird to the number of frying pieces it will produce. A small fryer, for instance, weighing about 1¾ pounds, should give you 11 or 12 pieces. If you cut up a larger chicken for a single fryer load of, say, 1¼ pounds, you should have 5 pieces. If you want your fryer load to be 1¾ pounds, you should have 7 pieces. But, regardless of the amount of chicken, always use the fixed quantity of oil.

Never use a batter to coat the chicken. It will be overcooked before the chicken is done. Always use the egg-milk wash, followed by (never mixed with) the seasoned flour. This latter is extremely flexible. You can flavor it to your own taste. To 1 cup of flour, add about 1 tablespoon of salt, about 1½ teaspoons of pepper, plus ½ teaspoon each of any one, two, or three dried herbs or spices from the following check-reminder list: ground allspice, basil, celery seed, ground cinnamon, ground clove, dill, ground ginger, ground juniper berries, marjoram, freshly ground nutmeg, oregano, rosemary, ground saffron, sage, tarragon, thyme, etc.

You will need the 6-quart specially designed pressure fryer-cooker described on page 21. (Do not, under any circumstances, attempt this recipe in a standard pressure cooker, which does not have the proper lid closure for this kind of superfast frying.) Prepare the egg-milk wash by beating together, in a bowl, the egg and milk. Hold it for the dipping of the chicken pieces. Make ready the seasoned flour by thoroughly mixing together, in a second bowl, the flour, salt, pepper, celery seed, marjoram and tarragon (or alternatives). Spread the mixture evenly across a large dinner plate. See that the chicken is correctly cut up, as described above, cut away all visible fat, then wash and completely dry each piece. Set aside. Pour the 6 cups of oil into the pressure fryer, set it over high heat and, using a deep-frying thermometer, bring it up to 350° F (175° C). Watch it carefully. The oil heats up very quickly and can easily overheat.

Meanwhile, dip each piece of chicken in the egg-milk wash, then roll it lightly in the seasoned flour, pressing the flour firmly in with the fingers, then shaking off the excess. The moment the oil is at the right temperature, gently lower into it the chicken pieces, one by one, using tongs, working fast, to avoid overcooking the first piece before the last is in. When all are in, set the timer on 2 minutes for light browning and sealing in the open pan.

The moment the timer rings, remove the thermometer, put on the lid with the pressure regulator already in its place on the vent pipe and screw down the lid tight. The working pressure of 5 pounds will be achieved within less than 1 minute, when the regulator will start gently hissing and/or jiggling. At once set the timer for 15 minutes. Turn down the heat to medium and then adjust it slightly, down or up, to keep the gentle hissing and/or jiggling going steadily.

When the timer rings again, turn off the heat and, with the tines of a two-pronged fork, tilt the pressure regulator to an angle so that the steam hisses out fast and the pressure reduces almost immediately. As soon as the hissing stops and the pressure is down, unscrew and remove the lid. Gently take out the pieces of chicken and drain and dry them on absorbent paper. Either serve them at once, very hot, or keep them warm in an oven while you fry a second batch.

Once you have prepared this chicken two or three times, you will begin to sense the possible variations in the timing. You can get darker or lighter brown on the crust by increasing or decreasing the time in the open pan. Do not change by more than ½ minute at a time, one way or the other. You can decrease or increase the internal cooking of the chicken by decreasing or increasing the time under pressure. Here, you can try going down or up in experimental steps of 2 minutes at a time, until you reach the perfect result to your own personal taste. Once you have found the best timing, it will always stay right, provided you keep the same quantity of chicken and cut it to the same size pieces. Also, your total load of chicken should never be more than 1¾ pounds, nor less than 1¼ pounds. If you overload the pan, there is not enough heat to go around all the pieces—if you underload, there is too much concentration of heat. But, if you stick to the rules, the results can be near to perfection each time.

A Good and Healthful Menu

Asparagus Bouillon (see page 36)
Southern Fried Chicken
   with succotash
Green tossed salad
Apple or peach pie
Coffee

The Ideal Wines

Luxurious

A white French Grand Cru Chablis from Burgundy
   or
A white California Pinot Chardonnay from the Napa Valley

Everyday

A white French Sylvaner from Alsace
   or
A California white Riesling from Monterey

Pressure-Fried, Texas-Style, Barbecue-Marinated Chicken

For 4
Marinate 8–12 hours, or overnight
Pressure-fry at 5 lb for 12 minutes

½ cup (115 g) finely minced onion
1 clove garlic, peeled and finely minced
One 8-oz (225 g) can tomato sauce
½ cup (1.25 dl) chili sauce
5 Tbs freshly squeezed lemon juice
2 Tbs Spanish sherry vinegar, or tarragon
   vinegar
2 Tbs Worcestershire sauce
1½ Tbs honey
1 Tbs chili powder
1 tsp dried oregano
1 tsp ground allspice
Salt, to your taste

Warning: This recipe can only be prepared in the specially designed pressure fryer-cooker described on page 21. Pressure frying must never be attempted in a standard pressure cooker, which does not have the proper lid closure required for this type of superfast frying.

Before starting this recipe, read the general advice on frying chicken under pressure in the Introduction to the previous recipe—also the general notes on pages 21 and 93. Once you are familiar with this barbecue marination technique, you can vary the times to suit your own tastes. The first, short cooking in the open pan controls the degree of browning and the crispness of the crust. The longer cooking under pressure controls the degree of doneness and the juiciness of the inside flesh of the chicken.

Freshly ground black pepper, to your
taste

1 drop or 2 Tabasco, more or less, to your
taste

2 lb (900 g) small or large frying chicken,
precisely cut up as described on page
140

One ¼-lb (115 g) stick butter

5 cups (1.25 liters) vegetable oil

You will need a 4-quart, specially designed pressure fryer-cooker as described on page 21. (Do not attempt this recipe in a standard pressure cooker without the special type of lid closure required for this type of pressure frying.) Prepare the barbecue marinating sauce by thoroughly mixing together, in a fairly large, covered refrigerator storage bowl, the onions, garlic, tomato sauce, chili sauce, lemon juice, vinegar, Worcestershire sauce, honey, chili powder, oregano, allspice, with salt, pepper and Tabasco, to your taste. Into this barbecue marinade, thoroughly immerse all the pieces of chicken, working them around for a couple of minutes so that they begin to absorb the sauce. Cover and set in the refrigerator for 8 to 12 hours, or overnight. Whenever convenient, move the chicken pieces around in the marinade.

When you are ready to start cooking, take out the chicken pieces, lightly shake off excess marinade and let them drain and dry on absorbent paper. At once pour the barbecue marinade into a saucepan, add the butter, sliced, then heat it all up to gentle simmering, keeping it lightly bubbling, uncovered, to concentrate and develop its flavors while you are frying the chicken. Pour the 5 cups of oil into the pressure fryer, set it over high heat and, using a deep-frying thermometer, bring it up to 350° F (175° C). As soon as it is at the right temperature, gently put in half the chicken pieces, one at a time, working fast to get them in as quickly as possible. Set your timer to brown and seal the pieces for ½ minute. Then at once put on the lid with the pressure regulator already in place on the vent and screw down tight. The pressure will come up to 5 pounds within less than 1 minute, when the regulator will start gently hissing and/or jiggling. Set your timer to 12 minutes, turn down the heat to medium and adjust it so as to maintain the gentle hissing and/or jiggling continuously. Meanwhile, turn on your oven to "keep-warm," 170° F (75° C), and set in it a serving platter to heat up.

When the timer rings, turn off the heat and, using the tines of a two-pronged fork, tilt the pressure regulator to an angle so that the steam escapes fast and the pressure reduces immediately. As soon as the hissing stops and the pressure is down, unscrew and take off the lid, gently lift out the chicken pieces and drain and dry them on absorbent paper. Then, while you fry the second batch, keep the first batch warm on the serving platter in the oven. Finally, taste the hot barbecue sauce, adjust its flavorings and seasonings to suit your personal taste and serve it with the chicken. Any leftover barbecue sauce will improve with keeping, for many days, in a covered jar in the refrigerator.

A Good and Healthful Menu

Texas ruby-red grapefruit halves
Barbecue-Marinated Chicken
with Brussels sprouts and boiled potatoes
Avocado and watercress salad
Pecan pie
Coffee

The Ideal Drink

Mexican beer

Pressure-Fried Superefficient Chicken à la Kievski

For 4
Pressure-fry at 5 lb for 8 minutes

10 oz (285 g) butter
4 fairly large chicken breasts from 2
   chickens, preferably with the first
   wing bone, or clavicle bone, still
   attached
2 Tbs freshly squeezed lemon juice
6 cups (1.5 liters) vegetable oil
¾ cup (1.85 dl) dry bread crumbs
3 Tbs finely minced fresh chives, or green
   scallion tops
Salt, to your taste
Freshly ground black pepper, to your
   taste
2 whole eggs, well beaten with a little salt

Warning: This recipe can only be prepared with the specially designed pressure fryer-cooker described on page 21. Pressure frying must not, under any circumstances, be attempted in a standard pressure cooker without the special closure on the lid that is essential for this type of superspeed frying.

This is probably the most famous of all Russian recipes around the world. It is dedicated to the Ukrainian city of Kiev, but it is virtually unknown there and was probably invented by a French chef in Paris in honor of some important Ukrainian diplomat or visitor. It is normally very tricky to prepare, since it involves enclosing a piece of spiced butter inside a chicken breast folded as if it were an envelope. If it is done dead right, the butter is still inside the chicken on your plate and, as you make the first cut, the butter is supposed to spritz into your face. But if anything goes wrong, the butter runs out during the cooking and all you have on your plate is an empty shell. This recipe is the most superefficient method ever devised for preparing perfect Chicken Kievski every time! But you must shape your sticks of butter at least 2 hours ahead and then freeze them until they are rock hard. To secure the chicken envelopes, you will need toothpicks, or small trussing pins, or miniature skewers, or they can be tied with thinnish string.

For general advice on pressure-frying chicken, see the previous two recipes and especially page 140. Additional notes are on pages 21 and 93.

You will need a 6-quart specially designed pressure fryer-cooker as described on page 21. (Do not, under any circumstances, attempt this recipe with a standard pressure cooker, which does not have the special lid closure that is essential for this type of superspeed frying.) At least 2 hours before you want to start cooking, quickly mold 8 neat butter sticks, each 2 inches (5 cm) long and ⅜ inch (1 cm) thick. Set them, not touching, on a tray, covered with aluminum foil and put them in the freezer to get rock hard. Remove all bits of bone and fat from the chicken breasts, except for the wing bones, which will form a sort of drumstick handle. For this purpose, remove all meat from the wing bone, leaving it bare and clean. (The wing bone is not absolutely essential.) Skin each breast, then wash and dry it. Place them between several thicknesses of wax paper on a heavy wooden board and pound them, with even, steady strokes, with a meat hammer, until they are enlarged, flexible, soft and thin. Then cut each breast in half crosswise, sprinkle it with lemon juice and set it aside.

Pour the 6 cups of oil into the pressure fryer, set it over high heat and, using a deep-frying thermometer, bring the oil up to 350° F (175° C). Watch it carefully. The oil will heat up very quickly and can easily overheat. Adjust the heat to hold the oil at the proper temperature while you complete the Chicken

Kievski. The "secret trick" is to work fast, so that the butter does not begin to melt. Spread the bread crumbs evenly on a large dinner plate. Lay the 8 breasts on a wooden board and sprinkle each with 1 teaspoon of the chives, plus salt and pepper, to your taste. Take the first butter stick out of the freezer and lay it in the center of the first breast. Fold the two sides over the butter, overlapping, then neatly tuck in the ends to form a completely sealed envelope. You must try to make it all tight enough to hold in the butter as it begins to melt. When you have a nice, flattish, oval shape, secure it with toothpicks, small trussing pins or skewers, or tie it with thinnish string. Then, at once, dip the envelope thoroughly in the beaten eggs and roll it in the bread crumbs, patting them on firmly with your fingers, then lightly shaking off any excess. Hold the envelope aside and repeat the operation with the next 7 breasts. Then, using a slotted spoon or tongs, gently lower them, one by one, but as quickly as possible, into the hot oil. Then put on the lid, with the pressure regulator already in place on the vent, and screw down tight. The working pressure of 5 pounds will be reached in less than 1 minute, when the regulator will begin gently hissing and/or jiggling. Set your timer for 8 minutes. Meanwhile, warm up a serving platter.

The instant the timer rings, turn off the heat and, using the tines of a two-pronged fork, tilt the pressure regulator to an angle, so that the internal steam hisses out quickly and the pressure reduces almost immediately. The moment the hissing stops and the pressure is down, unscrew and remove the lid. Gently lift out the Chicken Kievski and drain and dry them briefly on absorbent paper. They must now move, as quickly as possible, from the stove to the dining table. Otherwise the internal butter will melt completely and may begin to run out. With these Chicken Kievski, at the first cut with the knife at table, you can practically guarantee a spritz of butter in the eye for each of your guests!

A Good and Healthful Menu

Black lumpfish caviar on toast canapés
Chicken à la Kievski
   with green peas and bulgur wheat kasha
Russian salad
Lemon-lime sherbet

The Ideal Wines

Luxurious

A French Champagne or
  a Russian Champanskaya

Everyday

A California Champagne
  or
A New York State Champagne

Chapter 14

ONE-DISH MEALS WITH
GAME ANIMALS

*Including Speed Meals Prepared in One Hour
or Less from Kitchen Start to Serving at Table*

Although "wild game" has always had a glamorous and romantic ring to it, in terms of great eating, the glamour was a bit exaggerated. Truly wild animals are extremely active and seldom find enough excess of food to grow fat and juicy. Their flesh is, shall we say, athletic—lean, muscular, tough. Today, thanks to much needed conservation laws to protect wildlife in all the United States, the word "wild" is almost entirely inaccurate. No hunter anywhere is allowed to sell the animal he shoots or traps. So, when you buy a game animal in a store, it is always a domestic version of the breed—reared in cages on a game farm. Only once in a long while does a hunting friend bring us a gift direct from the mountains or woods. Then, we are especially grateful for our pressure cooker, in which the superheated steam loosens and softens the tough flesh. Here, then, are the best of all possible recipes for domestic or wild hare, rabbit or venison.

German Hasenpfeffer—Sweet-Sour Jugged Hare or Rabbit

For 4
Advance marination overnight
*Cook under pressure at 10 lb for 21 minutes
    (or at 15 lb for 16 minutes)*

3 lb (1.4 kg) hare (or rabbit), cleaned,
    skinned, cut into serving pieces
2 medium yellow onions, peeled and
    sliced
2 whole bay leaves
2 tsp whole juniper berries
18 whole black peppercorns

The classic German recipe for "peppered hare" (hare cooked in a spicy sauce) was carried to England centuries ago where it became "jugged hare," hare slowly simmered (sometimes for days) in a lidded ceramic pot known as a "jug." Much later, the British colonists brought jugged hare to Massachusetts, from where it spread all over the new country. This version is from Wisconsin, where the German influence is still strong, and, if you can't find a hare, you can do it almost equally well with a rabbit.

1½ cups (3.75 dl) tarragon white wine
  vinegar
1½ cups (3.75 dl) dry white wine
½ cup (60 g) flour
Up to 4 Tbs olive oil
2 medium butternut squash, peeled and
  cut into 2- to 3-inch (5 to 7.5 cm)
  chunks
4 medium white turnips, peeled, left
  whole
Salt, to your taste
1¼ cups (3.15 dl) sour cream
About a dozen gingersnaps, crumbled

You will need a pressure cooker of at least 4-quart capacity. Pack your pieces of hare preferably into a ceramic crock, or a lidded refrigerator storage bowl, interleaving them with the onions, the bay leaves, crumbled, the juniper berries and peppercorns. Then pour in the vinegar and wine plus, if necessary, enough cold water so that the meat is completely covered by the liquid. Keep all this in a very cool place—the refrigerator, if you must, but that is really a bit too cold—overnight, or for a full 24 hours.

Finally, carefully remove the pieces of meat from the marinade, thoroughly dry them and lightly coat them with the flour. Heat up the pressure cooker, without its base rack, to medium-high frying temperature, lubricate its bottom with 3 tablespoons of the oil and, when it is quite hot, quickly sauté the pieces of meat until they are nicely browned all over. Add more oil if needed. Turn off the heat. Neatly pack all the pieces of hare into the bottom of the pressure cooker. Place the squash and turnips on top. Strain out all the aromatic solids from the liquid in the marinating container and add them to the pressure cooker, with salt to taste. Measure 1½ cups of the remaining marinade liquid and pour it into the pot. Put on the lid, bring the steam pressure up to 10 pounds and cook for exactly 21 minutes.

When the timer rings, turn off the heat and allow the pressure to reduce gradually of its own accord. Lift out the pieces of meat and vegetables and keep them warm in a covered serving bowl. Quickly strain the sauce from the pressure cooker, discarding the aromatic solids and putting the liquid back into the pot. Work into it, gently heating it up and stirring all the time, the sour cream and the gingersnaps. When this aromatic sauce is nicely smooth and has the consistency roughly of heavy cream, pour it over the meat on the platter and serve at once.

A Good and Healthful Menu

Clam-Stuffed Cherry Tomatoes (page 51)
German Hasenpfeffer
  with butternut squash and white turnips
Salad of Belgian endive with orange sections
Banana Brandy Custard (page 213)
Coffee or Darjeeling tea

The Ideal Wines

Luxurious

A great Italian red Barolo from the Piedmont region
  or
A California red Barbera from the Napa Valley

Everyday

An Italian red Barbaresco from Piedmont
  or
A California red Barbera from Sonoma

Rabbit Ragout with Red Burgundy

For 4
Advance marination overnight
Cook under pressure at 10 lb for 12 minutes, plus 9 more
  (or at 15 lb for 9 minutes, plus 7 more)

3 lb (1.4 kg) rabbit, cleaned and cut into
  serving pieces
3 medium carrots, scraped and sliced
2 medium yellow onions, peeled and
  sliced
2 cloves garlic, peeled and finely minced
Enough chopped fresh basil leaves to fill
  1 Tbs, or 1 tsp dried
The same amount tarragon
The same amount thyme
¼ cup (60 ml) brandy
1 bottle good Burgundy
Freshly ground black pepper, to your
  taste
Up to ½ cup (60 g) flour
Up to 6 Tbs (90 g) butter
Salt, to your taste
¼ lb (115 g) salt pork, washed, desalted
  under running cold water and diced
4 medium carrots, scraped, left whole
8 small white boiling onions, peeled, left
  whole
4 medium boiling potatoes, peeled, left
  whole

This is, in principle, another version of the "jugged" method of cooking from the previous recipe. The bland meat is again made aromatic by soaking with spices, and is tenderized by the superheated steam. Finally, it is glamorized by a rich sauce. The cooking times below are calculated on the basis of a 3-pound rabbit at 7 minutes per pound at 10 pounds pressure (or 5½ minutes per pound of meat at 15 pounds pressure). If your rabbit is larger or smaller, you will have to adjust the times.

You will need a pressure cooker of at least 4-quart capacity. As in the previous recipe, marinate the rabbit overnight in a mixture of the sliced carrots, yellow onions, garlic, basil, tarragon, thyme, brandy, wine, with pepper to taste. Keep it all reasonably cool.

When you want to start cooking, carefully lift out the pieces of rabbit, dry them thoroughly and dredge them in the flour. Heat up the pressure cooker, without its base rack, to medium-high frying temperature, melt in it 3 tablespoons of the butter and, when it is quite hot, quickly sauté and lightly brown the rabbit pieces. Add more butter, if needed. Turn off the heat. Neatly pack all the rabbit pieces in the bottom of the pressure cooker and hiss over them the red wine marinade with all its solids. Add salt to taste. Put on the lid, bring the pressure up to 10 pounds and cook for exactly 12 minutes.

When the timer rings, turn off the heat and let the pressure reduce gradually of its own accord. Carefully take out the rabbit pieces and reserve them. Strain the marinade sauce from the pot, and discard the solids, but reserve the liquid. Heat up the pressure cooker again to medium-high frying temperature, put into it 2 more tablespoons of the butter with the salt pork and, when they are hot, add the whole carrots, white onions, potatoes, and sauté them until they are flecked with brown. Now put back the rabbit pieces and sauté them for the second time, but very lightly, so that they just absorb the flavors without further browning. After 2 or 3 minutes of moving them around, turn off the heat.

Now hiss in the strained liquid, put the lid back on, again bring the pressure up to 10 pounds and cook for exactly another 9 minutes.

When the timer rings again, turn off the heat and reduce the pressure immediately. Have ready a warmed, covered serving dish and put the pieces of rabbit and the vegetables into it. Keep them warm in an oven at 165° F (75° C). Boil the sauce down hard in the pressure cooker to reduce it and bring out its flavors. When it shows the first signs of thickening, usually in 5 to 7 minutes, pour it over the rabbit and serve.

A Good and Healthful Menu
Tiny Cocktail Marinated Mushrooms (page 50)
Rabbit Ragout with Red Burgundy
Salad of sliced pickled beets, green pepper rings and romaine
  lettuce
Vanilla ice cream
Coffee or tea

The Ideal Wines
Luxurious

A fine French red Burgundy from Beaune
or
A fine California red Cabernet Sauvignon from the Alexander
  Valley

Everyday

A French red regional Burgundy
or
A California red Cabernet Sauvignon from Sonoma

Quick Blanquette of Rabbit in a Cream Sauce

For 4
Cook under pressure at 10 lb for 13 minutes
   (or at 15 lb for 10 minutes)

Up to 4 Tbs olive oil
3 lb (1.4 kg) young rabbit, cleaned,
   skinned and cut into serving pieces
Enough chopped fresh parsley leaves to
   fill ½ cup (1.25 dl)
Enough chopped fresh leaves of thyme to
   fill 1 Tbs, or 1 tsp dried
1 small yellow onion, peeled, left whole,
   with 2 whole cloves stuck into it
1 clove garlic, finely minced
Salt, to your taste
Freshly ground black pepper, to your
   taste
1 bottle dry white wine
12 small boiling potatoes, peeled, left
   whole
9 Tbs (130 g) butter
Up to 12 Tbs all-purpose white flour
12 medium-sized fresh white
   mushrooms, wiped clean, stems
   trimmed, then sliced in hammer
   shapes
3 cloves shallots, finely minced
½ cup (1.25 dl) heavy cream
The freshly squeezed juice of ½ a lemon
Up to 1 Tbs white wine vinegar
2 egg yolks

The trick in this recipe is the high-heat searing of the rabbit pieces, which loosens the muscles, eliminates the need for advance marination and cuts down substantially on the cooking time.

You will need a pressure cooker of at least 6-quart capacity. Heat it up, without its base rack, to high frying temperature, lubricate its bottom with 3 tablespoons of oil and, when it is very hot, almost smoking, very quickly sear the rabbit pieces on all sides. They should be in contact with the hot oil for such a short time that they do not brown darkly, but just form a slight crust on their outsides, sealing tight their inner juices. It all goes like lightning. Add more oil, if needed. Then turn off the heat, take out all the rabbit pieces and pour off any excess oil. Now neatly pack the rabbit back into the pressure cooker, sprinkle with half the parsley and the thyme, put in the onion with its two cloves, the garlic, plus salt and pepper to taste. Wet everything down with as much of the wine as is needed just to cover the rabbit. On top, place the potatoes. Put on the lid, bring the steam pressure up to 10 pounds and cook for exactly 13 minutes.

Meanwhile, begin the preparations for the cream sauce. In a saucepan, gently melt 4 tablespoons of the butter and then work into it 8 tablespoons of the flour. When the mixture is creamy and smooth, hold it warm, covered, over very low heat. In a smallish sauté pan, melt 3 more tablespoons of the butter and quickly sauté the mushrooms and shallots, continuing until the hissing subsides to show that the mushrooms have given up their water and have absorbed some of the butter. Hold them, warm, covered, over low heat. Preheat your oven to 170° F (75° C) and set in it to get warm a covered serving dish for the rabbit and potatoes.

When the timer rings for the rabbit, turn off the heat and let the pressure reduce gradually of its own accord. Gently lift out of the pot and transfer to the serving dish all the potatoes and pieces of rabbit and keep them warm, covered. Also fish out and discard the onion with its 2 cloves. Now complete the sauce. Begin working the cream into the butter-flour mixture. At the same time, heat the mixture almost to the boil, but not quite. It should become very thick. If not, gradually work in more flour. Now begin thinning it by working in 1 cup of the hot liquid from the pressure cooker. When it is all thoroughly blended, begin stirring this mix back into the liquid remaining in the pressure cooker, working gradually, tablespoon by tablespoon, making sure that it is quickly blended in and that no lumps are forming. Heat up the pressure cooker so that its sauce is just below boiling, but do not let it bubble. Now work in the lemon juice, 1 teaspoon vinegar, the remaining parsley, plus the mushrooms and shallots from the sauté pan. Finally, work the egg yolks, one at a time, into the sauce in the pot. Beat the first yolk, in a small mixing bowl, with a few tablespoons of the hot sauce. Then quickly work the mixture into the main sauce, stirring vigorously to avoid any danger of lumping. Repeat with the second yolk. Your objective is to achieve a sauce with the consistency of heavy cream. The final step is to taste and adjust the seasonings if necessary, including a few drops more vinegar, for a slight, refreshing tartness. Last of all, melt in 2 more tablespoons of butter, pour the sauce over the rabbit and serve at once.

A Good and Healthful Menu

Clams on the half-shell with lemon wedges
Quick Blanquette of Rabbit in a Cream Sauce
Corn bread
Bibb lettuce with grapefruit sections
Lime-Fluff Custard with Walnuts (page 216)
Coffee or tea

The Ideal Wines

Luxurious

A noble French red Chambertin from Burgundy
   or
A noble California red Cabernet Sauvignon from the Napa Valley

Everyday

A French red Côte de Beaune-Villages from Burgundy
   or
A California red Cabernet Sauvignon from Santa Clara

Venison Stew with Red Wine

For 4
Advance marination for 24 hours
Cook under pressure at 10 lb for 40 minutes
(or at 15 lb for 30 minutes)

2½ lb (1.1 kg) boneless, entirely lean, venison stew meat, cut evenly into 1½-inch (3.5 cm) squares
3 medium yellow onions, peeled and sliced
1 whole fresh lemon, sliced, including the rind
2 whole bay leaves
1 Tbs whole juniper berries
Enough chopped parsley leaves to fill ½ cup (1.25 dl)
Enough chopped fresh thyme leaves to fill 2 Tbs, or 2 tsp dried
Freshly ground black pepper, to your taste
1¾ cups (4.4 dl) good red wine
Up to 4 Tbs good olive oil
Salt, to your taste

We don't eat venison every week or even every month, but once in a while it does make a memorable and deeply satisfying meal. You can usually find lean venison meat cubed for stewing at fancy butchers in most of the major cities. During the cooking, you should busy yourself preparing the vegetables. The ideal accompaniment is a dish of boiled chestnuts, perhaps with Brussels sprouts, or one of the seasonal squashes.

You will need a pressure cooker of at least 3-quart capacity. Starting the day before your party, begin the essential marination of the venison. (See the detailed instructions in the Hasenpfeffer recipe on page 146). Put the squares of meat into a deep ceramic crock or a lidded refrigerator storage bowl, interleaving them with the onions, lemon slices, the bay leaves, crumbled, the juniper berries, half the parsley, thyme, and pepper to taste. Then pour in the red wine, gently, down the side of the crock so as not to disturb the layers. Leave it in a cool place—but not too cold—for 24 hours.

When you are ready to go, carefully lift the squares of venison out of the marinade and thoroughly dry them. Save the marinade. Heat up the pressure cooker, without its base rack, to medium-high frying temperature, lubricate its bottom with 3 tablespoons of oil and, when it is good and hot, quickly sauté the venison squares until they are lightly browned on all sides. Add more oil if necessary. When the browning is done, pack the venison squares neatly on the bottom of the pressure cooker, and hiss over them the marinade with all its solid, aromatic components, plus salt to taste. Put on the lid, bring the steam pressure up to 10 pounds and cook for exactly 40 minutes.

When the timer rings, turn off the heat and let the steam pressure reduce gradually of its own accord. You can, if you prefer, strain the stewing sauce before pouring it over the venison. Since we like a spicy stew, we never do any straining.

A Good and Healthful Menu

Mushroom Bouillon (page 37)
Venison Stew with Red Wine
   with Brussels sprouts and boiled chestnuts
French bread
Salad of watercress and avocado slices with fresh lime juice
Fig Pudding (page 222)
Coffee or tea

The Ideal Wines

Luxurious

A great French château red from the Pomerol district of Bordeaux

or

A great California red Zinfandel from the Napa Valley

Everyday

A French red Cahors from the Southwest

or

A California red Zinfandel from the Livermore Valley

Haunch or Steak of Venison Braised in California Cabernet Sauvignon

For 4
Advance marination overnight
Cook under pressure at 10 lb for 47 minutes
*   (or at 15 lb for 35 minutes)*

1 small, about 3½-lb (about 1.6 kg)
    haunch of venison, with its bones, or
    a boneless, lean 3-lb (1.4 kg) venison
    steak, making sure that neither is too
    large for your pressure cooker
3 medium yellow onions, peeled and
    sliced
3 cloves shallots, finely minced
1 clove garlic, finely minced
2 whole bay leaves
½ tsp ground cloves
Freshly ground black pepper, to your
    taste
¼ cup (60 ml) brandy
¼ cup (60 ml) olive oil
1½ cups (3.75 dl) good red wine
Up to 4 Tbs (60 g) butter
¼ lb (115 g) salt pork, washed, desalted
    under running cold water, diced
Up to 2 Tbs flour
1 cup (2.5 dl) slightly sweet white wine
Enough chopped fresh leaves basil to fill
    1 Tbs, or 1 tsp dried
The same amount tarragon
The same amount thyme
Salt, to your taste

When you buy a haunch or steak of venison, you never quite know the age of the animal. So the cooking time will vary according to the maturity or youth of the meat—the younger it is, the less time is necessary. Our times are based on reasonably tender, young meat. When you open up the pressure cooker after the cooking, it is always wise to taste a sliver of the venison. If it seems undercooked, it is the simplest matter to put back the lid, bring back the pressure and continue cooking for a few more minutes.

Incidentally, we find that the particular character of a fine red wine made in California, from the transplanted-from-Europe Cabernet Sauvignon grapevine, goes outstandingly well with venison, both for the cooking and for the drinking at table.

You will need a large pressure cooker of at least 8 quarts, or more. The day before, start marinating the venison. (See detailed instructions in previous recipe and under Hasenpfeffer on page 146.) Put the haunch or steak into a ceramic crock or lidded refrigerator storage bowl, closely surrounding it with the onions, shallots, garlic, the bay leaves, crumbled, the ground cloves, and only a very little pepper. Now sprinkle on gently, so as not to disturb the arrangement of the spices, the brandy and oil. Finally, pour in, at the side, the red wine. Cover the crock and leave it in a coolish place for about 12 hours, to allow the brandy and oil to do their work with the spices. Then turn and slosh the meat around, so that it is thoroughly wetted by the wine.

When you are ready to start the cooking, carefully lift out the venison, scrape all the adhering spices back into the crock, and thoroughly dry the meat. Heat up the pressure cooker, without its base rack, to medium-high frying temperature, melt in it the butter and salt pork. When it is all good and hot, quickly sauté the venison until it is lightly browned on all sides. Lift it out and set it aside. Work just enough of the flour into the remaining fat to absorb most of it and then begin blending in, tablespoon by tablespoon, the white wine. When that is all in, pour and mix in 1 cup of the marinade. Turn off the heat and put back the meat. Sprinkle over it the rest of the marinade with all its solid components, the basil, tarragon, thyme, plus more pepper, and salt to taste. Put on the lid, bring the pressure up to 10 pounds and cook for exactly 47 minutes.

When the timer rings, turn off the heat and let the pressure reduce gradually of its own accord. Take out the venison and keep it warm, covered, for a few minutes. You may strain the sauce from the pot, if you wish. Since we like our venison spicy, we do not. Boil down the sauce hard for a few minutes to reduce it and magnify its flavor, then serve it at table separately in a warmed sauceboat.

A Good and Healthful Menu

Cream of lentil soup
Haunch or Steak of Venison Braised in Cabernet Sauvignon
    with stewed apples and puree of chestnuts
A long, crusty French loaf
Tossed green salad
A platter of cheeses
Bananas baked and flamed with rum
Coffee or tea

The Ideal Wines

Luxurious

A noble California red Cabernet Sauvignon from the Napa Valley

Everyday

A fine California red Cabernet Sauvignon from the Santa Clara Valley

Chapter 15

ONE-DISH MEALS WITH
LOW-BUDGET MEATS

Pressure Tenderizes the Inexpensive Cuts

The price structure of the allegedly "relatively inexpensive foods" seems to have become quite topsy-turvy. Fish was once a low-cost buy. It is now just about the same price as prime meat. Some of the so-called "organ or variety meats," once neglected and virtually given away, have now become "gourmet specialties," at prices to match their new prestige. The budget shopper hardly knows which way to turn.

Yet some things seem to stay in the good value line forever and ever. One example is a heart—of a cow, a calf, or a pig (not the baby heart of a lamb, which can be very expensive). The flesh of a heart is top-quality nutritive protein, but the problem is that, because the heart is an extremely hardworking muscle, it can be quite tough. So can a beef kidney, if you don't treat it right!

But nothing—absolutely nothing—stays tough under the powerful ministrations of the superheated steam in a pressure cooker. It softens the inexpensive cuts, producing the wonderful effect of long, slow simmering—the final richness of flavor, glutinous smoothness of texture, velvety tenderness, achieved in minutes instead of hours. Here are a few of our favorite recipes. They demonstrate the principles involved. Once you have mastered these, you will be able to invent your own variations.

Beef Hearts Sliced in Aromatic Cream
For 4
Advance marination for 24 hours
Cook under pressure at 10 lb for 20 minutes
  (or at 15 lb for 15 minutes)

One 3-lb approx. (about 1.4 kg) beef
  heart, cut lengthwise into ⅜-inch (1
  cm) slices, all fat and tough inner
  tubes cut away, the slices well
  washed
1 quart (1 liter) buttermilk, for marinating
4 Tbs (60 g) butter
½ lb (225 g) fresh mushrooms, trimmed,
  wiped clean, sliced into hammer
  shapes
2 Tbs olive oil
4 cloves shallots, finely minced
Enough chopped fresh leaves of rosemary
  to fill 1 Tbs, or 1 tsp dried
Salt, to your taste
Freshly ground black pepper, to your
  taste
1 quart (1 liter) sour cream
½ cup (1.25 dl) dry Madeira wine
4 medium boiling potatoes, peeled, sliced
  ⅜ inch (1 cm) thick

The secrets of the success of this dish are the correct buying and proper marination of the heart. Beef hearts normally come in sizes from about 3 pounds up to about 6 pounds. The smaller they are, the better. Two small ones are always preferable to a single large one. Then, during the overnight marination, the acids of the buttermilk start the softening and sweetening process of the flesh. Finally, the cooking in a combination of Madeira wine and sour cream completes the flavoring and softening cycle. The result, we think, is a dish that is attractive for its own sake, quite apart from its relatively low cost. The sour cream clots and thickens with the Madeira to form an excellent sauce.

The day before, put the heart slices slightly overlapping in a lidded refrigerator bowl and pour over them enough of the buttermilk just to cover. Refrigerate them overnight. First thing in the morning, turn the slices over to make sure that they are thoroughly wetted on all sides.

For the final preparation, you will need a pressure cooker of at least 6-quart capacity. First, remove the heart slices from the marinade, wash them under running cold water, pat them dry and set aside. Heat up the pressure cooker, without its base rack, to medium-high frying temperature, melt in it the butter and, when it is quite hot, lightly sauté the mushrooms for about 2 to 3 minutes. Lift them out with a slotted spoon and reserve them on absorbent paper. Add the oil to the butter remaining in the pressure cooker and, when it is quite hot, quickly and lightly brown the heart slices on both sides. Turn off the heat. Arrange a neat layer of the overlapping heart slices on the bottom of the pressure cooker and put the sautéed mushrooms, shallots and rosemary around and between them, adding salt and pepper to taste. Thoroughly mix together in a bowl the sour cream and Madeira, then spoon half of this mixture over the heart. Arrange the slices of potato as a second layer on top, with more salt and pepper. Cover them with the remaining sour cream mixture. Heat up the liquids just to boiling, put on the lid, bring the steam pressure up to 10 pounds and cook for exactly 20 minutes.

When the timer rings, reduce the steam pressure immediately. Cut off and taste a small piece of the heart. It should be quite tender. If not, return it to pressure and cook it for another 5 minutes. Serve it, with its "clotted cream" sauce, on very hot plates.

A Good and Healthful Menu

Clam-Stuffed Cherry Tomatoes (see page 51)
Beef Hearts Sliced in Aromatic Cream
  with steamed sliced potatoes
Salad of avocado and romaine lettuce

Custard tarts
Coffee or tea

The Ideal Wines   *Moderately Priced*

A French red Côtes du Rhone
   or
A California red Napa Pinot Noir

Beef Kidney Stew
For 4
Marinate kidneys overnight
Cook under pressure at 10 lb for 20 minutes
*   (or at 15 lb for 15 minutes)*

2 beef kidneys, each about 1 to 1½ lb (450
    to 675 g), skinned, cut up into bite-
    size pieces, all inner membranes
    removed, pieces well washed
1 quart (1 liter) buttermilk
4 Tbs (60 g) butter
2 medium yellow onions, peeled and
    sliced
6 cloves shallots, minced
½ lb (225 g) small, button mushrooms,
    trimmed, wiped clean, left whole
4 medium tomatoes, skinned and
    chopped
1 clove garlic, finely minced
1¼ tsp dry mustard
2 whole bay leaves
1 Tbs whole, dried juniper berries
Enough chopped fresh basil leaves to fill
    1 Tbs, or 1 tsp dried
The same amount marjoram
2 tsp brown sugar
½ cup (1.25 dl) sweet port wine, or sweet
    white wine, or sweet apple cider
2 cups (5 dl) clear beef bouillon (see page
    35, or use canned)
Salt, to your taste
Freshly ground black pepper, to your
    taste
Up to 2 Tbs white wine vinegar
1 cup (2.5 dl) sour cream

If you have never tasted the pleasures of well-prepared kidneys because you are prejudiced and squeamish about which foods are or are not edible, this is where you should break out of your gastronomic prison. The "secret trick" in the perfect preparation of all kidneys is the advance marination. The mild lactic acid of the buttermilk is drawn into the tiny tubes of the kidneys, cleansing and sweetening them. In the morning, the buttermilk is expelled from the tubes by hot water, leaving them virgin pure. The kidneys can then be refrigerated for later use, or prepared immediately. One taste of such kidneys, properly cooked, will make you a kidney devotee for the rest of your life. Of course, if enough people learn this trick, the demand for kidneys will rise so sharply that they will no longer be inexpensive!

The day before, put the kidney pieces into a covered storage dish, pour over them enough of the buttermilk to cover them and refrigerate them overnight. In the morning, give them a good stir or two, to encourage the absorption of the buttermilk. When you are ready to deal with them, half fill a large saucepan with water, heat it up to a rolling boil, strain the kidneys from the buttermilk and quickly rinse them under running cold water, then dump them, all at once, into the boiling water. Immediately turn off the heat and drain the kidneys. Cool them under cold water to prevent them from cooking. Now you can refrigerate them for later use, or prepare them at once.

For the preparation, you will need a pressure cooker of at least 4-quart capacity. Heat it up, without its base rack, to quite-gentle frying temperature. Melt in it the butter and, when it is gently hot, put in, to simmer rather than fry, the onions, shallots, mushrooms and kidney pieces. Stir everything around fairly continuously and let the butter be absorbed for no more than 3 or 4 minutes. Remember that overcooked kidneys become leathery. Stop the action by adding the tomatoes, stirring to mix them in. Also add, in this order, stirring in each ingredient before adding the next, garlic, dry mustard, the bay leaves, crumbled, the juniper berries, basil, marjoram, brown sugar, sweet wine, beef bouillon, and salt and pepper to taste. Finally, stir in 1 tablespoon of the vinegar and taste. There should be a delicate and subtle sweet-sour flavor to the liquid. If necessary, dribble in a dash or two more vinegar until you achieve the perfect balance. Gently heat up everything just to the boil, put on the lid, bring the steam pressure up to 10 pounds and cook for exactly 20 minutes.

When the timer rings, turn off the heat and let the steam pressure reduce gradually of its own accord. Work into the stew as much of the cup of sour cream as is needed to make the sauce creamy in taste and texture. Then gently heat it up, but not to boiling. Serve it at once in very hot, wide bowls over a bed of sliced boiled potatoes, or nicely chewy spaghetti.

A Good and Healthful Menu

Chinese Cucumber Submarines (see page 47)
Beef Kidney Stew
   with Georgia Hopping John (see page 65) and potatoes or
   spaghetti
Salad of romaine lettuce and grapefruit sections, with fennel
   seeds and French dressing
Lime-Fluff Custard with Walnuts (see page 216)
Coffee or Formosa black oolong tea

The Ideal Wines

Moderately Priced

A French Côte de Beaune-Villages from Burgundy
   or
A California red Petite Sirah from the Livermore Valley

Beef Tongue in Aromatic Port Wine

For 4 to 6
Boil the tongue the day before
Cook under pressure at 10 lb for 60 minutes, plus 2 minutes more
   (or at 15 lb for 45 minutes, plus 1 minute more)

1 fresh beef tongue of about 3 lb (1.4 kg),
   thoroughly washed, left whole
Enough chopped fresh leaves of parsley
   to fill ¼ cup (60 ml)
3 whole bay leaves
1 medium carrot, scraped and sliced
1 medium yellow onion, peeled and
   sliced
12 whole allspice berries
8 whole cloves
¼ cup (60 ml) white wine vinegar
Salt, to your taste, about 1 Tbs
Freshly ground black pepper, to your
   taste
3 Tbs (45 g) butter
6 cloves shallots, minced

The advantage of boiling the tongue the day before is that it absorbs the aromatic flavors of its cooking liquor if it is left soaking in the refrigerator overnight. But, if you are in a great hurry, you can do without the icing on the cake and start boiling your tongue about 1½ hours before serving it to your guests. Yes—this is entirely good enough to be a party dish!

You will need a pressure cooker of at least 6-quart capacity. The day before, put into it, without its base rack, the tongue and pour over it 2 cups of freshly drawn cold water. Gently heat it up. While you are waiting for it to come to the boil, add the aromatic ingredients: parsley, 2 bay leaves, crumbled, the carrots, onion, allspice berries, cloves, vinegar and about 1 tablespoon salt and a few grinds of pepper. The moment the water boils, put on the lid, bring the steam pressure up to 10 pounds and cook for exactly 1 hour.

When the timer rings, turn off the heat and let the steam pressure reduce gradually of its own accord. Carefully and

1 Tbs Italian tomato paste
¾ cup (1.85 dl) clear beef bouillon (see
    page 35, or use canned)
¾ cup (1.85 dl) sweet port wine
1 tsp grated orange rind
¼ tsp ground cinnamon
¼ tsp ground clove
½ cup (115 g) red currant jelly

gently lift the tongue out of its boiling liquor (saving the liquor, of course) and let it cool on a platter. As soon as it is cool enough to handle, skin it completely and cut away and discard any bones and bits of fat from the root end of the tongue. Transfer the boiling liquor from the pressure cooker to a covered storage dish, put the skinned tongue back into it and refrigerate everything overnight, so that the tongue will absorb the aromatic flavors. Before the final cooking, the following day, let the tongue come to room temperature.

On the final day, gently lift the tongue out of its soaking liquor, dry it, lay it on a cutting board and cross-slice it, each slice about ⅜ inch thick, from end to end. Reserve the slices at room temperature. Heat up the pressure cooker, without its base rack, to medium-high frying temperature, melt in it the butter and, when it is nicely hot, very lightly and quickly sauté the shallots for hardly more than a minute or two. At once turn down the heat to simmering and blend in the tomato paste, plus ½ cup each of the beef bouillon and port wine. Adjust the heat so that it all bubbles fairly hard, reducing and thickening the sauce. Now work in the orange rind, cinnamon, ground cloves, the remaining bay leaf, crumbled, plus salt and pepper to taste. As the sauce bubbles hard and thickens, work in more of the bouillon and port wine. Blend and melt in the red currant jelly. When the sauce is right for flavor and texture, pour it out, for the moment, into a heatproof jug. Without bothering to rinse out the pressure cooker, neatly arrange, across and around its bottom, the overlapping slices of tongue. Pour the sauce over it. Heat it all up just to boiling, put on the lid, bring the steam pressure up to 10 pounds and cook for exactly 2 minutes.

When the timer rings, turn off the heat and reduce the steam pressure immediately. Serve the tongue at once, on very hot plates.

A Good and Healthful Menu

Carrot and celery sticks with salted olive oil
Beef Tongue in Aromatic Port Wine
    with French bread
A tossed green salad
Cheese with fruit
Coffee or Formosa black oolong tea

The Ideal Wines

Moderately Priced

A French red Cahors from the Southwest
    or
A California red Zinfandel from Monterey

Ragout of Chicken Gizzards and Hearts

For 4 to 6
Cook under pressure at 10 lb for 26 minutes
(or at 15 lb for 20 minutes)

3 Tbs (45 g) butter
1 lb (450 g) chicken gizzards, well
    washed, then dried
1 lb (450 g) chicken hearts, also washed
    and dried
2 medium yellow onions, peeled and
    minced
3 Tbs flour
1½ cups (3.75 dl) dry white wine
2 cups (5 dl) clear chicken bouillon (see
    page 35, or use canned)
3 Tbs Italian tomato paste
1 clove garlic, finely minced
Enough chopped fresh leaves of basil to
    fill 1 Tbs, or 1 tsp dried
The same amount tarragon
The same amount thyme
1 whole bay leaf
Salt, to your taste
Freshly ground black pepper, to your
    taste
2 medium white turnips, peeled and cut
    into large dice
3 stalks celery, with some leaves, the
    leaves chopped, the stalks cut into 1-
    inch (2.5 cm) chunks
3 medium carrots, scraped and sliced
3 medium potatoes, peeled and cut into
    large dice

This is surely one of the lowest-of-all low-budget dishes. We recently prepared it, carefully noting every penny we spent for every ingredient. We ended up serving a sizable group of friends at an average cost of forty-four cents per person.

You will need a pressure cooker of at least 6-quart capacity. Heat it up, without its base rack, to medium-high frying temperature, melt in it the butter and, when it is quite hot, lightly and quickly sauté the gizzards and hearts. After the first couple of minutes, add the onions and, when they are just limp and transparent, sprinkle on and work in the flour. When almost all the butter has been absorbed by the flour, begin working in (tablespoon by tablespoon at first) the white wine. Then add the chicken bouillon, tomato paste, garlic, basil, tarragon, thyme, the bay leaf, crumbled, plus salt and pepper to taste. Bring the liquid up to gentle simmering, then add the turnips, celery stalks with chopped leaves, carrots and potatoes. As soon as the liquid returns to the boil, put on the lid, bring the steam pressure up to 10 pounds and cook for exactly 26 minutes.

When the timer rings, reduce the steam pressure immediately. You can, if you wish, thicken the sauce of this ragout. We never do. We serve it, with its natural liquor, in very hot, wide bowls.

A Good and Healthful Menu

Anchovies on toast
Ragout of Chicken Gizzards and Hearts
    on a bed of brown rice
Tossed green salad
Melon halves filled with fresh fruits
Coffee or tea

The Ideal Wines

Moderately Priced

A French white Pouilly-Fumé from the Loire
    or
A California white Blanc de Blancs from the Livermore Valley

Calves' Hearts Filled with Apples, Oranges, Peaches and Pine Nuts

For 4
Oven baking for 20 minutes
Best cooked at 10 lb for 45 minutes
(or at 15 lb for 33 minutes)

¼ lb (115 g) dried apple rings, coarsely
    chopped
¼ lb (115 g) dried peach halves, coarsely
    chopped
½ cup (1.25 dl) pitted and skinned
    orange sections
3-oz (90 g) jar baby cocktail pearl onions,
    drained
3 oz (90 g) pine nuts
1 clove garlic, finely minced
¼ cup (60 g) coarsely diced green pepper
Enough chopped fresh leaves parsley to
    fill ⅓ cup (80 ml)
Enough chopped fresh leaves basil to fill
    1 Tbs, or 1 tsp dried
The same amount rosemary
The same amount thyme
1 tsp whole celery seed
¼ cup (60 ml) melted butter
Salt, to your taste
Freshly ground black pepper, to your
    taste
Up to 1 cup (2.5 dl) orange juice
2 calves' hearts, each about 1¼ to 1½ lb
    (550 to 675 g), washed, all fat
    trimmed off, inner tubes and tough
    wall valves cut out
Up to 3 Tbs olive oil
½ cup (1.25 dl) dry white wine
The freshly squeezed juice of ½ lemon
6 thin slices salt pork, rinsed and desalted

So far, in this chapter, we have only mentioned the low cost and the pleasure of eating such things as hearts, kidneys, tongues and the other so-called "variety meats." But they carry another big plus. If you look them up in the nutrition guides, you will find them to be full of protein, calcium, essential copper and phosphorus, iron, carotene, B vitamins, ascorbic acid, etc.—more than in prime rib roast or sirloin steak.

You will need a pressure cooker of at least 6-quart capacity and an open roasting pan for your oven. First, in a fair-sized mixing bowl, combine the ingredients for the stuffing: apples, peaches, orange sections, onions, pine nuts, garlic, green pepper, parsley, basil, rosemary, thyme, celery seed, melted butter, and salt and pepper to taste. Blend it all thoroughly. If it needs wetting down, add a tablespoon or two of the orange juice. Stuff it firmly into the calves' hearts—carefully filling every odd corner. Close the openings with string or trussing pins.

Heat up the pressure cooker, without its base rack, to medium-high frying temperature, lubricate its bottom with 2 tablespoons of the oil and, when it is good and hot, quickly brown the hearts on all sides. Add more oil, if needed. When the job is done, turn off the heat, lift out the hearts momentarily, put in the base rack and set the hearts on top of it. Now hiss in ½ cup of the remaining orange juice, the white wine and lemon juice. Heat up these liquids just to the boil, put on the lid, bring the steam pressure up to 10 pounds and cook for exactly 45 minutes.

About 10 minutes before the timer is due to ring, preheat your oven to 375° F (190° C) and have your open roasting pan hot and ready. When the timer does finally ring, turn off the heat under the pressure cooker and let the steam pressure reduce gradually of its own accord. Transfer the hearts to the roasting pan and cover each of them with 3 slices of the salt pork. Let them bake and crisp in the oven for just about 20 minutes. Finally, deglaze the oven roasting pan with the liquid from the pressure cooker to form a natural sauce. To serve the hearts, remove the strings or trussing pins and the salt pork slices, then cut each heart in half lengthwise, giving each diner an equal share of the aromatic stuffing. Pour the sauce over each serving.

A Good and Healthful Menu

Black and green olives
Calves' Hearts Filled with Apples, Oranges, Peaches and Pine
    Nuts
A tossed escarole salad
Raspberry sherbet
Coffee or tea

The Ideal Wines

Moderately Priced

A French château red from the Médoc district of Bordeaux
    or
A California red Cabernet Sauvignon from Sonoma

Chapter 16   ONE-DISH MEALS WITH FISH

From Baltimore Bouillabaisse to Scandinavian

Fiskpudding

Let us be frank about it. We do not think that the cooking of fish is the strongest point of the pressure cooker. If it's a matter of simple salmon steak or a plain filet of sole, the super-heated steam poaching is so much "almost instantaneous" that, by the time you have brought up the pressure and lowered it, you have not really saved enough time to make the operation worthwhile. Also, unless you watch it with the eye of a hawk, there is the danger of overcooking and mushing the fish. For these good and solid reasons, we have omitted all simple cooking of single fish from this chapter.

But in the more complicated concoctions of mixed fish (and especially when there are fishbones involved), the pressure cooker is worth its weight in golden efficiency. It draws the glutinous richness out of the bones in a way that never happens with standard simmering. The fish stew (below) develops a velvety luxury in its liquid texture. So does the cioppino—that marvelous San Francisco specialty of shellfish, olive oil and tomatoes. Then there are the European pies, puddings and terrines of fish, a kind of fishy version of a layered and spiced meat loaf, some of them firm enough to be sliced and served either as an appetizer, a main dish or a sandwich. They have not become popular in the United States, probably because their preparation and slow cooking involve a good deal of kitchen time. With the pressure cooker, they can be speeded up. They are so flexible and can be so dramatically spiced and textured, that they ought to become as popular as the pizza or the hero.

Quickest-and-Simplest-of-All Clam Chowder

For 4

Best cooked at 15 lb for 1 minute
*   (or at 10 lb for 1½ minutes)*

6 oz (170 g) salt pork, washed, desalted and diced

3 medium yellow onions, peeled and chopped

4 medium boiling potatoes, peeled and coarsely diced

1 quart (1 liter) light cream (or milk, if you worry about calories)

Two 8-oz (225 g) cans minced clams, separated from their juice, both reserved

4 Tbs (60 g) butter

Salt, to your taste

Freshly ground black pepper, to your taste

For our superspeed version, we use canned minced clams with their juice, but they cannot stand up to the pressure cooking with hot steam, which tends to toughen them to little bits of leather. So, we cook the broth and vegetables with pressure and then just heat up the clams by simmering them in the open cooker for a last minute or two before serving.

You will need a pressure cooker of at least 3-quart capacity. Heat it up, without its base rack, to medium-high frying temperature, spread across its bottom the salt pork dice and keep stirring them around to prevent them from sticking until they begin to give up their liquid fat. Then put in the onions and sauté them until they are just limp and transparent. Do not let them brown. Stir in the potatoes and hiss in the light cream. Heat it up gently to the lightest simmering, put on the lid, bring the pressure up to 15 pounds and cook for exactly 1 minute.

When the timer rings, reduce the pressure immediately. Add to the pot all the clam juice and the butter. When the broth is again lightly simmering and the butter is melted, put in the clams, all at once, and stir them around until they are just hot—no longer than that—usually in 2 to 3 minutes. Taste, adding salt and pepper, as needed. Serve instantly, before the clams have a chance to toughen, in very hot bowls, with either oyster crackers floating on top, or large chunks of crusty white bread.

A Good and Healthful Menu

Quick Terrine of Veal with Mushrooms
    (see page 50)
Clam Chowder
Tossed green salad
Chocolate cake
Jasmine tea or coffee

The Ideal Wines

Moderately Priced

A French dry white Vouvray from the Loire
    or
A California dry white Pinot Blanc from the Napa Valley

Baltimore Bouillabaisse—An American Fish Stew

For 4
Cook under pressure at 10 lb for 7 minutes, plus 4 more
*   (or at 15 lb for 5 minutes, plus 3 more)*

4 Tbs best quality olive oil (very
    important—it gives its flavor to the
    entire stew)
3 medium yellow onions, peeled and
    chopped
The white parts of 2 leeks, washed,
    desanded and chopped
4 medium ripe tomatoes, chunked
Enough chopped fresh leaves parsley to
    fill ½ cup (1.25 dl)
2 whole bay leaves
1 clove garlic, minced
½ tsp saffron filaments
Enough chopped fresh leaves of thyme to
    fill 1 Tbs, or 1 tsp dried
Salt, to your taste
Freshly ground black pepper, to your
    taste
2 lb (1 kg) assorted fish backbones and
    heads, all chunked by the fishman,
    the eyes and gills removed from the
    heads
2 cups (5 dl) dry white wine
½ lb (225 g) lump crabmeat
½ lb (225 g) chunked lobster meat
1 lb (450 g) sea bass, chunked, bones left
    in
1 lb (450 g) cross section red snapper,
    bone in, chunked
6 small clams, in their shells, well washed
    and scrubbed
24 mussels, in their shells, well washed
    and scrubbed, beards pulled off
12 scallops
1 cup (225 g) green scallions, coarsely
    chopped

Bouillabaisse is a famous fish stew made on the shores of the Mediterranean. It takes its special character from the particular fish that swim in that region and cannot really be reproduced elsewhere. But a fine fish stew, without claiming to be exactly bouillabaisse, can be made anywhere where fishermen bring in their catch. We picked Baltimore for our version because it has at its doorstep the fishy riches of Chesapeake Bay and the Eastern Shore. But we have had memorable fish stews at every port on every coast and, more surprising, also inland: with mountain trout in Colorado, with Great Lakes fish in Milwaukee and—wondrous concoction—with river catfish in Missouri. So, wherever you are, you can adapt this recipe to your local supply.

You will need a large pressure cooker of at least 6-quart capacity. First, make the aromatic base for your stew. Heat up the pressure cooker, without its base rack, to medium frying temperature, put into it the oil and when it is fairly hot, quickly sauté, just until they are limp not browned, the onions and leeks. The instant they are done, hiss in the tomatoes, half the parsley, the bay leaves, crumbled, the garlic, saffron, thyme, plus only a little salt and pepper. When all this is mixed to an aromatic mush, usually in about 5 minutes, add the fishbones and heads, the wine and 2 cups of freshly drawn cold water. This will make the aromatic stock in which the "eating fish" will later be cooked. Heat it all up just to the boil, put on the lid, bring the steam pressure up to 10 pounds and cook for exactly 7 minutes.

When the timer rings, reduce the pressure immediately. With a pair of tongs and a wooden spoon, lift out and discard all the fishbones and heads, but leave the aromatic mush of vegetables in the stock. Now quickly put in the crabmeat, lobster meat, sea bass, red snapper, clams, mussels and scallops, with a quick taste of the broth to decide whether there should be a little more salt and pepper. Put on the lid, again bring up the steam pressure to 10 pounds and cook for exactly 4 more minutes, not a second longer, or you will overcook the fish.

When the timer rings again, turn off the heat, reduce the pressure immediately and serve instantly, in hot, deep bowls. The clams and mussels will be open. Use them, in the shells, to decorate each serving. Sprinkle on top the bright green parsley and scallions. Give each diner a side plate for the bones, which are an essential part of the character, flavor and glutinous richness of a great fish stew. Offer large chunks of French bread for mopping-up operations.

A Good and Healthful Menu

Black and green olives
Baltimore Bouillabaisse
with French bread

Russian salad
Baked apples
Coffee or tea

The Ideal Wines   *Luxurious*

A strong French "Yellow Wine" from the Jura Mountains
or
A powerful California Pinot Chardonnay from the Napa Valley

Everyday

A fruity French white Sancerre from the Loire
or
A fruity California white dry Sémillon from the Livermore Valley

Quick San Francisco Crab Cioppino—Another Great Fish Stew

For 4 to 6
Cook under pressure at 10 lb for 5 minutes, plus 5 more
   (or at 15 lb for 4 minutes, plus 4 more)

6 Tbs Italian olive oil
4 medium carrots, scraped and sliced
4 stalks celery, with some leaves, the
   leaves chopped, the stalks sliced
3 medium yellow onions, peeled and
   coarsely chopped
1-lb (450 g) can imported Italian peeled
   plum tomatoes
1-lb (450 g) can tomato sauce
2 cloves garlic, finely minced
½ tsp dried oregano
Enough chopped fresh parsley to fill 1
   cup (2.5 dl)
Enough chopped leaves fresh rosemary to
   fill 1 Tbs, or 1 tsp dried
½ tsp dried sage
The same amount thyme, fresh or dried
Salt, to your taste, usually about 1½ tsp
Freshly ground black pepper, to your
   taste
1½ cups (3.75 dl) dry white wine
¾ lb (340 g) lump crabmeat
1 lb (450 g) large shrimp, shelled
1 lb (450 g) cod or halibut, boned and cut
   into 2-inch (5 cm) squares
12 small clams, in their shells, washed
   and scrubbed
1 green pepper, cored and coarsely
   chopped

Originally, this marvelous combination of fresh shellfish with an Italian cioppino, or chopped sauce of garlic, onions, spices, tomatoes and wine, was the unique specialty of the Italian neighborhoods of San Francisco around Fisherman's Wharf and North Beach. But, it was so good they couldn't keep it a secret. First, it spread all around the Bay Area—now it is all over the country—one of the truly great regional dishes of America. Superheated steam pressure draws out and combines the flavor juices quite wonderfully in the shortest time.

You will need a large pressure cooker of at least 6-quart capacity. Heat it up, without its base rack, to medium-high frying temperature, put in the oil and, when it is fairly hot, add the carrots, celery with its leaves and onions, sautéing them around until they are all just gilded and soft, usually in 3 to 4 minutes. Turn off the heat. Now add the tomatoes, tomato sauce, garlic, oregano, ½ cup of parsley, rosemary, sage, thyme, and about 1½ teaspoons salt, plus pepper to taste. Pour in the first cup of wine, heat it up just to boiling, put on the lid, bring up the steam pressure to 10 pounds and cook for exactly 5 minutes.

When the timer rings, reduce the pressure immediately. Now pack into the pot the crabmeat, shrimp, cod or halibut, clams and green pepper. Put back the lid, bring the pressure to 10 pounds and cook for another 5 minutes.

When the timer rings again, once more reduce the pressure immediately. Don't stir the pressure cooker but lift it in your two hands and gently shake it to encourage the clams to open. Add the remaining ½ cup of wine. Taste the broth and adjust the seasoning, if needed. Also taste bits of the various fish and, if any of them are still the slightest bit underdone, continue simmering in the pressure cooker, uncovered, for 2 or 3 minutes more. In this way, you can bring everything to near perfection. Serve in deep, hot bowls, with the remaining bright green parsley sprinkled over the top and plenty of crusty sourdough bread for mopping-up operations. Naturally, each diner should have a spare plate for stray bones and shells. Even at the most formal dinner table, cioppino is always a kind of delightfully informal, use-your-fingers picnic.

A Good and Healthful Menu

Thin sticks of raw fennel
San Francisco Crab Cioppino
Sourdough bread
Peaches in port wine
Coffee or tea

The Ideal Wines

Moderately Priced

A California red Barbera from the Napa Valley
or
A California rosé of Grenache from Sonoma
or
A California dry white or Moscato Canelli from the Alexander Valley

Superb Spoon Bread with a Terrine of Smoked Fish

For 4
Make the terrine the day before
Cook the bread at 10 lb for 34 minutes

For the Terrine

½ lb (225 g) smoked salmon, either Nova Scotia, or Scottish, or belly lox
A full ½ lb (225 g) flaked flesh of smoked trout, after bones and skin have been removed and discarded
½ pint (2.5 dl) heavy whipping cream
4 Tbs finely diced sweet purple onion
2 Tbs (30 g) butter
About 4 oz (115 g) caviar (see note, opposite)

For the Spoon Bread

1½ cups (225 g) cornmeal
1½ cups (3.75 dl) boiling water
1½ cups (3.75 dl) light cream
1½ tsp salt
2 whole eggs
3 Tbs (45 g) butter, melted
1 Tbs (15 g) butter, firm

We admit that we're cheating a bit on this one. The terrine of smoked fish is not cooked in a pressure cooker. It isn't cooked at all. But it makes such a magnificent combination with our pressure-cooker-cooked Southern Spoon Bread—either as an appetizer for a party dinner, or as a main course for an informal lunch or supper—that we can't resist including it among the fish specialties. The terrine must be made ahead and allowed to set in the refrigerator overnight. Then, it can be unmolded just before being brought to the table.

The central filling layer of caviar can be as luxurious or as inexpensive as you choose. For a superparty, it can be the real black beluga caviar—or the relatively inexpensive Scandinavian black lumpfish caviar—or the simple, but handsomely colored American red salmon roe caviar. Take your pick.

Spoon bread steam-poached in a pressure cooker does not have a crackly-crisp crust, but it makes up for that with a luxurious richness, a smooth softness. Eat it with a spoon accompanied by large dollops of the smoked fish terrine. A memorable marriage!

Prepare the terrine the day before in a handsome, 3-pint mold. Pass the smoked salmon through a Cuisinart chopper-churner (or one of the other slightly similar machines), or an electric blender, or a food mill, or meat grinder, or pound it by hand in a mortar, or rub it through a sieve, until it is a smooth paste. Set it aside in a covered bowl. Do the same with the smoked trout and set it aside in a separate, covered bowl. Beat the heavy cream—electrically or by hand—until it is completely stiff, then divide it into 2 equal parts. Using a rubber spatula, with light, lifting strokes, fold the first half of the cream into the smoked salmon paste with 2 tablespoons of the onion dice. Do the same with the second part of the cream into the trout paste with the rest of the diced onion. Very lightly butter the inside of your mold. Spoon into it all the salmon cream and smooth it down to a level surface. Spread the 4 ounces of caviar evenly across this surface, so that it becomes the central layer of the terrine. Now, extremely carefully and gently, so as not to disturb the caviar, spoon in all of the trout cream. Smooth it to a level surface on which the unmolded terrine will eventually stand. Cover it completely and tightly with foil and put it to set in the refrigerator overnight.

You can start the spoon bread about ¾ of an hour before you intend to serve the terrine. You will need at least a 4-quart pressure cooker and an open baking pan about 2½ inches deep and just large enough so that it will fit into the pot with about ¾ inch to spare all around. Put the cornmeal into a largish mixing bowl and pour over it, all at once, the absolutely boiling water. This very slightly cooks the cornmeal. Stir thoroughly for a couple of minutes, then begin working in the cream and the salt. Beat it with a wooden fork to make it all very smooth. Now lightly beat the eggs in a separate small bowl and then work them into the corn mix. Finally, blend in the melted butter. Use the firm butter thoroughly to lubricate the inside of the baking pan, then spread in the spoon bread mix. Completely and tightly cover the pan with aluminum foil. Pour 1½ cups of hot water into the pressure cooker, put in the base rack and set the spoon bread pan on it. Put on the lid but not the control weight, heat up the water so that it gently steams through the open vent pipe for exactly 5 minutes. Then put on the control weight, bring the pressure up to 10 pounds and cook for exactly 34 minutes more.

While this is in progress, carefully unmold the smoked fish terrine onto an ice-cold serving platter. When the timer rings, turn off the heat and reduce the pressure immediately. Lift the baking pan out of the pot, remove the aluminum foil and serve the spoon bread from the baking pan, with good helpings of the fish terrine. Eat everything with a spoon.

A Good and Healthful Menu

Asparagus Bouillon (page 36)
Spoon Bread with a Terrine of Smoked Fish
Grilled stuffed tomatoes
Bananas baked with rum
Coffee or tea

The Ideal Wines

Luxurious

A noble French white Bâtard-Montrachet from Burgundy
   or
A noble California white Pinot Chardonnay from Monterey

Everyday

A French white Muscadet de Sèvre-et-Maine from the Loire
    or
A California white Pinot Blanc from Santa Clara

Scottish Leftover Fish Pie

For 2
Cook under pressure at 15 lb for 15 minutes
    (or at 10 lb for 20 minutes)

2½ cups (570 g) boned, flaked, cold
    cooked fish; in Scotland cod or
    haddock are used, but any firm-
    fleshed fish will do
1 Tbs freshly squeezed lemon juice
1 tsp Scotch whisky
2 medium potatoes, boiled, peeled and
    mashed in advance
2 Tbs (30 g) melted butter
Enough chopped fresh leaves of parsley
    to fill ¼ cup (60 ml)
Freshly ground nutmeg, to your taste
Salt, to your taste
Freshly ground black pepper, to your
    taste
1 whole egg
⅓ cup (80 ml) light cream
1 Tbs (15 g) firm butter

This is one of the oldest and best ways of reheating leftover cold, flaked fish. The flavor and texture vary, of course, with the different kinds of fish and you can also change, as you please, the aromatic spicing of the mashed potatoes.

You will need a pressure cooker of at least 4-quart capacity and a 6-cup mold or soufflé dish of a shape to fit inside the pressure cooker with about ¾ inch (2 cm) to spare around it. Put the flaked fish into a mixing bowl and toss it lightly with the lemon juice and whisky. In a second mixing bowl, blend together the mashed potatoes, melted butter, parsley, a few grinds of nutmeg, with salt and pepper to taste. Now lightly work the potato mix into the fish. Thoroughly beat the egg into the cream and stir it at once into the fish mixture. Liberally butter the inside of the mold or soufflé dish, transfer the fish pie mix into it and tightly cover it with aluminum foil. Pour ¾ cup hot water into the pressure cooker, put in the base rack and set the fish pie on it. Put on the lid, bring the steam pressure up to 15 pounds and cook for exactly 15 minutes.

When the timer rings, turn off the heat and reduce the pressure immediately. Test the pie for doneness. A bright silvery knife plunged into its center should come out dry. If not, give it another 2 or 3 minutes at pressure. This pie is juicy and good just as it comes out of the dish, but you can, if you wish, glamorize it with one of our sauces from Chapter 4.

A Good and Healthful Menu

Mushroom Bouillon (page 37)
Scottish Fish Pie
Salad of tomatoes and scallions marinated with oil and vinegar
Cheesecake
Coffee or tea

The Ideal Wines

Moderately Priced

A French white Hermitage from the Rhone
    or
A New York State white Delaware from the Finger Lakes

Scandinavian Fiskpudding

For 2
Cook under pressure at 5 lb for 15 minutes
(or at 10 lb for 11 minutes)

¼ cup (60 g) raw rice, well washed
1¼ cups (3.15 dl) light cream
2 cups (450 g) boned, flaked, cold cooked
  fish; most often used among the
  Scandinavians are fresh or salt cod,
  haddock or smoked fish, but almost
  any kind will do
Salt, to your taste
Freshly ground black pepper, to your
  taste
1 whole egg, lightly beaten
2 Tbs (30 g) melted butter
1 Tbs (15 g) firm butter

The Scandinavians don't use this recipe only for leftover fish. They seem to like it so much, they often prepare it with fresh fish, or salt cod, or smoked fish. There are dozens of possible variations—all of them excellent and inexpensive.

You will need a pressure cooker of at least 3-quart capacity and a 4-cup mold or metal baking pan of a shape to fit inside the pot with about ¾ inch to spare all around. First, put into the pressure cooker, without its base rack, the rice and cream. Heat it up gently to simmering, stirring most of the time, until the rice is richly soft. Turn off the heat. Now lightly work into the creamed rice the fish, with salt and pepper to taste. Next, thoroughly stir in the lightly beaten egg and the melted butter. Liberally butter the mold or baking pan and transfer the fish pudding mix into it. Cover the mold tightly with aluminum foil. Rinse out the pressure cooker, put in its base rack, pour in ¾ cup of hot water and set the mold on the rack inside the pot. Put on the lid, bring up the steam pressure to 5 pounds and cook for exactly 15 minutes.

When the timer rings, turn off the heat and let the pressure reduce gradually of its own accord. Check the doneness of the pudding. A bright, silvery knife plunged into the center should come out dry. If not, give it 2 or 3 minutes of extra cooking at pressure. It should all be stiff enough to slice and serve on hot plates, either alone, or with one of our sauces from Chapter 4. The Scandinavians would use extra melted butter as sauce. This pudding is excellent cold, or it can be sliced about ⅜ inch thick and lightly browned in butter.

A Good and Healthful Menu

Chinese Pork-Stuffed Mushrooms (page 48)
Scandinavian Fiskpudding
Salad of lentils with dill
Pineapple in white wine
Coffee or tea

The Ideal Wines

Moderately Priced

A French white Côtes de Provence from the South
  or
A California white Folle Blanche from the Napa Valley

Pressure-Fried, Crackly-Crispy-Juicy Fish Fillets with Butter-Chive-Lemon Sauce

For 4
Pressure-fry at 5 lb for 2 minutes

¼ lb (115 g) butter
1½ cups (175 g) all-purpose white flour
1½ lb (675 g) fish fillets, fresh, of course, by far the best, but if you insist on frozen, they must be completely thawed before you begin this recipe
1 large egg, separated
3 Tbs olive oil
1 tsp granulated white sugar
Salt, to your taste
¾ cup (1.85 dl) milk
¼ cup (60 g) finely minced onion
Enough fresh tarragon leaves, in season, finely chopped, to fill 2 Tbs, or 2 tsp dried
Freshly ground black pepper, to your taste
Enough chives, fresh or frozen, finely snipped, to fill 2 Tbs
¼ cup (60 ml) finely chopped parsley
1 whole fresh lemon
6 cups (1.5 liters) vegetable oil

Warning: This recipe can only be prepared in the specially designed pressure fryer-cooker described on page 21. Pressure frying cannot be done in a standard pressure cooker, which does not have the special lid closure for this type of super-speed frying. For general advice on pressure-frying techniques, see the Introduction to chicken frying on page 140.

You will need a 6-quart specially designed pressure fryer-cooker as described on page 21. (Do not, under any circumstances, attempt this recipe in a standard pressure cooker, which does not have the proper lid closure required for this type of superspeed pressure frying.) Bring out the butter to soften at room temperature. Spread ½ cup of the flour evenly across a large dinner plate. Cut the fish fillets into 2-inch by 2-inch (5 cm by 5 cm) squares, all exactly the same size, then coat them with the flour on the plate and hold them aside to dry. Next, prepare the batter. Sift the remaining 1 cup of flour into a fair-sized mixing bowl. Put the egg yolk into a separate, smaller mixing bowl and lightly beat into it the olive oil and sugar, with about 1 teaspoon salt, more or less, to your taste. Now lightly work this mixture into the flour in the bowl, until you have a smooth paste. Next, work in the milk, dash by dash, not necessarily using it all, but only enough to achieve a thickish cream. Now stir into it the minced onion and tarragon, with about 1 teaspoon pepper, more or less, to your taste. If the batter thickens, add a dash more milk. Then set it all aside, uncovered, stirring it occasionally, to mellow and ripen.

Finally, among the advance preparations, the butter sauce takes only a few seconds. Put the now-softened butter into a smallish mixing bowl and lightly cream into it 1 tablespoon each of chives and parsley, with the juice of half the lemon, plus salt and pepper, to your taste. The lemon flavor should be fairly strong. If not, add a few more spritzes of juice from the other half of the lemon. Then hold this sauce at room temperature. Turn on your oven to "keep warm," 150° F (65° C), and heat up in it the serving platter. Now we are ready for the frying.

Pour the 6 cups of oil into the pressure fryer, set it on high heat and, using a deep-frying thermometer, bring it up to 350° F (175° C). Watch it carefully. The oil heats up very quickly and can easily overheat. Meanwhile, check the batter. If it has again thickened, stir in a dash or two more milk to restore it to a thickish cream. Quickly beat the egg white stiff and fold it into the creamy batter. This is now the lightest frying batter in the world and can be used for any kind of fish. The moment the oil has reached the right temperature, dip each square of fish into the batter and, using a slotted spoon or tongs, gently lower it into the oil. Work quickly, so that the minimum time elapses between the first and last pieces going in. Let them all brown and seal in the open pan for exactly 2½ minutes. Preferably using a wooden fork, make sure that the fish squares do not stick together.

The instant the timer rings, remove the thermometer and put on the lid with the pressure regulator already in place on the vent and screw down the big knob tight. The working pressure of 5 pounds will be reached in less than 1 minute, when steam will start gently hissing and/or the regulator will begin to jiggle. At once set your timer to 2 minutes. Turn down the heat to medium and adjust it, slightly down or up, so that the gentle hissing and/or jiggling continues.

The moment the timer rings again, turn off the heat and use the tines of a two-pronged fork to tilt the pressure regulator to one side, so that the steam escapes quickly and the pressure is reduced almost immediately. When the hissing stops and the pressure is down, unscrew and remove the lid. Carefully lift out the fish squares and let them drain and dry on absorbent paper. Then transfer them to the warm serving platter. Dot each square with the butter-chive-lemon sauce and sprinkle all the remaining chopped chives and parsley over the top. Decorate the platter, to your taste, with lemon wedges and sprigs of parsley.

A Good and Healthful Menu

Small spicy sausages, served hot
Crispy Fish Fillets with Butter-Chive-Lemon Sauce
Green beans and boiled potatoes
Salad of scallions and sliced tomatoes
Blueberry pie
Darjeeling tea

The Ideal Wines

A white French Graves from Bordeaux
or
A white California Pinot Chardonnay from Monterey

Everyday

A white French Sancerre from the Loire
or
A white California Pinot Blanc from the Napa Valley

Pressure-Fried, Rolled, Stuffed Flounder with Delicate and Gentle Mustard Sauce

For 4
Pressure-fry at 5 lb for 6 minutes

1 batch mustard sauce from recipe on
    page 41
1 large whole egg, slightly beaten
1 cup (2.5 dl) milk
¼ cup (60 g) finely minced onion
2 Tbs (30 g) butter
½ cup (1.25 dl) soft white bread crumbs

Warning: This recipe can only be prepared in one of the specially designed pressure fryer-cookers described on page 21. Pressure frying must never be attempted in a standard pressure cooker, which does not have the proper lid closure that is essential for this type of superspeed frying.

For general advice on the techniques of pressure frying, see the Introduction to the basic fried chicken recipe on page 140—also the recipe for Crispy Fish Fillets on page 170. After you have prepared this recipe a couple of times and have be-

½ cup (115 g) finely chopped fresh
  mushrooms
¼ cup (60 ml) finely chopped parsley
1 finely minced clove garlic
1 large egg yolk, lightly beaten
Enough fresh dill, in season, finely
  chopped, to fill 1 Tbs, or 1 tsp dried
1 teaspoon salt, more or less, to your taste
Freshly ground black pepper, to your
  taste
Up to 2 Tbs freshly squeezed lemon juice
4 boneless fresh flounder fillets, each
  weighing about 6 oz (170 g)
1 cup (2.5 dl) dry bread crumbs
5 cups (1.25 liters) vegetable oil

come familiar with it, you will, of course, be able to vary the stuffing in many different ways, to suit your personal tastes.

You will need a 4-quart specially designed pressure fryer-cooker as described on page 21. (Do not, under any circumstances, attempt this recipe in a standard pressure cooker, which does not have the proper lid closure for this type of superspeed pressure frying.) Perhaps several hours ahead, prepare the mustard sauce, according to the recipe on page 41, and let it stand to mellow and ripen at room temperature. It will be warmed up just before serving. Next, make the egg-milk frying wash by beating together, in a smallish mixing bowl, the whole egg with the milk. Let it stand, covered. Next, prepare the stuffing by working together, in a largish mixing bowl, the minced onion, butter, soft bread crumbs, chopped mushrooms, parsley, minced garlic, egg yolk, dill, with 1 teaspoon salt and pepper, to your taste. Then mix in 1 tablespoon of lemon juice and taste again. There should be a delicate yet clear flavor of lemon. If not, add more lemon juice, dribble by dribble, until you have the stuffing exactly to your taste.

Wash each fish fillet and dry it completely. Lightly sprinkle each with salt and pepper. Spoon about a quarter of the stuffing onto each fillet, or a bit less, according to the length and width of each one. Then roll them up, jelly roll style, tying each securely with thinnish string. Spread the dry bread crumbs evenly on a large dinner plate. Give the egg-milk wash a final beat or two, dip each flounder roll in it and then, so to speak, roll each roll in bread crumbs. Pat the crumbs with your fingers into a firm, not-too-thick covering. Let the rolls dry while you prepare the fryer.

Pour the 5 cups of oil into the pressure fryer, set it over high heat and, using a deep-frying thermometer, bring it up to 350° F (175° C). Watch it carefully. The oil will heat up very quickly and can easily overheat. While waiting for the oil, set the mustard sauce to warm up gently, but do not, of course, let it come anywhere near to boiling. It should be just hot to the tip of the finger. The moment the oil is at the right temperature, gently lower into it, using a slotted spoon or tongs, one at a time, the 4 flounder rolls. Let them brown and seal in the open pan for precisely 1 minute.

The instant the timer rings, take out the thermometer and put on the lid, with the pressure regulator already in place on the vent, and screw down the main big knob tight. The working pressure of 5 pounds will be reached in less than 1 minute, when steam will begin gently hissing and/or the regulator will begin to jiggle. At once set your timer for 6 minutes and turn down the heat to medium, adjusting it slightly, down or up, to maintain the gentle hissing and/or jiggling continuously.

The instant the timer rings again, turn off the heat and, using the tines of a two-pronged fork, slightly tilt the pressure regulator to an angle so that the steam hisses out quickly and the pressure is reduced almost immediately. As soon as the hissing stops and the pressure is down, unscrew and take off the lid. Gently lift out the flounder rolls and let them drain and dry briefly on absorbent paper. Then set them out on the warm serving platter, accompanied by the delicate and gentle mustard sauce.

A Good and Healthful Menu   Quick Veal Terrine (see page 50)
Rolled, Stuffed Flounder with a Gentle Mustard Sauce
Puree of fennel and boiled potatoes
A green tossed salad
Café Bénédictine Custard (see page 215)
Formosa oolong tea

The Ideal Wines   *Luxurious*

A white French Meursault from Burgundy
    or
A California white Riesling from the Napa Valley

Everyday

A white French Pouilly-Fumé from the Loire
    or
A white California Fumé Blanc from the Napa Valley

Chapter 17

ONE-DISH SAVORY
CUSTARDS AND SOUFFLÉS

Filled with Cheese, Meats, Shellfish or
Aromatic Vegetables

If there is one very special pleasure in food preparation with the pressure cooker—something that you cannot do as well with any other kitchen tool—it is the making of feathery-fluffy egg custards, steam-baked at 5 pounds pressure, often in under 10 minutes. (If you must, they *can* be done at 10 pounds or 15 pounds pressure, but they will never be quite as luxuriously perfect.) Done slowly, they are, quite simply, the best custards we have ever tasted. You can fill them with savory ingredients (in this chapter) and use them as main dishes for lunches or suppers, or as opening courses for party dinners. Or you can fill them with sweet and fruity ingredients as luscious desserts (in Chapter 21). Here are a few recipes to teach you the basic principles. Once you have mastered these, you will be able to invent your own variations. If you have leftover cooked meat, fish or a vegetable, here is the simple and dramatic way of converting it back into a main course—remembering always that the eggs and milk (or light cream) of the custard add the highest-quality protein to the meal.

Basic Principles of All Steam-Baked Custards—Practical Advice

The process of preparing a custard is so simple—nothing more than the gentle solidification of milk or cream by the albumen of eggs—that you would think you could do it with your eyes shut and your hands tied behind your back. Yet, because eggs react so quickly and sensitively to uncontrolled heat, you have to learn and follow a few precise rules if you are going to achieve consistent and complete success. Here are some of the variable factors which you must watch for and control if you want a superbly smooth and velvety result from every custard recipe in this book. . . .

1. Always heat the milk or cream to a temperature which feels quite hot (but not painfully burning) to the tip of your finger. If you have an available thermometer, it should read

about 125° F (about 50° C). The timing under pressure in all our recipes is based on this degree of heating of the milk. If you start with cooler milk, you will, naturally, need a longer steam-baking time under pressure and your custard will be less smooth. Also, to avoid recooling the milk during the mixing, the eggs and flavoring ingredients should be at room temperature.

2. Break the eggs into a small bowl and lightly beat them with a fork just to mix the yolks and whites. The moment the milk has reached its proper temperature, incorporate the eggs, but with a fork rather than with a wire whisk and *never* with a rotary beater. You want to mix the eggs and milk thoroughly, but you do not want to froth them. Only after the egg is completely mixed in do you work in the other ingredients, according to the recipe. Again, avoid foam or froth.

3. To avoid unnecessary cooling of the custard mix, warm the custard cups or baking dish by holding them, for a few seconds, under hot running water in the sink, then dry them, butter them and pour or spoon the custard into them. Always add *hot* water to the bottom of the pressure cooker, so that the steaming begins as quickly as possible.

4. What went wrong? The two complaints we hear most often are: "When I took the cover off my custard, the center was still runny," or, "My custard was set all right, but it was sort of floating in water." The first, obviously, means insufficient cooking. The second is the inevitable result of overcooking. When it is cooked too long, egg protein shrinks and squeezes the whey from the meshlike custard combination of the egg and the milk. The custard then becomes rubbery and floats in the liquid. So you must get your timing approximately right between moderately narrow limitations and you must understand the factors which affect that timing. First is the temperature of the ingredients as described above. Second is the type of custard cup or dish in which you steam-bake your custard. Metal is the best conductor of heat, and, therefore, if you use aluminum, copper, enameled iron, stainless steel or tin, your custard will be set in the fastest possible time. Pyrex, or other heatproof glass, will require more cooking by several minutes. Heatproof white china soufflé dishes are slower still. Slowest of all are thick stoneware dishes. The third time factor is the shape and size of your custard—how deep and wide it is—the distance from its outer edge to its center. The longer that distance, the longer the cooking time. That is why, if you make a 1-quart custard mix, you can steam-bake it just about twice as fast in four 8-ounce custard cups as you can if you pour the whole of it into a 1-quart soufflé dish. On the other hand, if you pour it as a fairly thin layer into a wide pie plate, then it will cook faster than in the soufflé dish, because the custard is now shallower.

5. Finally, when the timer rings and, after reducing pressure, you take off the lid of the cooker and the inside cover of the custard, never remove it from the cooker until you have

tested for doneness by plunging into the center a bright knife, which must come out dry and clean. If not, continue steam-baking the custard under pressure for another 3 or 4 minutes—carefully noting down the extra time in the margin of the recipe. One sure service you can count on from your pressure cooker is that, once you know the timing for a particular recipe, with your equipment on your stove, you can go on repeating that timing with the absolute certainty of getting completely consistent results. If you have a timing problem at all, it need only be on the first try.

An Alsatian Ham and Cheese Quiche Without a Crust

For 4
Cook under pressure at 5 lb for 12 minutes
(or at 10 lb for 9 minutes)
(or at 15 lb for 6 minutes)

3 whole eggs, lightly beaten
1¼ cups (3.15 dl) light cream, heated until it feels quite hot to the tip of your finger, but not scalded
1 medium yellow onion, peeled and diced
2 Tbs flour
Salt, to your taste
Freshly ground black pepper, to your taste
1 cup (225 g) coarsely diced boiled ham, lean only
¾ cup (170 g) coarsely grated Gruyère cheese
2 Tbs (30 g) butter
4 slices Canadian-style bacon, fried until crisp, in 1 Tbs of the butter, then coarsely crumbled

The Alsatian quiche savory pie of cheese, ham and egg custard seems to have become the all-American symbol of a luscious beginning to a party meal, a light main course for lunch or supper, or a lazy Sunday-morning breakfast. The only trouble, for calorie counters, is the buttery-flaky crust. Here is an Alsatian quiche without the crust. Instead of being baked in an oven for about 40 minutes, it is set in superheated steam in 12 minutes. It is made—and comes to table, handsomely—in a shallow pie plate or au gratin dish, preferably of metal (aluminum, copper, enameled iron, stainless steel or tin). If you use a Pyrex or heatproof china plate, allow 2 or 3 more minutes cooking time. Obviously the plate must be of a size to fit inside your pressure cooker, with about ½ inch space all around. (See the basic notes on the preparation of custards on page 174).

You will need a pressure cooker of at least 6-quart capacity and a pie plate to fit inside, as described above. First, lightly beat together in a mixing bowl the eggs and cream, then work in the onion and flour, with salt and pepper to taste. Next, stir in the ham and ½ cup of the grated cheese. Liberally butter the inside of the pie plate. Give the mix in the bowl a final quick stir and pour it into the plate. Sprinkle the top surface with the remaining ¼ cup of grated cheese. Tightly cover the pie plate with aluminum foil. Pour ¾ cup (1.85 dl) of hot water into the pressure cooker, put in the base rack and stand the plate on it. Put on the lid, bring the steam pressure up to 5 pounds and cook for exactly 12 minutes.

When the timer rings, turn off the heat and reduce the steam pressure immediately. Check the quiche for perfect doneness by sticking in a bright, silvery knife, which should come out clean and dry. If not, return the quiche to pressure for 2 or 3 more minutes. When it is dead right, sprinkle the crisp bacon on top, rush it to table and serve at once in pie-shaped wedges on very hot plates.

Glutinous Italian Beef and Tomato Spaghetti Sauce alla Bolognese

Quick New England Clam, Oyster and Shrimp Chowder

Superspeed Pork Chop Dinner with Browned Potatoes, Glazed
Figs, Cheesed Vegetable and Nut-Filled, Steam-Baked Apples

Amazingly Quick Alsatian Sauerkraut,
and Corn-Stuffed Pork Chops
with Pickled Peaches

An Alsatian Ham and Cheese Quiche Without a Crust

Chinese Cucumber Submarines, Chinese Beef-Rice
Baby Meatballs and Clam-Stuffed Cherry Tomatoes

French Cherry Custard, and Peppermint and Pistachio Fluffy Custard

**A Good and Healthful Sunday Brunch
Menu**

Fresh fruit with orange juice
Alsatian Ham and Cheese Quiche
Hot biscuits with bitter orange marmalade
Unlimited coffee or tea

Quick Crab Custard

For 2
Cook under pressure at 5 lb for 15 minutes
(or at 10 lb for 11 minutes)
(or at 15 lb for 8 minutes)

2 whole eggs, lightly beaten together
1 cup (2.5 dl) light cream, heated until it
  feels quite hot to the tip of your
  finger, but not scalded
6 oz (170 g) smallish, carefully picked
  over fresh crab lumps, canned or
  frozen flakes, or Alaskan king crab
2 slices Canadian bacon, fried crisp and
  crumbled, or lean ham
1 Tbs blanched, slivered, unsalted
  almonds, lightly toasted
3 medium-sized fresh mushrooms, well
  shaped and white, thinly sliced
  through their caps and trimmed
  stems
Salt, to your taste
2 tsp corn or peanut oil

So far, we have discussed only the ease and pleasure of steam-baked egg custards. There is, also, their nutritional value. Here, for example, you have the proteins of the eggs and fish, the calcium of the milk, the minerals and vitamins of bacon, mushrooms and nuts. . . .

We use metal individual custard cups in which the custard cooks in the fastest time. If you use heatproof glass, the cooking time will be about 3 or 4 minutes longer. You could also double this recipe and cook the custard in a baking dish but then the extra time might be as much as 10 minutes. See basic notes on all custards on page 174.

You will need a pressure cooker of at least 3-quart capacity and 2 or 3 individual custard cups, according to their size. Put the eggs into a fairly large mixing bowl and lightly beat the heated cream into them with a fork. Now stir in the crabmeat, bacon, toasted almonds, mushrooms, and salt, to your taste. Lightly oil the insides of the custard cups and, giving the mixture a final good stir, pour it into the cups. Cover each completely and tightly with aluminum foil. Pour ¾ cup (1.85 dl) of hot water into the pressure cooker, put in the base rack and stand the cups on it. Put on the lid, bring the steam pressure up to 5 pounds and cook for exactly 15 minutes.

When the timer rings, turn off the heat and reduce the pressure immediately. Test the custard for doneness by plunging in a bright, silvery knife, which should come out dry and clean. If not, give the custard 2 or 3 more minutes cooking at pressure. Then unmold onto very hot plates.

A Good and Healthful Menu

A chicken liver pâté with melba toast
Quick Crab Custard
Tossed green salad
Apple slices and orange sections dribbled with kirsch cherry
  liqueur
Coffee or Lapsang souchong smoky tea

The Ideal Wines

Luxurious

A French white Châteauneuf-du-Pape from the Rhone
  or
A California white Riesling from the Livermore Valley

Everyday

A French white Crépy from the mountains of the Savoy
    or
A California white Sauvignon Blanc from Santa Clara

Quick Chicken Liver Soufflé
For 4
Cook under pressure at 10 lb for 16 minutes
    (or at 15 lb for 12 minutes)

5 Tbs (75 g) butter
8 Tbs flour
1 cup (2.5 dl) milk
1 smallish yellow onion, peeled and
    finely diced
Salt, to your taste
Freshly ground black pepper, to your
    taste
4 eggs, separated, each yolk kept
    separate, the whites put together
¾ lb (340 g) chicken livers, washed, dried
    and quite coarsely chopped on a
    cutting board

If you have never before attempted a true soufflé, this is the one with which to begin. It is easy, sure and marvelously quick—16 minutes of steaming instead of the usual 45 minutes in an oven—and you don't have the tense worry of looking at it every few minutes to see whether or not it is rising properly.

You will need a pressure cooker of at least 2½-quart capacity, and a 6-cup soufflé dish of a shape to fit inside the pot with at least ¾ inch of space all around. First, set a saucepan on medium heat and melt in it 4 tablespoons of the butter. As soon as it is liquid—before it has had time to heat up—thoroughly work in the flour and keep stirring and heating until it all just begins to bubble gently. Pour in, quite quickly, stirring continuously, the cup of milk. Continue heating and stirring, thoroughly scraping the bottom and sides of the saucepan, until it begins to thicken. At the same time, add the onion, with salt and pepper to taste. When the mixture is quite thick, take it off the heat and add, one at a time, the 4 egg yolks. Break up each yolk and work it in vigorously to avoid any danger of lumping. When all the yolks are blended in, continue the gentle heating, stirring continuously, but do not let it come anywhere near to boiling. Now work in the chopped chicken livers. Turn off the heat and let the mixture rest, covered.

Beat the egg whites until they form stiff peaks. Now, preferably using a rubber spatula, lightly and quickly fold the beaten egg whites into the main mixture, using lifting rather than stirring strokes. Don't try to mix it all completely or you will push out too much of the air that you have beaten in. White streaks are O.K. Thoroughly butter the inside of the soufflé dish and pour the mixture into it. The dish should be just about half full. Cover the top of the soufflé dish tightly with aluminum foil. Pour ¾ cup (1.85 dl) of hot water into the pressure cooker, put in the base rack and set the soufflé dish on top of it. Place a heatproof plate on the aluminum foil over the soufflé dish. Put on the lid, bring the steam pressure up to 10 pounds and cook for exactly 16 minutes.

When the timer rings, turn off the heat and reduce the pressure immediately. Test the soufflé for doneness. When you press your finger on the top surface, it should spring back. If not, return it to pressure and cook it for another 2 or 3 minutes. The moment it is perfectly done, serve it instantly on very hot plates.

A Good and Healthful Menu   Salad of just-cooked green beans with sliced raw mushrooms
                                          lightly dressed with oil and vinegar
                                      Quick Chicken Liver Soufflé
                                      Corn bread
                                      Chocolate mousse
                                      Coffee or tea

The Ideal Wines   *Moderately Priced*

A French red Beaujolais from the district of Moulin-à-Vent
     or
A California red Napa Gamay

Gruyère Cheese Soufflé Custard with Anchovies and White Grapes

For 2
Cook under pressure at 5 lb for 15 minutes
*   (or at 10 lb for 11 minutes)*
*   (or at 15 lb for 8 minutes)*

1 whole egg, lightly beaten
¾ cup (1.85 dl) light cream, heated until
    it feels quite hot to the tip of your
    finger, but not scalding
¾ cup (170 g) grated Gruyère cheese (see
    opposite)
¾ tsp dry mustard
A grind or 2 of nutmeg
Salt, to your taste
Freshly ground black pepper, to your
    taste
1 Tbs (15 g) butter
2 flat fillets boned anchovies, cut into
    dice squares
½ cup (115 g) white seedless grapes,
    washed and halved lengthwise

This will be a conversation piece when served as a main dish for a light lunch or supper, or as a first course for a party dinner. The "secret trick" is to get from your local specialty cheese shop the real, imported, Switzerland Gruyère from the village of Gruyère in the Gruyère Valley. It gives an almost-dry nuttiness, with not the slightest trace of oiliness, to this luxurious and smooth soufflé custard.

We use metal individual cups, in which the custard cooks in the fastest time. If you use heatproof glass, the cooking time will be about 3 or 4 minutes longer. You could also double this recipe and cook the custard in a baking dish, but then the extra time might be as much as 10 minutes. See basic notes on all custards on page 174.

You will need a pressure cooker of at least 3-quart capacity and 2 or 3 individual custard cups, according to size. First, in a mixing bowl, lightly beat together with a fork the egg and heated light cream. Then mix in ½ cup of the cheese, the dry mustard, nutmeg, with salt and pepper to taste. Butter the insides of the cups and, giving the custard mixture a final good stir, pour it into the cups and lightly sprinkle the top surface with some of the remaining cheese. Cover them completely and tightly with aluminum foil. Pour 1 cup (2.5 dl) of hot water into the pressure cooker, put in the base rack and stand the custard cups on it. Put on the lid, bring the steam pressure up to 5 pounds and cook for exactly 15 minutes.

When the timer rings, turn off the heat and reduce the pressure immediately. Test the custard for doneness. A bright, silvery knife plunged into the center should come out dry and clean. If not, put it back under pressure and continue cooking for another 2 or 3 minutes. When it is dead right, unmold the custards onto hot plates, and decorate with bits of anchovy and the grape halves. Then serve immediately.

A Good and Healthful Menu

Stuffed Mushrooms (see page 48)
Gruyère Cheese Soufflé Custard with Anchovies and White Grapes
Salad of red-tipped lettuce vinaigrette
Pears marinated in sweet white wine
Coffee or Darjeeling tea

The Ideal Wines

Moderately Priced

A French white Roussette de Seyssel from the Alps
or
A California white Riesling from the Napa Valley

Vegetarian Soufflé Custard with Rice

For 2
Cook under pressure at 5 lb for 15 minutes
      (or at 10 lb for 11 minutes)
      (or at 15 lb for 8 minutes)

¼ cup (60 g) brown rice
½ cup (1.25 dl) clear chicken bouillon
2 whole eggs, lightly beaten
¾ cup (1.85 dl) milk, heated until it feels quite hot to the tip of your finger, but not scalding
2 Tbs (30 g) melted butter
½ cup (1.25 dl) grated Parmesan cheese
⅓ cup (75 g) thin slices of the tenderest inner stalks of a head of fennel (or, if unavailable, use celery)
⅓ cup (75 g) small green peas, just scalded, still crisp and brightly green
⅓ cup (75 g) crisp slivers of green bell pepper
Enough chopped fresh dill fronds to fill 2 Tbs, or 1 tsp dried
Salt, to your taste
Freshly ground black pepper, to your taste
Medium-sweet paprika, for color and taste
2 tsp firm butter
Enough parsley, leaf only, chopped, to fill 1 Tbs

Don't be fooled by the simplicity of these ingredients. This is a healthy and solid main dish. The cheese provides excellent protein, the vegetables give their minerals and vitamins and the brown rice is a good source of essential fiber.

We use metal individual custard cups, in which the custard cooks in the fastest time. If you use heatproof glass, the cooking time will be about 3 or 4 minutes longer. You could also double this recipe and cook the custard in a baking dish, but then the extra time might be as much as 10 minutes. See basic notes on all custards on page 174.

You will need a pressure cooker of at least 6-quart capacity to hold as many individual custard cups as are needed for the mix, possibly 4 to 6 cups, according to size. First, cook the rice in the normal way, in the chicken bouillon until perfectly done. Next, in a mixing bowl, lightly beat together with a fork the eggs and the heated milk. Then beat in the melted butter, cheese and cooked rice. Now, stir in gently the fennel, green peas, green pepper, dill, salt and pepper to taste, plus paprika, for a delicate pink color and its sweet-flowery-peppery flavor. Butter the insides of the custard cups and, giving the contents of the mixing bowl a final good stir, fill the cups, each no more than ¾ full, since they will soufflé up during the cooking. Cover each of them completely and tightly, with aluminum foil. Pour ¾ cup (1.85 dl) of hot water into the pressure cooker, put in its base rack and set the custard cups on top of it. Put on the lid, bring the pressure up to 5 pounds and cook for exactly 15 minutes.

When the timer rings, turn off the heat and reduce the pressure immediately. Check the custard for doneness. A bright, silvery knife plunged into the center should come out dry and clean. If not, continue cooking under pressure for 2 or 3 minutes longer. When it is perfect, it should be stiff enough to unmold onto a hot serving platter. Then decorate with bright green sprinklings of chopped parsley and serve at once on very hot plates.

A Good and Healthful Menu

Clear Asparagus Bouillon (see page 36)
Vegetarian Soufflé Custard with Rice
Salad of Bibb lettuce vinaigrette
Strawberry tarts
Coffee or winey Keemun tea

The Ideal Wines

Moderately Priced

A French pink Tavel from the Rhone
    or
A California Rosé of Cabernet from the Alexander Valley

Chapter 18

ONE-DISH VEGETARIAN

Pressure Preserves Freshness of Flavor

We are not vegetarians at heart, but we often choose to be for weeks or months at a time. Suddenly, for no easily explainable reason, we turn against meat and long for the crisp, refreshing succulence and sweetness of vegetables as the main dish of our meal. In the spring, especially, when the new, young, brilliantly colored buds and flowerets and leaves and stalks come into the markets, we dine with joy on vegetables alone. And this is where the pressure cooker—set to its maximum speed—is the supreme kitchen tool for preserving the just-picked freshness. Here are a few of our favorite and most successful recipes. Each illustrates a basic principle of preparation. Once you have mastered it, you will be able to invent your own recipes.

Cheese and eggs are, of course, the classic protein accompaniments to vegetables. But vegetables also mix very well with each other. We offer below some basic examples of our typical conglomerations, mélanges, mishmashes, mix-ups—call them whatever you like—of vegetables in season and in stock in our refrigerator crisper. You can prepare these recipes with your own choice of vegetables. But you must solve the problem of timing. Obviously, if you put a slow-cooking vegetable together with a fast-cooking one, the slow one must be cut into smaller pieces and the fast into larger, to make sure that both will be done perfectly at the same time when the lid is opened. You can get help on this from our Vegetable Cutting, Cooking and Timing Chart on page 190, which tells you what size to cut a particular vegetable in order to bring it within a chosen cooking time. With the help of this chart, you will be able to make up your own combinations of vegetables for your part of the country and your personal taste.

Steam-Baked Eggs with Parmesan Cheese and Diced Zucchini

For 2
Cook under pressure at 5 lb for 15 minutes
(or at 10 lb for 11 minutes)
(or at 15 lb for 8 minutes)

2 eggs, lightly beaten together
¾ cup (1.85 dl) light cream, heated until it feels quite hot to the tip of your finger, but not scalded
⅓ cup (80 ml) grated Parmesan cheese
Medium-sweet paprika, to your taste
Salt, to your taste
Freshly ground black pepper, to your taste
1 medium zucchini, washed, skin left on, fairly finely diced, enough to fill about ¾ cup (170 g)
1 Tbs (15 g) butter

When we are in a hurry, we prepare this in individual metal custard cups (aluminum, copper, enameled iron, stainless steel or tin), which give the fastest cooking time and allow the custard to be unmolded easily onto your plate. If you use heat-proof glass cups, the cooking time will be about 3 or 4 minutes longer. You could also double this recipe and cook the custard in a baking dish, but then the extra time might be as much as 10 minutes. Also, we sometimes prepare it for a lazy Sunday-morning breakfast in a lidded, earthenware casserole which, because it is a relatively poor conductor of heat, takes the longest cooking time of all—but produces a custard of a marvelous delicacy and lightness. See basic notes on all custards on page 174.

You will need a pressure cooker of at least 2½-quart capacity and as many custard cups as are needed to divide the mix, possibly 3 or 4, according to size. First, lightly beat together with a fork, in a fair-sized mixing bowl, the eggs and heated cream. Then work in the grated cheese and paprika to give it all a delicately rosy color, with salt and pepper to taste. Finally, stir in the diced zucchini. Butter the custard cups and, giving the egg mixture a final good stir, pour it into the cups. Completely and tightly cover each with aluminum foil. Pour ¾ cup (1.85 dl) of hot water into the pressure cooker, put in the base rack and stand the cups on it. Put on the lid, bring the steam pressure up to 5 pounds and cook for exactly 15 minutes.

When the timer rings, turn off the heat and reduce the pressure immediately. Test the custard for doneness by plunging into the center a bright, silvery knife, which should come out dry and clean. If not, cook under pressure for 2 or 3 minutes more.

A Good and Healthful Menu

Red salmon caviar on melba toast
Steam-Baked Eggs with Parmesan and Zucchini
Tossed green salad
Strawberry shortcake
Coffee or tea

The Ideal Wines

Luxurious

A German white from the Steinberg on the Rhine
        or
A California white Pinot Chardonnay from the Napa Valley

Everyday

A German white from the village of Nierstein on the Rhine
        or
A California white Pinot Chardonnay from Santa Clara

Our Whole-Meal Vegetable Casserole à la Belle Saison

For 4 to 6
Cook under pressure at 15 lb for 10 minutes
*   (or at 10 lb for 13 minutes)*

6 Tbs (90 g) butter
4 medium raw potatoes, peeled and cut
    into ½-inch (1.2 cm) cubes
2 medium yellow onions, peeled and
    sliced
½ cup (115 g) sliced leeks, white parts
    only
½ cup (115 g) coarsely chopped scallions,
    green tops and white bulbs
½ lb (225 g) green beans, trimmed and
    cut into 1-inch (2.5 cm) chunks
3 medium green peppers, cored and cut
    into 3-inch (7.5 cm) squares
3 medium carrots, scraped and sliced ½
    inch (1.2 cm) thick
½ cup (115 g) sliced celery
1 cup (225 g) fresh shelled peas
4 medium ripe tomatoes, peeled, pitted
    and coarsely chunked
1 clove garlic, finely minced
Enough chopped fresh leaves of basil to
    fill 1 Tbs, or 1 tsp dried
The same amount tarragon
The same amount thyme
Salt, to your taste
Freshly ground black pepper, to your
    taste
¼ cup (60 ml) dry white wine
8-oz (225 g) can tomato sauce
½ cup (1.25 dl) heavy cream

We call this à la Belle Saison because we find that every time of the year is a "beautiful season" if you choose the vegetables which are at their best at that time. Even the root parsnips and turnips of midwinter have their special pleasures in our vegetable casseroles. So the trick here is to vary the ingredients to fit the seasons and your taste.

Since this is as good cold as it is hot, we make it in substantial quantities in a large pressure cooker of at least 6-quart capacity. Heat it up, without its base rack, to medium frying temperature, melt in it 3 tablespoons of the butter and, when it is fairly hot, put in item by item all the vegetables which you have previously prepared (preferably in the following order: potatoes, onions, leeks, scallions, green beans, green peppers, carrots, celery, peas, tomatoes). As each one goes in, stir everything around gently with a wooden spoon, so that it all becomes coated with butter. Add the remaining tablespoons of butter, one by one, as needed. Then add the garlic, basil, tarragon, thyme, plus salt and pepper to taste. After about 3 or 4 minutes of gentle simmering in the butter, pour in the wine, heat it up just to boiling, put on the lid, bring the steam pressure up to 15 pounds and cook for exactly 10 minutes. Meanwhile, beat together in a bowl the tomato sauce and the cream.

When the timer rings, reduce the steam pressure immediately. Stir into the vegetables the cream-tomato sauce and warm it all up over gentle heat, in the open pot, stirring it carefully to avoid mashing the vegetables. When everything is good and hot—and the cream-tomato sauce is thoroughly distributed—serve the vegetable casserole at once on very hot plates with big chunks of crusty French bread.

A Good and Healthful Menu

Oysters on the half-shell with lemon wedges
Vegetable Casserole à la Belle Saison
French bread
Cherry pie
Coffee or Darjeeling tea

The Ideal Wines

Luxurious

A French white Meursault "Les Charmes" from Burgundy
    or
A California white Pinot Chardonnay from the Napa Valley

Everyday

An Italian white Frascati from the Rome region
    or
A California white Pinot Blanc from the Livermore Valley

Broccoli-Gruyère Soufflé Casserole

For 2
Cook under pressure at 15 lb for 2 minutes
Oven baking for 30 minutes

½ cup (1.25 dl) dry white wine, or clear
  chicken bouillon
½ bunch young broccoli, about 1 lb
  (450 g), well washed, the heads left
  whole, stems trimmed
2 Tbs (30 g) butter
2 Tbs flour
Up to ¾ cup (1.85 dl) light cream
Salt, to your taste
Freshly ground black pepper, to your
  taste
¼ lb (115 g) Switzerland Gruyère cheese,
  grated
2 eggs, separated

This can, of course, be done with green beans, Brussels sprouts, carrots, cauliflower, etc. The basic trick is to undercook the vegetable in the pressure cooker, so that it does not mush inside the soufflé in the oven.

You will need a pressure cooker of at least 3-quart capacity and a 6-cup soufflé dish for the oven. Pour the wine or bouillon into the pressure cooker, put in the base rack and neatly arrange the whole heads of broccoli on it. Put on the lid, bring the steam pressure up to 15 pounds and undercook the broccoli in no more than 2 minutes.

When the timer rings, turn off the heat and reduce the pressure immediately. Lift out the broccoli heads, carefully break them up into their flowerets and set aside. Empty the liquid out of the pressure cooker and use it, without its base rack, as the open saucepan in which to prepare the white sauce. Gently melt the butter and blend in the flour. Meanwhile, warm the cream. After about 3 minutes of steadily stirring the butter and flour add, all at once, the first ½ cup of the warmed cream. Stir continuously until it becomes quite thick. At the same time, add salt and pepper to taste. At this point, the sauce will be much too thick. Gradually dribble and work more cream into it, dash by dash, until you have thinned it to the consistency of quite-thick cream. Mix in the grated cheese. Turn off the heat and work in, one by one, the egg yolks—stirring quickly to avoid lumping. Let the sauce cool slightly while you beat the egg whites. Preheat your oven to 350° F (175° C). Beat the egg whites until they hold stiff peaks and then, preferably using a rubber spatula, fold them lightly and quickly into the sauce. Thoroughly butter the inside of the soufflé dish, neatly put in the broccoli flowerets and pour the soufflé fluff over the top. Set the dish in the center of the oven and bake it, without opening the oven door, for 30 minutes. Test the soufflé for doneness by pressing the top surface with your finger—it should be springy. If not, give it another 5 minutes in the oven. When we are in our vegetarian mood, this makes a quite-sufficient main course.

A Good and Healthful Menu

Tiny Cocktail Marinated Mushrooms (page 50)
Broccoli-Gruyère Soufflé Casserole
  with buttered egg noodles
Salad of Belgian endive and chopped red pimento with oil and
  vinegar
Walnut ice cream
Coffee or Earl Grey tea

The Ideal Wines *Luxurious*

A German white Bernkasteler from the Moselle Valley
> or
A California white Pinot Blanc from Monterey

Everyday

A German white Franconian Würtzburger Sylvaner in a classic
flagon
> or
A California white Fumé Blanc from Santa Clara

Our Whole-Meal, Green-and-Yellow Vegetable Soup

For 4
Cook under pressure at 15 lb for 6 minutes
(or at 10 lb for 8 minutes)

3 medium potatoes, peeled and cut into
¼-inch (7 mm) dice
3 medium carrots, scraped and cut into
¼-inch (7 mm) dice
2 tart apples, peeled, cored and sliced
about ⅛ inch (3 mm) thick
8 scallions, both green tops and white
bulbs trimmed and chopped
2 medium green peppers, cored and cut
into ¼-inch (7 mm) dice
5 stalks celery, with their leaves, the
stalks thinly sliced, the leaves
chopped
1 medium bunch parsley, fairly coarsely
chopped
1 medium bunch watercress, coarsely
chopped
2 medium purple onions, peeled and
fairly finely chopped
12 smallish fresh mushrooms, wiped
clean, trimmed and sliced into
hammer shapes
Enough chopped fresh leaves basil to fill
1 Tbs, or 1 tsp dried
The same amount rosemary
The same amount thyme
Salt, to your taste
Freshly ground black pepper, to your
taste
4 cups (1 liter) clear beef bouillon (see
page 35, or use canned)
Up to 1 pint (5 dl) light cream (or milk, if
you are calorie-conscious)

This is the basic rule for preparing a nutritive, savory and sustaining one-dish soup using, first, any vegetables you may have in your refrigerator crisper and, second, those that are at their seasonal peak in the markets. The ingredients list is quite flexible—you can substitute your own combinations and variations.

You will need a large pressure cooker of at least 6-quart capacity. Remove its base rack and pile all the vegetables into the pressure cooker (preferably in layers in this order: potatoes, carrots, apples, scallions, green peppers, celery stalks and leaves, parsley, watercress, purple onions, mushrooms). Sprinkle on top the basil, rosemary, thyme, plus salt and pepper to taste. Finally, pour in the beef bouillon. Heat it up just to boiling, put on the lid, bring the steam pressure up to 15 pounds and cook for exactly 6 minutes.

When the timer rings, reduce the pressure immediately. The soup is likely to be quite thick. Thin it with as much of the light cream as you need to give it the richness and texture you like. Then reheat it, without the lid, but do not let it boil. Check the seasonings and serve it in very hot bowls, each with a slice of lemon and a good dollop of butter floating and melting on top.

1 whole fresh lemon, sliced very thinly
    with the rind left on
About 4 Tbs (60 g) butter

A Good and Healthful Menu	Clams on the half-shell with wedges of lemon Green-and-Yellow Vegetable Soup Steamed Date Pudding (see page 221) Coffee or tea

The Ideal Wines	*Luxurious*
	
	A German white from the village of Forst on the Rhine
	    or
	A California white Riesling from the Alexander Valley
	
	Everyday
	
	An Italian white Soave from the Venice region
	    or
	A California Napa Pinot Blanc

Ratatouille à la Niçoise—a Savory Mediterranean Mélange of Vegetables

About 1 quart
Best cooked at 15 lb for 10 minutes
    (or at 10 lb for 13 minutes)

1 medium eggplant, cut into 1-inch (2.5
    cm) cubes
4 medium tomatoes, peeled and cut into
    eighths
2 medium zucchini, unpeeled, cut into
    ½-inch (1.2 cm) chunks
3 medium green peppers, cored, cut into
    ¾-inch (2 cm) squares
1 medium yellow onion, peeled and
    sliced
2 cloves garlic, finely minced
1 whole bay leaf
Enough chopped fresh leaves of thyme to
    fill 1 Tbs, or 1 tsp dried
About 1 tsp salt
About ½ tsp freshly ground black pepper
A pinch or two red cayenne pepper
⅓ cup (80 ml) good olive oil
¼ cup (60 ml) dry white wine

Ratatouille seems now to be almost as well known in the United States as it is in its hometown, the Mediterranean city of Nice on the border between France and Italy. The dish is simply a slow-cooked, marvelously flavorful coarse puree of mixed vegetables and olive oil which for centuries has been associated with the south of France and the region of Provence. Ratatouille can be served hot as an accompaniment to a main dish, as a main dish in itself, cold as an appetizer or as a salad. In the pressure cooker the hours of slow simmering are out—the ratatouille is ready to serve in just over half an hour.

Since it is so excellent cold and keeps for days in a covered jar in the refrigerator, we believe in making a fair quantity. When you take off the lid after the cooking, there will always be a lot of vegetable juice in the bottom of the pot. The liquid must be boiled off hard, generally for about 7 to 10 minutes, until the puree is thick enough to be lifted with a fork. This concentration of the flavors is the "secret trick" of a great ratatouille.

You will need a pressure cooker of at least 6-quart capacity. Take out its base rack and put all the ingredients into it, in layers, in the order listed opposite. Put on the lid, bring the pressure up to 15 pounds and cook for exactly 10 minutes.

When the timer rings, turn off the heat and reduce the pressure immediately. Gently stir all the vegetables around with a wooden spoon. Your final mixture should be gooey, but not liquid. The pool of juices and wine on the bottom should be boiled off by bubbling it quite hard, in the open pan. Stir, now and then, and scrape the bottom of the pot. Do not deliberately mash the ratatouille. Finally, when the bottom is almost dry, taste and check once more for seasoning. Then serve at once, hot, or let it get cold in a covered serving dish in the refrigerator. Ratatouille keeps for several days. It is an irresistible snack.

A Good and Healthful Menu   Mixed nibbles of salted nuts
Ratatouille à la Niçoise
Southern pecan pie
Coffee or tea

The Ideal Wines   *Luxurious*

A French white Bellet from Nice
or
A California white Pinot Chardonnay from the Alexander Valley

Everyday

A French white Estandon from Provence
or
A California white Folle Blanche from the Napa Valley

Chapter 19

MORE BASIC RECIPES:
VEGETABLE SIDE DISHES

The pressure cooker is a superb tool for cooking fresh vegetables. If they are in really good condition, and the timing of the steam pressure is exactly right, they come out with a springtime ambience, as if they had just been picked and prepared at once in a farm kitchen filled with the savors and scents of the rich surrounding earth. Precise timing is the secret. Overcooking, even for a minute or two, can give a vegetable the feel and flavor of a soggy bath sponge.

Yet there can be a reasonable flexibility about the timing and this is explained on the Vegetable Cutting, Cooking and Timing Chart on page 190. Obviously, the key to the perfect cooking of any vegetable is the time it takes for the heat to penetrate from the outside skin to the center of the flesh. Therefore, you can vary the timing by carefully cutting your vegetable into larger or smaller pieces—all of uniform shape and size. This is what the chart shows you. For example, if you peel a medium potato and put it whole into the pressure cooker at 15 pounds, the potato will be cooked in just about 10 minutes. If you cut the same potato in halves, at 15 pounds, it will be cooked in 6 minutes. If you slice it an inch thick, at 15 pounds, it will take 4 minutes. And so on, for various other cutting sizes—as shown along the horizontal line for potatoes on the chart.

The value of this information is twofold. First, if you are preparing a meat dish with a fixed, preset timing, you can add vegetables to that dish cut exactly to a shape and size so that they will be perfectly cooked in the same time as the meat. For example, in the sautéed chicken one-dish meal on page 125, where the essential time for the chicken is 5 minutes, the chart shows that you could replace the whole medium carrots by whole cauliflower or whole medium onions and have them perfectly cooked exactly in time with the chicken.

Second, the chart enables you to combine various vegetables (each with a different basic cooking time) in the same pressure cooker by simply cutting the slower-cooking vegetables into

189

Vegetable Cutting, Cooking and Timing Chart

		Minutes to Cook at 15 Pounds		
	Up to Pressure	1	2	3
Artichoke				
Asparagus	whole			
Beans, green	whole			
Beets		¼" slices	¼" slices	
Broccoli	flowerets	whole stalks		
Brussels Sprouts		whole	whole	
Cabbage	chopped or coarsely shredded	quarters		
Carrots, large	¼" slices or large dice	quarters	quarters or halves, lengthwise	1" slices or cubes
Cauliflower		flowerets		
Celery	1" slices	whole, halves, lengthwise, or slices		
Chestnuts, in skins				
Fennel		1" slices	quarters or halves, lengthwise	halves, lengthwise
Leeks	1" slices		whole	
Onions, medium yellow	¼" slices		1" slices or quarters	halves, lengthwise
" white boilers				
Parsnips	quarters	halves, lengthwise		
Potatoes	¼" slices or large dice			1" cubes
Squash, acorn (halves)			1" cubes	
" butternut			1" cubes	
" yellow	1" slices	halves, lengthwise		
" zucchini	halves, lengthwise, or slices			
Sweet Potatoes	large dice or ¼" slices		1" cubes or slices	quarters
Tomatoes	halves	whole, cored		
Turnips, white	¼" slices			halves or quarters

4	5	6	7	8	9	10
						whole
					whole————→	
			whole			
	whole					
					whole	
whole						
	whole					whole, large
				whole		
1″ slices		halves, lengthwise (medium)				whole (medium)
			quarters			
whole						

smaller pieces. For example, the chart shows that carrots cut into 1-inch chunks can be combined with fennel bulbs, halved, with potatoes in 1-inch cubes, plus turnips quartered . . . and that all of them will be perfectly cooked together at 15 pounds in 3 minutes.

Finally, here are a few basic rules which apply to all the recipes and all the vegetables listed in this chapter. . . .

1. Always peel potatoes. When they are steamed in their jackets, they tend to become a bit mushy.

2. We do not bother with spinach in the pressure cooker. It goes so fast, anyway, that there is virtually no saving of time.

3. There must, of course, be a minimum quantity of liquid in the pressure cooker to produce the steam. But we keep away from water as much as possible. It adds nothing in the way of flavor. Our vegetables are uplifted by the use of clear beef bouillon, clear chicken broth or dry white wine— always with a good spritz of lemon juice in it and a fair sprinkling of salt. We *always* bring the liquid to the boil before putting in the vegetables, so as to keep the steaming down to the minimum possible time. Put in the vegetable the instant the liquid boils, and move quickly to put on the lid and the pressure control weight immediately. Because we are sure of what we do, we seldom use more than ¼ cup (60 ml) of liquid and our vegetables taste all the better for this minimum. If, at first, you feel unsure of yourself, then by all means begin by using ½ cup of liquid. But your vegetables will be that much more soggy.

4. Properly pressure-steamed-cooked vegetables are so beautiful that they really require no sauce. If you want to enrich them slightly, put a small dab of butter on the hot little pile of vegetables on your plate and let it melt into them. Or melt the butter in a tiny saucepan, stir in a little salt and pepper, then dribble it over the vegetables. Or use our Butter-Lemon Sauce from page 193. Or any of our sauces from Chapter 4.

5. The cooking times we give in the following recipes are based on the freshest, youngest vegetables we can find in the markets and, therefore, we think they represent a fair average. If you live in the country and have access to just-picked vegetables, then your cooking times will have to be a half-minute or so shorter. But, if you are dealing with old and tired vegetables, then you will have to allow that extra half-minute or so. For perfect results, you will have to get to know your own vegetables in your own markets. Remember that it is always best to choose the shorter time and undercook rather than overcook. Remember, also, that you can always speed up slow-cooking vegetables by cutting them according to the chart on pages 190–191.

Asparagus with Butter-Lemon Sauce

For 4
Cook under pressure at 15 lb for 1 minute

For the Butter-Lemon Sauce

8 Tbs (115 g) butter
1 Tbs chopped fresh, dried or frozen
     chives
Enough chopped fresh leaves parsley to
     fill ¼ cup (60 ml)
Salt, to your taste
Freshly ground black pepper, to your
     taste
The freshly squeezed juice of a lemon
¼ cup (60 ml) dry white wine, or clear
     chicken bouillon
A good spritz of lemon juice
2 lb (1 kg) young, thinnish, nicely
     straight spears of asparagus, washed
     and prepared, as opposite

We take the time and trouble to prepare our asparagus spears carefully. First, we always break the stalks by hand—never cut them—because then they will snap automatically at the exact point where the inedibly woody part joins the softer green. We get rid of every speck of sand by repeatedly washing them under running cold water. With a sharp vegetable parer, we remove the scales (where sand hides) and, if the skin of the lower part of the green stalks seems thick and tough, we thinly peel it off. Finally, we dig the sand out of the crevices of the tips with a soft brush and again rinse under running water. We object to hollandaise, or any other dominant sauce that overpowers the delicate freshness of young asparagus. This is absolutely our favorite way of preparing and serving it.

Use a minimum 2½-quart pressure cooker. First, use a separate, small saucepan to get the sauce started. Over gentle heat, melt the butter and work into it the chives, parsley, and salt and pepper to taste. Then begin spritzing and stirring in the juice of the lemon until you have a distinctly lemony flavor. This can be kept warm, covered, over very low heat. Stir it once more and finally check its taste just before serving it. This sauce is ideal with many vegetables.

With its base rack in place, pour into the pressure cooker the wine or bouillon, a good spritz of lemon juice and a nice sprinkling of salt. Bring it rapidly just to boiling, then instantly lay in the asparagus, put on the lid, bring the steam pressure up to 15 pounds and cook for exactly 1 minute. (If the asparagus spears are quite thick, make the cooking time a few seconds longer.)

When the timer rings, reduce the pressure immediately. Lift out the asparagus with tongs and pour the butter-lemon sauce over the neatly arranged tips.

French-Cut Green Beans as They Do Them in Provence

For 4
Including oven baking for 10 minutes
Cook under pressure at 15 lb for 1 minute

¼ cup (60 ml) dry white wine, or clear
     chicken bouillon
A good spritz freshly squeezed lemon
     juice
Salt, to your taste
1½ lb (675 g) French-cut green beans,
     fresh or frozen

"French-cut" beans are, as you almost certainly know, thinly sliced lengthwise. You can get them at supermarkets ready cut in frozen packages, or fancy kitchen equipment shops can supply a small, hand-turned machine that will do the job in double-quick time. If you have dexterous hands, you can do the cutting on a board with nothing more than a sharp kitchen knife. The advantage is that the beans cook in almost no time at all and remain beautifully crisp on the tongue.

4 smallish ripe tomatoes, coarsely diced
½ cup (115 g) finely diced, dark-smoked
    ham
1 clove garlic, finely minced
2 Tbs good olive oil
Freshly ground black pepper, to your
    taste

You will need a minimum 2½-quart pressure cooker, and a 1-quart casserole to go into the oven. Pour the wine or bouillon into the pressure cooker, with a spritz of lemon and a sprinkling of salt. Put in its base rack and heat up the liquid just to the boiling point. Watch carefully to make sure that none of the liquid gets boiled away. The moment it bubbles, working fast, spread the beans on the rack, put on the lid, bring the steam pressure up to 15 pounds and cook for exactly 1 minute. If the beans are large, old and tired, give them ½ minute more. Preheat your oven to 375° F (190° C) and set the casserole in it to heat up.

The moment the timer rings, reduce the steam pressure immediately. With a slotted spoon, transfer the beans to the hot oven casserole and gently mix with them the tomatoes, ham, garlic, oil, with more salt if you like, plus pepper. Set the casserole, open, in the oven and leave it until everything is thoroughly hot, usually in about 8 to 10 minutes.

Green Lima Beans with Baby Pearl Onions and Brown Rice
For 4
Cook under pressure at 15 lb for 20 minutes

½ cup (115 g) raw brown rice
4-oz (115 g) jar baby pearl cocktail
    onions, drained, their juice reserved
10-oz (285 g) frozen package small green
    lima beans
Enough chopped fresh leaves parsley to
    fill ¼ cup (60 ml)
Enough chopped fresh leaves thyme to fill
    1 Tbs, or 1 tsp dried
2 cups (5 dl) clear chicken bouillon (see
    page 35, or use canned)
Salt, to your taste
Freshly ground black pepper, to your
    taste
4 Tbs (60 g) butter

Use a minimum 3-quart pressure cooker. Take out its base rack and put into it all the above ingredients, in order. Mix everything thoroughly with a wooden spoon. Dot the top surface with bits of the butter. Heat up the bouillon just to boiling, put on the lid, bring the steam pressure up to 15 pounds and cook for exactly 20 minutes.

When the timer rings, reduce the pressure immediately. Taste a few grains of the rice to make sure it is properly done. If not, give it a few minutes more under pressure. When the rice is perfect, if there is liquid left, boil it off fast without the lid. Correct the seasonings and serve very hot.

Yellow Wax Beans with Baby Pearl Onions and a Delicate Touch of Mustard
For 4
Cook under pressure at 15 lb for 2 minutes

2 lb (1 kg) yellow or wax beans, topped
    and tailed, then cut or snapped into
    ½-inch (1.2 cm) pieces

Use a minimum 2½-quart pressure cooker. Take out its base rack and put into it the list of ingredients in order. Add a teaspoon or two of the onion juice—just enough to give a very slight onion flavor. Stir everything together with the mustard. Dot the surface with bits of the butter. Heat up the bouillon

8-oz (225 g) jar baby pearl cocktail
onions, drained, their juice reserved
Salt, to your taste
Freshly ground black pepper, to your
taste
½ cup (1.25 dl) clear chicken bouillon
(see page 35, or use canned)
1½ Tbs prepared mustard, preferably
imported French or German from
Dijon or Düsseldorf
3 Tbs (45 g) butter

just to boiling, put on the lid, bring the steam pressure up to 15 pounds and cook for exactly 2 minutes.

When the timer rings, reduce the pressure immediately. Drain off the bouillon, saving it for some other use. Taste to check the seasonings and serve at once.

Beets in the Polish Style with Sour Cream
For 4
Cook under pressure at 15 lb for 10 minutes

½ cup (1.25 dl) sweetish wine
A good spritz freshly squeezed lemon
juice
Salt, to your taste
2 bunches fresh beets, washed and cut
(see note, opposite)
3 Tbs (45 g) butter
1 Tbs brown sugar
1 Tbs red wine vinegar
Freshly ground black pepper, to your
taste
1 cup (2.5 dl) sour cream

When you cut whole beets off the bunch, always leave about ½ inch of stem at one end and the root at the other. Otherwise, if you expose the inner flesh, they may become waterlogged during the cooking. After cooking, of course, roots and stems are removed with the skins. The trick is always to undercook beets, so that they remain crisply chewy. On days when you are in a terrible rush, you can, with some compromise, prepare this recipe with canned, precooked and skinned, whole beets. Or you can do your cooking ahead, then mix in the sour cream and reheat just before serving.

Use a minimum 2½-quart pressure cooker. Take out the base rack and pour in the wine with a good spritz of lemon juice and a fair sprinkling of salt. Put back the rack and heat up the wine just to boiling, then, working quickly to prevent the wine from boiling away, stack in the beets, put on the lid, bring the steam pressure up to 15 pounds and cook for exactly 10 minutes. Large, old or stale beets may need a minute or two longer.

When the timer rings, reduce the steam pressure immediately. The moment the beets are cool enough to handle, skin them and dice them, or chop them. Remove the base rack and drain the liquid from the pressure cooker. Put the beets back into it with moderately low heat and add the remaining ingredients, lightly stirring in each addition, including more salt, if needed. Gently warm it all up (but do not let it boil), then taste it for final seasoning and serve it at once.

Broccoli with Butter-Lemon Sauce

For 4
Best cooked at 15 lb for 1 minute

½ cup (1.25 dl) dry white wine, or clear
    chicken bouillon
The juice of ½ a lemon
Salt, to your taste
One 2-lb (1 kg) bunch of broccoli,
    washed; do not divide up the
    flowerets; leave them in bunches at
    the head of each stalk, cut away the
    old, thick stalks, slash the softer,
    green stalks into quarters
Freshly ground black pepper, to your
    taste

For the Butter-Lemon Sauce

See recipe on page 193

This recipe is almost exactly the same as the one for Asparagus with Butter-Lemon Sauce on page 193. Prepare the sauce as described there. Allow for slight variations in the cooking time (generally not more than 30 seconds) according to the age and freshness of the broccoli.

Use a minimum 2½-quart pressure cooker. First, prepare the Butter-Lemon Sauce as described on page 193 and keep it gently warm in a covered pan. Take out the base rack from the pressure cooker and pour in the wine or bouillon, with a spritz or two of lemon juice and a sprinkling of salt. Put back the base rack and heat up the liquid just to boiling, then, working fast to avoid it boiling away, stack in the broccoli, put on the lid, bring the steam pressure up to 15 pounds and cook for exactly 1 minute.

When the timer rings, reduce the steam pressure immediately. Drain the broccoli, break it up into its flowerets, chunk the stalks, dress it with the Butter-Lemon Sauce, add more salt and pepper, if you like, then serve it at once.

Brussels Sprouts with Italian Chestnuts and California Thompson Seedless Grapes

For 4
Precook the chestnuts
Cook under pressure at 15 lb for 4 minutes

½ cup (1.25 dl) clear chicken bouillon
    (see page 35, or use canned)
1½ Tbs freshly squeezed lemon juice
Salt, to your taste
About 2 lb (1 kg) nicely fresh and green
    Brussels sprouts, trimmed, soaked
    for a few minutes in salted water,
    then washed under running water
3 Tbs (45 g) butter
2 cups (450 g) precooked chestnuts (see
    opposite)
2 cups (450 g) Thompson seedless grapes,
    picked over and well washed
1 clove garlic, finely minced
1 tsp whole caraway seed
Enough chopped fresh leaves parsley to
    fill ¼ cup (60 ml)
Enough chopped fresh leaves rosemary to
    fill 1 Tbs, or 1 tsp dried
The same amount tarragon
Freshly ground black pepper, to your
    taste
Up to 1 cup (2.5 dl) sour cream

Cook the chestnuts the day before, according to the recipe on page 199. Or use hot roasted ones from the man on the street corner. Or use the French canned kind.

Use a minimum 4-quart pressure cooker. Remove its base rack and pour in the chicken bouillon, lemon juice, and a fair sprinkling of salt. Heat up the liquid just to boiling, then, working fast to avoid too much of the bouillon being boiled away, stack in the Brussels sprouts, put on the lid, bring the steam pressure up to 15 pounds and cook for exactly 4 minutes.

When the timer rings, reduce the steam pressure immediately. Now, with the pressure cooker open at medium-low heat, add the remaining ingredients, carefully combining each before the next is added and including more salt, if needed. Finally, work in enough of the sour cream to make a sauce of the consistency of heavy cream. Heat it all up, stirring every few minutes, but do not let it boil. When it is all thoroughly hot, serve it.

Cabbage with Grated Parmesan Cheese

For 4
Cook under pressure at 15 lb for 8 minutes

½ cup (1.25 dl) clear chicken bouillon
    (see page 35, or use canned)
2 tsp freshly squeezed lemon juice
Salt, to your taste
1 medium-to-small cabbage (say, about 2
    lb [1 kg]), tough outer leaves and
    stalk trimmed off, well washed, then
    quartered
1 tsp whole caraway seed
4 Tbs (60 g) butter
½ cup (1.25 dl) Parmesan cheese, grated
Enough chopped fresh leaves parsley to
    fill ¼ cup (60 ml)
Enough chopped fresh leaves tarragon to
    fill 1 Tbs, or 1 tsp dried
Freshly ground black pepper, to your
    taste

Use a minimum 2½-quart pressure cooker. Take out its base rack and pour in the chicken bouillon, with a good squirt of lemon juice, and a fair sprinkling of salt. Rapidly heat it up just to boiling, then, working fast so that as little as possible of the bouillon will boil away, stack in the cabbage quarters, sprinkle over them the caraway seed, put on the lid, bring the steam pressure up to 15 pounds and cook for exactly 8 minutes.

When the timer rings, reduce the steam pressure immediately. Drain off the excess liquid and at once melt the butter onto the cabbage quarters. Then sprinkle on the grated Parmesan, parsley, tarragon, remaining lemon juice, with more salt, if needed, and pepper. Gently stir it all around, to make sure that everything is amalgamated and melted into the cabbage, then serve it at once.

Luxurious Red Cabbage

For 4
Cook under pressure at 15 lb for 4 minutes

3 Tbs (45 g) butter
4 slices Canadian bacon, cut into ½-inch
    (1.2 cm) squares
2 medium yellow onions, peeled and
    thinly sliced
1 small red cabbage (say, about 1½ lb
    [675 g]), tough outer leaves and stalk
    trimmed off, well washed, then
    chopped or shredded
2 tart cooking apples, peeled, cored and
    thinly sliced
½ cup (115 g) seedless raisins
2 Tbs brown sugar
Salt, to your taste
Freshly ground black pepper, to your
    taste
¼ cup (60 ml) red wine
¼ cup (60 ml) cider vinegar
½ cup (115 g) black currant jelly

Use a minimum 3-quart pressure cooker. Heat it up, without its base rack, to medium-high frying temperature, melt in it the butter and, when it is fairly hot, quickly sauté the squares of Canadian bacon until they are nicely browned. As soon as they start to gild, add the onions and let them, also, become lightly golden. The moment this is achieved, stop the action by adding the cabbage, apples, raisins, sugar, plus salt and pepper to taste. Pour in the red wine and cider vinegar, turn up the heat and bring it just to boiling, put on the lid, bring the steam pressure up to 15 pounds and cook for exactly 4 minutes.

When the timer rings, reduce the steam pressure immediately. Gently stir and melt into the cabbage the black currant jelly. Let it all simmer, uncovered, for 3 or 4 minutes, stirring often, until the jelly has combined with the juices to form the sauce. If it remains too thin, boil hard for a minute or two to evaporate the excess liquid, until the sauce shows signs of thickening. Then serve at once.

Young Carrots Candied with Maple Syrup

For 4
Cook under pressure at 15 lb for 3 minutes

¼ cup (60 ml) dry white wine
2 tsp freshly squeezed lemon juice
Salt, to your taste
12 young carrots, scraped and trimmed
3 Tbs (45 g) sweet butter
2 Tbs pure maple syrup
Freshly ground black pepper, to your
    taste

Use a 2½-quart pressure cooker. Take out its base rack and pour in the wine, lemon juice and a small sprinkling of salt. Put back the base rack and quickly heat up the wine just to boiling, then, working fast to avoid boiling it away, stack in the carrots, put on the lid, bring the steam pressure up to 15 pounds and cook for not a second more than 3 minutes.

When the timer rings, reduce the pressure immediately. The moment the carrots are cool enough to handle, cut them lengthwise, first into halves, then into quarters, then eighths, finally into thickish matchsticks. Remove the base from inside the pot, pour off all the liquid, set the pressure cooker over low frying heat and put in it the butter. As soon as it is melted, work the maple syrup into it. Lightly toss the carrot sticks in this hot mixture, so that each is thoroughly coated and glazed, while being reheated. At the same time, lightly salt and pepper them to taste. When you see the golden glaze on the carrots, serve them instantly.

Squashed Cauliflower with Nutmeg

For 4
Including frying for about 10 minutes
Cook under pressure at 15 lb for 5 minutes

½ cup (1.25 dl) dry white wine
1 Tbs freshly squeezed lemon juice
Salt, to your taste
1 smallish, nicely white, tightly headed
    cauliflower (say, about 2 lb [1 kg]),
    well washed, left whole, a single ring
    of outer leaves left on
A thickish crust of bread
Up to 3 Tbs good olive oil
1 clove garlic, finely minced
½ cup (1.25 dl) grated Parmesan cheese
Freshly ground black pepper, to your
    taste
Freshly ground nutmeg, to your taste

Use a minimum 2½-quart pressure cooker, and a medium-sized sauté or fry pan. First, take the base rack out of the pressure cooker and put in the wine, with a good dribble or two of the lemon juice and a fair sprinkling of salt. Put back the base rack and rapidly bring the liquid just to boiling, then, working fast to minimize its boiling away, set the whole cauliflower on the rack with the crust of bread alongside it, at once put on the lid, bring the steam pressure up to 15 pounds and cook for exactly 5 minutes. (The bread, incidentally, is an old French trick for absorbing and getting rid of the unpleasant odors of the cauliflower.) Meanwhile, set the sauté pan over medium frying temperature and heat up in it 2 tablespoons of the oil. It must become fairly hot, but certainly not smoking or anywhere near it.

When the timer rings, reduce the steam pressure immediately. Lift out the cauliflower and immediately sprinkle it with the remaining lemon juice. Remove its outer leaves and break it up into its separate flowerets. Put these, with the garlic, into the hot sauté pan and quickly sprinkle over them the grated cheese, more salt to your taste, a fair grinding of pepper and plenty of grated nutmeg. Now, working fast with a wooden fork, squash the cauliflower down to a coarse mash and press it together until it forms a single, solid pancake about ½ inch (1.2 cm) thick. Turn up the heat and fry this pancake until it has a brown, crisp crust on both sides. Add more oil if needed. Use a large, reasonably flexible spatula to turn the pancake over without breaking it. When it is done, drain it for a few seconds on absorbent paper, then serve it on a hot platter and cut it into pie-style wedges. It should be crackly on the outside, lusciously juicy inside.

Chestnuts Poached in Beef Broth and Madeira Wine

For 4
Presoak chestnuts overnight
Cook under pressure at 15 lb for 30 minutes

2 cups (about 1 lb [450 g]) Italian dried chestnuts (see note, opposite)
1 cup (2.5 dl) clear beef broth (see page 35, or use canned)
1 cup (2.5 dl) dry Madeira wine
4 Tbs (60 g) butter
¼ tsp ground cinnamon
¼ tsp ground cloves
A few grinds nutmeg
Salt, to your taste
Freshly ground black pepper, to your taste

Shelling and peeling fresh chestnuts is always a nuisance. You can avoid it by buying the Italian preshelled and peeled, dried chestnuts—usually in Italian markets or fancy food stores. Whole cooked chestnuts are an outstanding alternative to potatoes. Or, if you want to mash them, give them an extra 5 minutes of cooking at 15 pounds, then serve them as a fluffy mound, or enrich them with butter and spices.

The day before, set the chestnuts to soak well covered in freshly drawn cold water. As they absorb some of the water and expand, add more water to keep them covered. Just before cooking them, drain and rinse them thoroughly under running cold water. They will, by now, probably have expanded to 2½ to 3 cups.

For the cooking, use a minimum 2½-quart pressure cooker. Take out its base rack and put in the soaked chestnuts. Pour over them the beef broth and Madeira. Heat it up rapidly just to boiling, put on the lid, bring the steam pressure up to 15 pounds and cook for exactly 30 minutes. (This time is for serving the chestnuts whole—if you intend to mash them, cook them for 35 minutes.)

When the timer rings, reduce the steam pressure immediately. Drain the chestnuts. If you are serving them whole, work the butter over and around them, so that it melts and coats them. At the same time, sprinkle on, to your taste, cinnamon, clove, nutmeg, salt and pepper. Or, if you prefer, mash them all together with a fork into a coarse, slightly lumpy, nutty puree.

Fennel Poached with a Touch of Dry Vermouth

For 4
Cook under pressure at 15 lb for 3 minutes

¼ cup (60 ml) clear beef bouillon (see page 35, or use canned)
¼ cup (60 ml) dry vermouth

Fennel, called finocchio in Italian markets (sometimes confused with anise), looks a bit like a deformed head of celery, with a big bulb at the bottom, short stalks and grassy-green fronds which are used as an herb in fish cookery. When chopped into a salad, fennel stalks add a strong licorice flavor.

A good spritz or two freshly squeezed
    lemon juice
Salt, to your taste
2 medium-sized knobs fennel, well
    washed, the green fronds cut off and
    saved for herbaceous uses, the less-
    tough parts of the short stalks
    chopped, the bulbs sliced ½ inch
    (1.2 cm) thick
4 Tbs (60 g) butter
Freshly ground black pepper, to your
    taste

It is much more gentle when poached in superheated steam as a hot vegetable to accompany fish or meat.

Use a minimum 2½-quart pressure cooker. Take out its base rack and pour in the bouillon, vermouth, lemon juice and a fair sprinkling of salt. Put back the base rack and rapidly heat up the liquids just to boiling, then, working fast to minimize any boiling away, pile onto the rack all the choppings and slicings of fennel, put on the lid, bring the steam pressure up to 15 pounds and cook for exactly 3 minutes.

When the timer rings, reduce the steam pressure immediately. Pour off any excess liquid and at once work the butter over and around the fennel so that all the bits and slices are nicely coated. At the same time add pepper, to your taste, and more salt, if you like.

Aromatic Mousse of Leeks

For 4
Cook under pressure at 15 lb for 5 minutes

½ cup (1.25 dl) clear chicken broth (see
    page 35, or use canned)
A couple of spritzes freshly squeezed
    lemon juice
1 bay leaf
1 whole clove
4 whole black peppercorns
Salt, to your taste
1 largish bunch (say, about 2 lb [1 kg])
    young leeks, the white parts no more
    than about ¾ inch (2 cm) thick, each
    quartered lengthwise, soaked,
    desanded and washed, the best parts
    of the green leaves cut into 2-inch (5
    cm) lengths
1 lb (450 g) medium potatoes, peeled and
    quartered
4 Tbs (60 g) softened butter
¾ cup (1.85 dl) heavy cream, lightly
    whipped until lightly stiff
3 oz (85 g) Switzerland Gruyère cheese,
    grated
Enough chopped fresh leaves of basil to
    fill 1 Tbs, or 1 tsp dried
Freshly ground black pepper, to your
    taste

Leeks, those fruity-nutty members of the onion family, are wonderful to eat and wonderfully flexible. You can stop this recipe halfway, dress the hot leek quarters in a white cream sauce, or a hollandaise, or an aromatic tomato sauce, and serve them as the accompanying vegetable to the main course of the meal. Or you can cool them in your refrigerator, dress them à la Française with oil and vinegar, then serve them as a classic, French-style salad appetizer. But, best of all, we like to puree them with butter and cream for this luxuriously rich, vegetable mousse.

The trick in handling the white parts of the leeks is to get absolutely all the sand out of them. Always quarter them, at least halfway down, then soak them in cold water for at least 10 minutes—finally rinsing them under strongly running cold water.

Use a minimum 3-quart pressure cooker. Take out its base rack and pour in the chicken bouillon, lemon juice, the bay leaf, crumbled, the clove, peppercorns and a fair sprinkling of salt. Put back the base rack, rapidly heat up the bouillon just to boiling, then, working fast to minimize the boiling away of the bouillon, stack in on the rack the leeks, including the green leaves, and the potato quarters, then at once put on the lid, bring the steam pressure up to 15 pounds and cook for exactly 5 minutes.

When the timer rings, reduce the steam pressure instantly. The moment the lid is opened, work in the butter so that it melts over and around everything. Now drain off any excess liquid from the pressure cooker and puree its entire solid contents, either through a Cuisinart chopper-churner (or one of the similar machines), an electric blender, or an electric or hand sieve or a food mill. Transfer the puree to a large mixing bowl and lightly blend into it, preferably using a rubber spatula with lifting rather than stirring strokes, the whipped cream, grated cheese, basil, plus salt and pepper, if needed. If it becomes too stiff, add a few dashes of the aromatic bouillon drained off from the pressure cooker. We usually serve this marvelous mousse as a separate course after the main dish. It is that good!

Small Onions Glazed with Slightly Burnt Butter

For 4
Cook under pressure at 15 lb for 10 minutes

½ cup (1.25 dl) clear chicken bouillon (see page 35, or use canned)
A couple spritzes of freshly squeezed lemon juice
Salt, to your taste
16 small white boiler onions, peeled, left whole
4 Tbs (60 g) butter
Freshly ground black pepper, to your taste

Use a minimum 2½-quart pressure cooker. Take out its base rack and pour in the bouillon and lemon juice, with a fair sprinkling of salt. Rapidly heat up the bouillon just to boiling, then, working fast to minimize the liquid boiling away, set all the onions on the bottom of the pressure cooker, instantly put on its lid, bring the steam pressure up to 15 pounds and cook for exactly 10 minutes. (Naturally, this time can vary by a minute or so either way, according to the size and solidity of the onions. Better to undercook them at first. You can always return them to pressure for a short extra minute or so.)

When the timer rings, reduce the steam pressure instantly. Drain off the remaining bouillon and now keep the pressure cooker going, uncovered, at medium-high frying temperature. Melt the butter around the onions, with more salt, if you like, plus a goodly grind of pepper. As the butter gets really hot, swish the onions around, until they are flecked with good black spots on all sides and there is a pleasant, nutty smell of burning. Naturally, the butter will also brown. When the sacrifice by fire has gone far enough, serve the onions at once and, if you can bear the calories, spoon a little of the brown butter over them.

Potatoes Creamed at a Shotgun Wedding

For 4
Cook under pressure at 15 lb for 1 minute

4 cups (1 kg) raw, peeled potatoes, in ½-inch (1.2 cm) cubes
1 medium yellow onion, peeled and finely minced
1 cup (2.5 dl) light cream
½ cup (1.25 dl) heavy cream
3 Tbs (45 g) butter
3 Tbs flour
Salt, to your taste

We have found, in general, that quite a few potato recipes do not work entirely satisfactorily in the pressure cooker. In the internal atmosphere of the superheated steam, potatoes can become soggy. But this recipe is always a superb success. It is a kind of shotgun wedding between the starch of the potato, the butter, cream and flour—all forced together into a perfect marriage by the power of the superheated steam. The final result is the creamiest potato we know.

Use a minimum 3-quart pressure cooker. Take out its base rack and put into it the potatoes, onion and light and heavy

Freshly ground black pepper, to your
    taste
¼ lb (115 g) sharp Cheddar cheese,
    grated
Enough chopped fresh leaves parsley to
    fill loosely ¼ cup (60 ml)

creams. Dot the surface with bits of the butter. Sprinkle the flour on top, and add salt and pepper to taste. Gently heat up the liquids just to the boiling point, put on the lid, bring the steam pressure up to 15 pounds and cook for exactly 1 minute.

When the timer rings, turn off the heat and allow the pressure to reduce gradually of its own accord, usually in about 4 or 5 minutes. The moment the lid is opened, gently and thoroughly stir in the grated cheese, so that the hot ingredients will melt it. Also make sure, with your wooden spoon, that all the creamy mixtures are completely blended around the potato cubes. Serve with the bright green parsley sprinkled over the top.

Potatoes Lionized
For 4
Cook under pressure at 15 lb for 7 minutes

4 Tbs (60 g) butter
2 lb (1 kg) small to medium potatoes,
    peeled and cut into quarters, but of
    roughly uniform size; then wash the
    pieces after cutting
3 medium yellow onions, peeled and
    sliced
Salt, to your taste
Freshly ground black pepper, to your
    taste
3 Tbs flour
¼ cup (60 ml) dry white wine
1 Tbs freshly squeezed lemon juice
¼ cup (60 g) finely minced scallions,
    white bulbs and green tops
Enough chopped fresh leaves parsley to
    fill 2 Tbs

"Lionized" is what our favorite young waitress insists on calling a side order of potatoes which, on the menu, is printed as *à la Lyonnaise*. Since the city of Lyons in central France has traditionally been the principal marketplace of French onions, anything Lyonnaise on a menu is always fairly solid with onions. This is another way with potatoes that goes excellently in the pressure cooker.

Use a minimum 2½-quart pressure cooker. Heat it up, without its base rack, to medium-high frying temperature, melt in it the butter and, when it is good and hot, quickly and lightly sauté the potatoes and sliced onions until they are gilded. At the same time add salt and pepper to your taste. Turn off the heat. Now absorb the remaining butter by sprinkling on and working in as much of the flour as is needed to form a thin paste, usually somewhere between 2 and 3 tablespoons, depending on the moisture that was in the onions and potatoes. Next, pour on the wine and lemon juice and gently stir them in. Heat up the liquids rapidly just to boiling, put on the lid, bring the steam pressure up to 15 pounds and cook for exactly 7 minutes.

When the timer rings, reduce the steam pressure immediately. Gently blend in the scallions. Taste for seasonings, adding more salt and pepper, if needed. Serve with the bright green parsley sprinkled over the top.

Sweet Potatoes with Apricots, Pears and White Grapes
For 4
Cook under pressure at 15 lb for 8 minutes

4 largish sweet potatoes, peeled and each
    cut into 6 slices

Use a minimum 4-quart pressure cooker. Take out its base rack and put into it the potato slices, slightly overlapping, with the apricot halves, pear slices and raisins fitted around and above the potatoes. Pour in the lime juice and the juice of

1 cup (225 g) dried apricot halves

1 cup (225 g) sliced pears, fresh or dried, cored if fresh but with the skin left on

½ cup (115 g) seedless white raisins

½ cup (1.25 dl) unsweetened lime juice

The freshly squeezed juice of 1 lemon

Up to ⅓ cup (80 ml) pure maple syrup

4 Tbs (60 g) butter

1 tsp ground cinnamon

Salt, to your taste

Freshly ground black pepper, to your taste

½ cup (115 g) seedless white grapes

the lemon. Heat up these liquids just to boiling, put on the lid, bring the steam pressure up to 15 pounds and cook for exactly 8 minutes.

When the timer rings, reduce the steam pressure immediately. Everything inside the pressure cooker will now be too tart and too liquid. Correct the tartness by stirring in as much of the maple syrup as is needed to give it all a delicately and pleasantly sweet-sour effect. Heat up everything, uncovered, to a merry bubbling to evaporate off the excess water which has come out of the fruit and the potatoes. At the same time, gently work in, bit by bit, the butter, cinnamon, and salt and pepper to taste. At the last moment before serving, work in the grapes very gently so as not to burst them. Let them warm up for a couple of minutes, then serve.

Buttered and Walnuted Acorn Squash with Maple Syrup

For 4
Cook under pressure at 15 lb for 7 minutes
Plus oven baking for about 30 minutes more

½ cup (1.25 dl) dry white wine

A couple good spritzes freshly squeezed lemon juice

Salt, to your taste

2 medium acorn squash, washed, cut in half lengthwise, the pulp and seeds dug out

Up to 4 Tbs (60 g) butter

Up to 4 Tbs pure maple syrup

4 Tbs fairly finely chopped walnut meats

4 tsp walnut oil, if you can find it at a fancy food or health store (quite optional)

Use a minimum 6-quart pressure cooker. You will also need an open, oven-baking platter large enough to hold 4 acorn squash halves side by side. First, take out the base rack from the pressure cooker and pour in the wine, with the lemon juice and a smallish sprinkling of salt. Put back the base rack and quickly heat up the wine just to boiling. While it is getting hot, stack the squash halves on the base rack with their cut sides facing downward. If necessary, stagger them diagonally one above the other. The instant the wine begins bubbling, put on the lid, bring the steam pressure up to 15 pounds and cook for exactly 7 minutes. Meanwhile, preheat your oven to 300° F (150° C).

When the timer rings, reduce the steam pressure immediately. Set the squash halves cut sides upward on the oven platter and begin filling their cups. It is really a matter of personal taste as to how much butter and maple syrup you put in each. How rich and sweet do you like your squash? Try our way the first time. Put into each of the 4 half squash cups: 2 teaspoons of butter, 2 teaspoons of maple syrup and 1 tablespoon of the chopped walnuts. (We often replace 1 teaspoon of the butter with a teaspoon of walnut oil.) Now, with a metal kitchen fork, lightly break up the flesh of the squash and work the butter, etc., into it. Put everything into the oven to melt together and develop flavor and richness, for about 25 to 30 minutes. At the last moment before serving, taste for seasoning and sprinkle on, if you like, a very little salt and pepper.

Tomatoes as They Do Them in Provence

For 4
Cook under pressure at 15 lb for 3 minutes

4 Tbs (60 g) butter
4 medium good and ripe, nicely firm
    tomatoes, washed and cut in half
4 flat anchovy fillets, finely minced
2 cloves garlic, finely minced
Enough chopped fresh leaves parsley to
    fill ⅓ cup (80 ml)
Salt, to your taste
Freshly ground black pepper, to your
    taste
Up to 8 Tbs crisp bread crumbs
¼ cup (60 ml) dry white wine

Use a minimum 6-quart pressure cooker. Heat it up without its base rack, to medium-high frying temperature, melt in it the butter and, when it is good and hot, put in the tomato halves, cut side down, letting them sizzle fairly strongly for no more than 2 minutes each. Remove them one by one and, with a small spoon, open up the central cavities of each tomato half, spooning out some of the juice and pits, simply dropping this into the butter on the bottom of the pressure cooker. Now fill the space you have opened up with the minced anchovies and garlic, with the chopped parsley equally divided among all the tomatoes. Save some of the parsley for later garnishing. Then salt and pepper the halves to your taste. Finally, fill up and cover each tomato half with the bread crumbs. Place the halves in the pressure cooker. Carefully pour the wine onto the bottom of the pot, heat it up just to boiling, put on the lid, bring the steam pressure up to 15 pounds and cook for exactly 3 minutes.

When the timer rings, reduce the steam pressure immediately. Serve each tomato half with some of the buttery-winey juices poured over it and a bright green sprinkling of the remaining parsley, plus more salt and pepper, if needed.

Aromatic Mousse of White Turnips (or Yellow Parsnips) with Sour Cream and Herbs

For 4
Cook under pressure at 15 lb for 4 minutes
Plus extra oven baking for about 15 minutes

¼ cup (60 ml) dry white wine
A couple of good spritzes freshly
    squeezed lemon juice
Salt, to your taste
8 medium-to-smallish, young white
    turnips (or about 6 usually slightly
    larger parsnips), washed, skins left
    on, the turnips quartered (each
    parsnip cut into 6 cross slices)
Up to ¾ cup (1.85 dl) heavy cream,
    whipped stiff
Enough chopped fresh leaves parsley to
    fill ⅓ cup (80 ml)
Enough chopped fresh leaves rosemary to
    fill 1 Tbs, or 1 tsp dried
The same amount tarragon
The same amount thyme
½ cup (115 g) coarsely chopped pecan
    nutmeats
Freshly ground black pepper, to your
    taste

The beauty of these refreshing and smooth vegetable purees is that they are studded with chopped fresh herb leaves. So don't stick strictly to the rosemary, tarragon and thyme mentioned in the ingredients list; use whatever fresh leaf happens to be available in the market—basil or chives, celery leaves or dill fronds, scallion tops or sorrel . . . Anything goes—as long as it is fresh and green and aromatically crisp on the tongue.

You will need a minimum 2½-quart pressure cooker and a covered serving dish, preheated in the oven at 160° F (70° C). First, take out the base rack from the pressure cooker and pour into it the wine, a good spritz of the lemon juice and a fair sprinkling of salt. Put back the base rack and heat up the wine just to boiling, then, working fast to avoid the wine boiling away, stack the turnip quarters (or parsnip slices) on the base rack, at once put on the lid, bring the steam pressure up to 15 pounds and cook for exactly 4 minutes. Meanwhile preheat your oven to 300° F (150° C). When the timer rings, reduce the steam pressure immediately. Take out the turnips (or parsnips), skin them and puree them, either through a Cuisinart chopper-churner (or one of the other similar machines), an electric blender, an electric or hand sieve, a food mill, or a plain old ricer. Put the puree into a largish mixing bowl and gently work into it (preferably using a rubber spatula, with lifting rather than stirring movements) as much of the whipped cream as you need to convert it all into a creamy-smooth mousse, a few more spritzes of lemon juice, enough parsley to dot it nicely with green (saving some for the final decoration), the rosemary, tarragon, thyme, pecans, plus more salt, if you like, with a final sprinkling of pepper. Pile it all into your serving dish and set it in the center of the oven to develop and intermingle the flavors for about 15 minutes. Just before serving, sprinkle more bright green parsley on top.

Steam-Baked Zucchini with Mushrooms and Scallions

For 4
Cook under pressure at 15 lb for 2 minutes

¼ cup (60 ml) dry white wine
1 Tbs freshly squeezed lemon juice
½ tsp dried oregano
Salt, to your taste
6 smallish zucchini, each about 4 to 6 inches (10 to 15 cm) long; wash them, do not peel, cut them across into ¾-inch (2 cm) chunks
4 Tbs (60 g) butter
½ cup (115 g) sliced white button mushrooms
¼ cup (60 g) finely minced scallions, white bulbs and green tops
Enough chopped leaves of parsley to fill 2 Tbs
Freshly ground black pepper, to your taste

Use a minimum 2½-quart pressure cooker. Take out its base rack and pour into it the wine, lemon juice, oregano and a fair sprinkling of salt. Put back the base rack and heat up the wine just to boiling, then, working fast to avoid the liquid boiling away, stack the zucchini chunks on the base rack, put on the lid, bring the steam pressure up to 15 pounds and cook for exactly 2 minutes.

When the timer rings, reduce the steam pressure immediately. Drain any excess liquid from the pressure cooker and pull out its base rack. At once blend in, gently, with a wooden spoon, the butter, so that it melts over and around the still-hot zucchini, coating every chunk. Keep the pressure cooker at simmering heat as you also gently work in all the remaining ingredients (preferably in the following order: mushrooms, scallions, parsley, more salt and pepper). As you serve, make sure that each portion of zucchini gets its fair share of the accompanying aromatic garnishings.

Chapter 20

MORE BASIC RECIPES: STEAMED BREADS

From Boston Brown to Savannah Spoon

When the Founding Fathers in the Massachusetts Bay Colony invented Boston brown bread, they probably did so because their dry-heat ovens were so inefficient and unworkable that it was much better to cook the bread in a closed steam pot hanging over the fire. The resulting rich, soft bread was so good that it has stayed with us for more than two hundred years. We wouldn't dream of serving Boston Baked Beans (see page 62) without its accompanying slices of luxurious, buttered, brown bread—now made better than the colonists ever knew it, with the help of superheated steam in a pressure cooker.

Other breads—corn, fruit or nut—can also be perfectly steam-baked in a matter of minutes. If variety is the spice of bread life, then there is a place both for the kind of bread that crackles out of a dry brick oven, and the steamed kind which replaces the crackle by the richness and softness of a velvet texture on the tongue.

Basic Principles—Practical Advice

1. The art of cooking has to follow nature's immutable laws. One of them is that raised dough bread must be steam-baked at the lowest possible pressure—never more than 5 pounds. The reason is simple. When you mix into your dough a leavening agent (such as, in the following recipes, baking powder, baking soda, or yeast), the rising of the dough is accomplished by the formation of thousands of tiny bubbles which expand with the heat, forcing the mixture outward and upward, so that, finally, when the baking is complete, there are hundreds of little air holes which make the lovely light texture of the bread. If these bubbles, at the beginning of their work, while the dough is still soft, are subjected to the heavy pressure of 15 pounds (or even 10 pounds), then the bubbles are crushed, the rising does not take place and you will finish up with bread that is inedibly heavy and unpleasantly soggy.

   You should not, therefore, attempt any of the following

pressure recipes unless you have a 5-pound control weight for your cooker. You can get one, quite easily, by writing to the manufacturer.

2. For all but one of the following recipes, you will need a metal bread or cake pan, or a metal mold (either with a cover, or to be covered with aluminum foil) of a shape and size to fit into your pressure cooker with at least ¾ inch (2 cm) space to spare all around and at least an inch between the top of the bread pan and the underside of the pressure lid, so as to allow proper circulation of the steam. We tested these recipes in many ways, in several different sizes of cooker, in various shapes, sizes and types of molds and pans. We finally decided to time and write the recipes for a standard, 3-quart cooker in which we placed a standard, aluminum pan of 6 inches diameter and 3 inches depth. We never filled it more than ⅔ full of the raw dough and, after the preliminary steaming without pressure to encourage the rising, the pan was entirely filled. You need not, however, be restricted by our method. You can use any size of cooker and any shape or size of pan, including ceramic or earthenware. You will simply have to recalculate the amount of the ingredients and the timing.

3. The timing, of course, is controlled by the shape and size of the loaf—in precise fact, by the distance from the outside edge to the dead center. The greater that distance, the longer the cooking time. So—even the same amount of dough, when put into a different shape of pan, may require a different timing. This is why our figures can only be an indication and not a fixed rule. But this question of timing is not really a severe problem and can only be a small nuisance to you at the first try of a recipe. As soon as you open up your pressure cooker, after the steam baking, you test the doneness of the bread by plunging a bright knife into the center. If it does not come out clean and dry, you continue the pressure for 3 or 4 minutes longer, carefully noting in the margin of the recipe how much extra time was required. Then, every time you repeat the recipe, with your particular bread pan, in your particular cooker, on your particular stove, you will get absolutely consistent results. A good, simple, first recipe with which to begin your experimenting is this one. . . .

Historic Boston Brown Bread

1 loaf, about 2 lb
Steam without pressure for 30 minutes,
*   then at 5 lb for 30 minutes*

2 whole eggs, lightly beaten
2 Tbs (30 g) butter, melted

This is one of the most truly American of all our foods. Apart from its being traditionally served with Boston Baked Beans (page 62), it is just about the best midnight snack we know—nicely buttered and with a glass of ginger ale, soda

⅔ cup (1.6 dl) unsulfured molasses
1 tsp baking soda
1 cup (2.5 dl) buttermilk
1 cup (115 g) all-purpose white flour,
    sifted
1 tsp double-acting baking powder
1 tsp salt
2 cups (225 g) whole wheat flour
1 cup (225 g) seedless white raisins
1 Tbs (15 g) butter, firm

water, white wine, or, bless the children, milk. See basic notes on steamed breads on page 206.

You will need a minimum 3-quart pressure cooker and a 6-cup baking pan to fit inside it (see page 207). First, in a largish mixing bowl, beat together the eggs, melted butter and molasses. In another bowl, stir the baking soda into the buttermilk. In still a third bowl, sift together the white flour, the baking powder and salt, then thoroughly blend into this mixture the whole wheat flour. Now, ¼ cup by ¼ cup, alternately work into the egg-molasses mix the buttermilk and the flours, beating them vigorously together. Finally, stir in the raisins. With the remaining butter, lightly grease the baking pan and fill it ⅔ full. Cover it completely and tightly with aluminum foil. Pour into the pressure cooker 2½ cups (6.25 dl) of hot water, put in its base rack and stand the baking pan on it. Put on the lid, but do not put the control weight on the vent. Adjust the heat so that a very small stream of steam blows out steadily through the vent for the first 30 minutes. Do not allow the steam either to blow hard or to die down.

When the timer rings, put the control weight on the vent, bring the steam pressure up to 5 pounds and continue cooking for 30 minutes.

When the timer rings again, turn off the heat and reduce the pressure immediately. Uncover the bread and check it for doneness, as described on page 207. If necessary, cook it under pressure a few minutes longer. When the bread is perfect, take the baking pan out of the cooker and invert it onto a rack. As soon as it is cool enough to handle, remove the loaf from the pan, letting it continue to cool and dry on the rack.

Basic Pressure Cooker Farmhouse Bread Without Pressure

2 loaves
Rising of dough up to 2 ½ hours
Steaming without pressure about 1 ½ hours

2 envelopes dried granulated yeast
¼ tsp sugar
½ cup (1.25 dl) warm water
¼ cup (60 ml) honey
2 Tbs corn or peanut oil
1 Tbs salt
Up to 8 cups (900 g) all-purpose white
    flour
2 cups (5 dl) lukewarm water
1 Tbs (15 g) butter

This recipe is adapted from one given us by Betty Wenstadt, who does food preparation research for the people who make the famous Presto pressure cooker. By a neat twist, the bread is steamed in a pressure cooker, but without pressure. You may feel, while the relatively slow steaming is in progress, that this is a strangely roundabout way of making a loaf of bread. But the final taste and texture are so unusually good that the quiet waiting seems entirely worthwhile.

This version uses white flour, but you can also work with other types, for example, cracked wheat, soy, wheat germ, whole wheat, etc. You will soon find the one you like best.

For each of these loaves, you will need a minimum 4-quart pressure cooker, and to avoid any buildup of pressure during the baking, you should remove the gasket ring from the lid. First, in a small bowl, mix the yeast with the sugar and add the warm water at precisely the right temperature. This is the key to success. If the water is only lukewarm, it will not start the yeast going. If it is too hot, it will kill the yeast stone dead. The right temperature is between 105° and 115° F (40°–45° C). The proof that you are right comes within 5 to 10 minutes, when bubbles form on the yeast water. If this does not happen, the yeast may be too old. Throw it all away and start over.

When the yeast is obviously working, pour the entire contents of the small bowl into a large bowl and work into it with a wooden spoon the honey, oil and salt. Now begin sprinkling the flour over the top, cup by cup, working each cupful in before adding the next. Alternate the additions of flour with good dashes of the lukewarm water, continuing until you have worked in the full 2 cups of water and 7 cups of the flour. Do not let the dough get too stiff. You are really aiming at a very thick batter. But, at the end, if the dough is not quite firm enough, add, tablespoon by tablespoon, as much of the last cup of flour as is needed. When it seems right, beat the dough thoroughly with your wooden spoon, then cover the bowl with a cloth and set it in a warm place to rise until it has doubled its bulk. This usually takes about an hour to an hour and a half, according to the temperature and weather.

Our own trick for assuring a consistent temperature in the "warm place" is to turn on our oven to 500° F (260° C), leave it on for exactly 60 seconds, then immediately turn it off, place the covered bowl of bread dough in the oven, close the door and wait for the dough to double its bulk.

When the dough has risen properly, punch it down and work it with your fingers to expel its air bubbles. Now divide the dough into 2 parts and hold the second part in a warmish place until you are ready to make the second loaf. Remove the base rack from your pressure cooker and lightly grease it. Now shape and spread the first half of the dough inside the pressure cooker. It should be ⅓ to ½ full. Then cover it with a cloth and set it so that the dough rises again in that essential "warm place" (we repeat our oven trick) until the pressure cooker is about ¾ full. This may take 40 to 50 minutes.

Now put the lid on the pressure cooker and set it on gentle heat on top of the stove. Do not put on its pressure control weight. Leave the steam vent open. Keep the heat gentle (if you have a temperature dial, the pointer should be at about 300° F [150° C]). After about 30 minutes, reduce your heat to gentle simmering (215° F [100° C]). There is a danger, at this point, that the bottom of the loaf might burn. So keep the heat very low. Continue the gentle steaming, from the moment when you first saw the steam at the vent, for another 45 minutes. Then open the lid and test the loaf with a bright knife, which should come out clean and dry if the bread is cooked through. If not, put back the lid and continue the steaming for another 15 minutes or so. Finally, when the loaf is done and as soon as it is cool enough to handle, take it out and let it dry on a rack. The bottom, which is beautifully golden now, of course, becomes the top. Then repeat the operation with the second batch of dough.

Almond, Brazil, Pecan and Walnut Bread

1 loaf, about 2 lb
Steam without pressure for 30 minutes,
*   then at 5 lb for 30 minutes*

1 whole egg, lightly beaten
½ cup (115 g) sugar
2½ cups (285 g) all-purpose white flour,
    sifted before measuring
2 tsp double-acting baking powder
1 tsp salt
1 cup (2.5 dl) milk
¼ cup (60 g) each coarsely chopped meats
    of almonds, brazil nuts, pecans and
    walnuts—or, if it is easier, the same
    total of mixed, nonsalted nutmeats
1 Tbs (15 g) butter for greasing bread
    mold

See basic notes on steamed breads on page 206.

You will need a minimum 3-quart pressure cooker and a 4-cup baking pan to fit inside it. First, in a large mixing bowl, beat together the egg and sugar. Resift the flour with the baking powder and salt. Now, ¼ cup by ¼ cup, blend into the egg-sugar mixture, alternately, the milk and the flour mixture, beating it all vigorously until you have a smooth dough. Finally, work in the chopped nuts. Lightly grease the baking pan and turn the dough into it but do not fill the pan more than ⅔ to allow for rising. Cover it completely and tightly with aluminum foil. Pour 2½ cups (6.25 dl) of hot water into the pressure cooker, put in its base rack and stand the baking pan on it. Put on the lid, but not the pressure control weight. Adjust the heat under the cooker so that a small stream of steam blows through the vent pipe. Keep the steam going, not too hard, but not dying down, for exactly 30 minutes.

When the timer rings, put the pressure control on the vent pipe, bring the steam pressure up to 5 pounds and cook for exactly 30 minutes longer.

When the timer rings again, turn off the heat and reduce the pressure immediately. Test the bread for doneness by sticking in a bright knife which should come out clean and dry. If not, put back the pan under pressure for another 5 minutes or so. When the bread is perfect, lift its pan out of the cooker, uncover it and invert it onto a rack. As soon as the bread is cool enough to handle, take it out of its pan, then continue to cool it and dry it on the rack.

Lemon-Orange Bread with Walnut Quarters

1 loaf, about 2 lb
Steam without pressure for 30 minutes,
*   then at 5 lb for 25 minutes*

The outer rinds of 2 lemons, finely
    minced
The outer rinds of 2 oranges, finely
    minced
¾ cup (170 g) sugar
1¾ cups (200 g) all-purpose white flour,
    sifted before measuring
2 tsp double-acting baking powder
1 tsp salt
1 whole egg, lightly beaten
½ cup (1.25 dl) milk

See basic notes on steamed breads on page 206.

You will need a minimum 3-quart pressure cooker and a 4-cup baking pan to fit inside it. First, in a 1½-pint saucepan, boil together ½ cup of water with the minced rind of the lemons and oranges, plus ½ cup of the sugar. Stir well and bubble quite hard until all the sugar is melted and you have a thickish sugar syrup. Turn off the heat and let it cool, covered. Resift the flour with the baking powder and salt. In a fair-sized mixing bowl, beat together the egg and the remaining ¼ cup of sugar. Now add and beat in, ¼ cup by ¼ cup, alternately, the milk and the flour mix. Finally, work in the warm syrup and walnuts. Lightly butter the baking pan and spread the dough

¾ cup (170 g) walnut halves, each cut
　　into 2 quarters
1 Tbs (15 g) butter to grease the bread
　　mold

in it, but no more than ⅔ full to allow for rising. Cover the pan completely and tightly with aluminum foil. Pour 2 cups of hot water into the pressure cooker, put in the base rack and stand the pan on it. Put on the lid, but not the control weight. Leave the vent pipe open. Adjust the heat so that a very small stream of steam blows steadily through the vent and continues, neither blowing harder, nor dying down, for 30 minutes.

When the timer rings, put the control weight on the vent pipe, bring the steam pressure up to 5 pounds and cook for exactly 25 minutes longer.

When the timer rings again, turn off the heat and reduce the steam pressure immediately. Test the bread for doneness by sticking in a bright knife which should come out clean and dry. If not, put back the pan under pressure for another 5 minutes or so. When the bread is perfect, lift its pan out of the cooker, uncover it and invert it onto a rack. As soon as the bread is cool enough to handle, take it out of its pan, then continue to cool it and dry it on the rack.

Savannah Spoon Bread

For 2
Steam without pressure for 5 minutes,
then cook at 10 lb for 34 minutes

¾ cup (170 g) cornmeal
¾ cup (1.85 dl) boiling water
¾ cup (1.85 dl) light cream
¾ tsp salt
1 whole egg
1½ Tbs (23 g) butter, melted
1 Tbs (15 g) butter, firm

We normally prepare this in a handsome, stainless-steel baking pan, 6 inches across and 2½ inches deep, which gives the fastest cooking time and is good-looking enough to come to table. If you use a pan of china, earthenware or heatproof glass, or if your bread is much thicker than 2 inches, you may need a few extra minutes of cooking time. Spoon bread, naturally, is served and eaten with a spoon. This version does not have a crackling crust, but it makes up for that with a superb, velvety softness.

You will need a minimum 2½- or 3-quart pressure cooker and a baking pan to fit inside it with at least ¾ inch space to spare all around. Put the cornmeal into a largish mixing bowl and pour over it, all at once, the absolutely boiling water. This very slightly cooks the cornmeal. Stir thoroughly for a couple of minutes, then begin working in the cream and the salt. Beat it with a wooden fork to make it all very smooth. Now lightly beat the egg in a separate small bowl and then work it into the cornmeal mix. Finally blend in the melted butter. Use the firm butter liberally to grease the inside of the baking pan, then spread in the spoon bread mix. Completely and tightly cover the pan with aluminum foil. Pour 1½ cups of hot water into the pressure cooker, put in the base rack and set the spoon bread pan on it. Put on the lid, but not the control weight. Leave the vent pipe open. Heat up the water so that it gently steams through the vent pipe (neither blowing too hard, nor dying down) for exactly 5 minutes. Then put on the control weight, bring the pressure up to 10 pounds and cook for exactly 34 minutes more.

When the timer rings, turn off the heat and reduce the pressure immediately. Check the center of the spoon bread to make sure it is set all the way through. If not, give it 2 or 3 extra minutes of cooking under pressure. When it is perfectly done, serve it directly from its pan.

Chapter 21

MORE BASIC RECIPES: SWEET DESSERT SOUFFLÉ CUSTARDS

Steam Produces the Fluffiest of Velvet

We have already spoken of the feathery-light, egg-custard marvels produced with such unique ease and speed by the pressure cooker. (See the Introduction on page 174 and the practical notes on page 174.) Custards as savory main courses for light lunches or suppers are in Chapter 17. A few custard desserts are included in the "complete meal" recipes on pages 95 and 116.

Here, now, are a few of our favorite recipes for party dessert custards which can be unmolded and decorated as a handsome centerpiece at the end of a party dinner for 2 or 20 guests.

Banana Brandy Custard

For 2
Cook under pressure at 5 lb for 12 minutes

1 whole egg, lightly beaten
¾ cup (1.85 dl) light cream, warmed until it feels hot to the tip of your finger, but not scalding
1 Tbs brown sugar
A pinch of salt
¾ oz (22 ml) good brandy
A half-ripe banana, mashed to a smooth puree
Up to 1 tsp butter for buttering the custard cups

We use metal individual custard cups, in which the custard cooks in the fastest time. If you use heatproof glass, the cooking time will be about 3 or 4 minutes longer. You could also double this recipe and cook the custard in a baking dish, but then the extra time might be as much as 10 minutes. See basic notes on all custards on page 174.

Use a minimum 2½- or 3-quart pressure cooker and as many individual custard cups as may be needed to hold the mix according to their size. Using a fork in a fair-sized mixing bowl, lightly beat together the egg and the heated cream. Then work in all the other ingredients (except the butter), in the order as listed opposite. Beat thoroughly each time before adding the next ingredient. Butter the custard cups and then, giving the mixture a final good stir, pour it in and tightly cover each cup with aluminum foil. Pour ¾ cup (1.85 dl) of hot water into the pressure cooker, put in the base rack and stand the cups on it. Put on the lid, bring the pressure up to 5 pounds and cook for exactly 12 minutes.

When the timer rings, turn off the heat and reduce the steam pressure immediately. Test the custard for perfect doneness by plunging into its center a bright, silvery knife which should come out dry and clean. If not, give it all another couple of minutes under pressure. Finally, let the custard cool slightly before serving it, either in its cups, or unmolded onto a platter. As a last, luxurious touch, you can dribble a few more drops of brandy over the top of each serving.

French Cherry Custard

For 2
Cook under pressure at 5 lb for 15 minutes

⅔ cup (150 g) sugar
20–30 fresh sweet cherries, pitted and
    destalked (or, out of season, canned,
    see opposite)
2 whole eggs, lightly beaten
1 cup (2.5 dl) light cream, heated until it
    feels quite hot to the tip of your
    finger, but not scalded
¼ tsp pure almond extract
2 tsp kirsch cherry liqueur, plus a little
    bit more for dribbling on at table, if
    you wish
½ tsp pure vanilla extract

We turn to this luscious dessert when fresh Bing cherries are in season. It can be made with canned sweet cherries, but their purplish color sometimes turns the bright yellow custard to a shade of bluish gray. We prepare this in metal custard cups (aluminum, copper, stainless steel or tin), which gives the fastest cooking time. If you use Pyrex or other heatproof glass cups, allow 2 or 3 minutes longer. You can also double the recipe and steam it in an aluminum baking pan or china dish, but then the time will be at least 10 minutes longer. See basic notes on all custards on page 174.

Use a minimum 2½-quart pressure cooker and as many custard cups as may be needed to hold the mix, according to their size. First, in a small, heavy saucepan, gently heat ⅓ cup of the sugar with 1 teaspoon of water, stirring it continuously, until the sugar melts into syrup, boils and then turns a walnut brown. Dribble this syrup into the bottom of the cups to form a sticky base. At once stick onto this base as many whole cherries as will fit in a single layer in the bottom of each cup. Then set the cups aside while you mix the custard. In a fairly large mixing bowl, lightly beat the eggs with a fork into the heated cream. Then work in the almond extract, cherry kirsch, vanilla, and as much of the remaining sugar as your sweet tooth demands. Beat it all lightly, then pour it at once over the cherries. Cover each cup completely and tightly with aluminum foil. Pour into the pressure cooker, with its base rack in place, ½ cup (1.25 dl) of hot water and stand the cups on the rack. Put on the lid, bring the pressure up to 5 pounds and cook for exactly 15 minutes.

When the timer rings, turn off the heat and reduce the pressure immediately. Test the custard for doneness by plunging into its center a bright, silvery knife, which should come out dry and clean. If not, give the custard a couple of minutes longer under pressure. Finally, unmold onto a serving platter. If you like, you can dribble on a little more kirsch liqueur.

Fluffy Custard with Café Bénédictine (or Other Sweet Liqueur)
For 2
Cook under pressure at 5 lb for 9 minutes

1 whole egg, lightly beaten
¾ cup (1.85 dl) light cream, heated until it feels quite hot to the tip of your finger, but not scalded
1 oz (30 ml) Café Bénédictine, or other liqueur (see list, opposite)
1 Tbs sugar
A pinch of salt
Butter for greasing custard cups

A blend of Bénédictine with coffee is one of the newest and nicest combinations to reach us from France, but there are at least a hundred other essences of fruits and herbs—some world famous, others hardly known at all. It would take many pages to list every one worth trying in a dessert custard. Here is our favorite "baker's dozen": orange Curaçao, cherry Heering, crème de banane, green Chartreuse, crème de fraises (strawberry), crème de menthe, peach, Williams pear, kümmel (caraway), black raspberry, apricot, almond cream, ginger liqueur. (See advice on timing in the Introduction to the previous recipe and basic notes on all custards on page 174.)

Use a minimum 2½- to 3-quart pressure cooker with as many individual custard cups as may be needed to hold the mix, according to their size. First, in a fair-sized mixing bowl, lightly beat together with a fork the egg and heated cream. Then work in 4 teaspoons of the Café Bénédictine and the sugar, plus the salt. Lightly butter the cups and, giving the custard mixture a final beat or two, pour it in. Completely and tightly cover each cup with aluminum foil. Pour into the pressure cooker, with its base rack in place, ¾ cup (1.85 dl) of hot water and set the cups on the rack. Put on the lid, bring the pressure up to 5 pounds and cook for exactly 9 minutes.

When the timer rings, turn off the heat and reduce the steam pressure immediately. Test the custard for doneness by plunging into its center a bright, silvery knife, which should come out dry and clean. If not, give it another couple of minutes of pressure. You may serve it in the cups or unmolded onto hot plates. Either way, dribble over each custard 1 teaspoon of the remaining Café Bénédictine.

Cheese and Honey Fluffy Custard
For 4
Cook under pressure at 5 lb for 15 minutes

1½ cups (3.75 dl) light cream, heated until it feels quite hot to the tip of your finger, but not scalded
3 whole eggs, lightly beaten
1 cup (225 g) cream-style, small-curd cottage cheese
¼ cup (60 ml) honey
Butter to grease the soufflé dish
A few grinds of nutmeg

This ultrasimple yet excellent recipe is adapted from one given us by Gretchen Zeismer, who does all the food research for the people who make the famous Mirro pressure cooker. You can also prepare it in individual custard cups and the cooking time is then brought down to about 2½ minutes.

You will need a minimum 4-quart pressure cooker and a 6-cup metal mold or soufflé dish to fit into the cooker with at least ¾ inch space to spare all around. First, in a fairly large mixing bowl, lightly beat together with a fork all the ingredients (except the nutmeg and butter) in the order listed, beating in each new ingredient before the next is added. Lightly butter the soufflé dish and, giving the custard mixture a final beat or two, put it in. Cover the dish, completely and tightly, with aluminum foil. Pour into the pressure cooker, with its base rack in place, 1 cup of hot water and stand the soufflé dish on the rack. Put on the lid, bring the pressure up to 5 pounds and cook for exactly 15 minutes.

When the timer rings, turn down the heat and reduce the pressure immediately. Check the doneness of the custard by plunging into its center a bright, silvery knife, which should come out dry and clean. If not, give the custard a couple more minutes at pressure. Finally, unmold it onto a hot serving platter and sprinkle it lightly with freshly ground nutmeg.

Lime-Fluff Custard with Walnuts

For 2
Cook under pressure at 5 lb for 12 minutes

2 eggs, separated
¾ cup (1.85 dl) light cream, heated until it feels hot to your finger, but not scalded
2 Tbs superfine-grind sugar
The grated rind of 1½ limes, plus up to 1 Tbs of the juice of 1 of them
A pinch of salt
3 Tbs finely chopped walnut meats
2 tsp butter, for buttering the custard cups
2 glacéed cherries (optional)

We use metal individual custard cups, in which the custard cooks in the fastest time. If you use heatproof glass, the cooking time will be about 3 or 4 minutes longer. You could also double this recipe and cook the custard in a baking dish, but then the extra time might be as much as 10 minutes. See basic notes on all custards on page 174.

You will need a minimum 2½-quart pressure cooker and as many custard cups as may be needed to hold the mix, according to their size. First, lightly beat with a fork the egg yolks and the heated cream. Then beat in the sugar, lime rind, 4 teaspoons of the lime juice and the salt. In a separate bowl, beat the egg whites until they form stiff peaks, then fold them, quickly and lightly, with 2 tablespoons of the chopped walnuts, into the egg-cream mix. Butter the custard cups and pour the fluffy mix into them. Cover them completely and tightly with aluminum foil. Pour 1 cup of hot water into the pressure cooker, put in the base rack and set the cups on it. Put on the lid, bring the pressure up to 5 pounds and cook for exactly 12 minutes.

The moment the timer rings, turn off the heat and reduce the pressure immediately. Test the custard for doneness by plunging into its center a bright, silvery knife, which should come out dry and clean. You may serve the custard in its dish, or you may unmold it onto a warm platter. Sprinkle the remaining chopped walnuts over the top. Decorate it, if you like, with thinly sliced glacéed cherries and dribble over it some of the remaining lime juice.

Fluffy Coconut-Fig Soufflé Custard

For 4
Cook under pressure at 10 lb for 16 minutes

2 large eggs, separated, plus 1 extra white
2 Tbs superfine-grind white sugar
1 tsp pure vanilla extract
A pinch of salt
1¼ cups (3.15 dl) light cream, heated
    until it feels quite hot to the tips of
    your fingers, but not scalded
3 Tbs flaked or grated coconut
4 Kadota figs, chopped finely
1 Tbs (15 g) butter for greasing the soufflé
    dish
Freshly ground nutmeg, to your taste

You will need a minimum 2½- or 3-quart pressure cooker and a 4-cup soufflé dish to fit into the cooker with at least ¾ inch to spare all around.

First, beat the egg yolks with the sugar, vanilla and salt. Then, gradually beat into this mixture the heated cream, with the coconut and figs. In a separate bowl, beat the egg whites to stiff peaks and then fold them, quickly and lightly, into the egg-cream mixture.

Butter the inside of the soufflé dish and, giving the custard fluff a final beat or two, pour it in, making sure that the dish is no more than ¾ full. Cover completely and tightly with aluminum foil. Pour into the pressure cooker, with its base rack in place, 1 cup of hot water and stand the dish on the rack. Place a heatproof plate on the aluminum foil over the soufflé dish. Put on the lid, bring the pressure up to 10 pounds and cook for exactly 16 minutes.

When the timer rings, turn off the heat and reduce the pressure immediately. Test the soufflé for doneness. When you press your finger on the top surface, it should spring back. If not, return it to pressure and cook it for another 2 or 3 minutes. The moment it is perfectly done, serve it instantly on very hot plates; sprinkle with a little grated nutmeg.

Peppermint and Pistachio Fluffy Custard

For 2
Cook under pressure at 5 lb for 11 minutes,
    then refrigerate for 4 hours

1 whole egg, lightly beaten
½ tsp pure vanilla extract
A good pinch salt
1 cup (2.5 dl) light cream, heated until it
    feels quite hot to the tip of your
    finger, but not scalded
5 Tbs (about 70 g) crushed peppermint
    stick candy, coarsely crumbled with a
    rolling pin between towels
3 Tbs shelled pistachio nuts, coarsely
    chopped
Butter for greasing the custard cups

We use metal individual custard cups, in which the custard cooks in the fastest time. If you use heatproof glass, the cooking time will be about 3 or 4 minutes longer. You could also double this recipe and cook the custard in a baking dish, but then the extra time might be as much as 10 minutes. See basic notes on all custards on page 174.

You will need a minimum 2½-quart pressure cooker and as many custard cups as may be needed to hold the mix, according to their size. First, in a fairly large mixing bowl, lightly beat together with a fork the egg and heated cream. Then work in the vanilla, salt, plus 4 tablespoons of the peppermint and 2 tablespoons of the pistachios. Butter the custard cups and, giving the mix a final beat or two, pour it in. Cover each cup completely and tightly with aluminum foil. Pour into the pressure cooker, with its base rack in place, ¾ cup of hot water and stand the cups on the rack. Put on the lid, bring the pressure up to 5 pounds and cook for exactly 11 minutes.

When the timer rings, turn off the heat and reduce the pressure immediately. Check the custard for doneness by plunging into its center a bright, silvery knife, which should come out dry and clean. If not, give the custard another couple of minutes at pressure. Finally, chill the custard cups, covered, for at least 4 hours in the refrigerator. Then unmold them onto a serving platter, decorate the custards with the remaining crushed pink peppermint candy and green pistachio nuts.

Cold Pumpkin Custard Mousse

For 2
Cook under pressure at 5 lb for 12 minutes,
*   then cool in the refrigerator for 2 hours*

¾ cup (1.85 dl) canned pumpkin, or you can cook and mash your own from fresh pumpkin
¾ cup (1.85 dl) light cream, heated until it feels quite hot to the tip of your finger, but not scalded
½ tsp ground cinnamon
½ tsp ground cloves
½ tsp ground ginger
The grated rind of a quarter of an orange
⅓ cup (75 g) brown sugar
¾ oz (22 ml) Williams pear brandy
2 whole eggs, lightly beaten
A pinch of salt

We use metal individual custard cups, in which the custard cooks in the fastest time. If you use heatproof glass, the cooking time will be about 3 or 4 minutes longer. You could also double this recipe and cook the custard in a baking dish, but then the extra time might be as much as 10 minutes. See basic notes on all custards on page 174.

You will need a minimum 2½-quart pressure cooker and as many custard cups as may be needed to hold the mix, according to their size. Thoroughly mash the pumpkin, then beat into it the cream, cinnamon, cloves, ginger, orange rind, brown sugar, pear brandy, eggs and salt. When the custard is thoroughly smooth, pour it into the lightly buttered cups and cover each completely and tightly with aluminum foil. Pour into the pressure cooker, with its base rack in place, ¾ cup of hot water and stand the cups on the rack. Put on the lid, bring the pressure up to 5 pounds and cook for precisely 12 minutes.

The instant the timer rings, turn off the heat and reduce the pressure immediately. Check the custard for doneness by plunging into its center a bright, silvery knife, which should come out dry and clean. If not, give the custard another couple of minutes at pressure. This pumpkin custard is best served cold, but not ice cold—so set it, still covered, in the refrigerator for a couple of hours or so. You may serve it in its cups, or unmold it onto a platter.

Chapter 22

MORE BASIC RECIPES:
STEAMED FRUIT PUDDINGS

Superheated Steam Brings Out
Natural Lightness

One of the most joyous and vivid memories of our childhood is of our grandmother's huge country kitchen with the gentle glub-glubbing sounds and the fruity-yeasty scents of a great steamed fig pudding (see page 222), tied in a knotted white cloth, slowly bubbling in its huge pot. We seem to remember that the bubbling went on all day and that the pudding was glorious when it was finally lifted out and unwrapped. One of our most favorite scenes in literature is in Charles Dickens' *Christmas Carol,* when the Cratchit family boils its fruit-filled Christmas pudding in the copper washtub. As our lives have grown faster-moving—as the pressures of the daily routine have increased—as there has been gradually less and less time for the simple joys—slowly steamed fruit puddings have literally disappeared from our tables.

Now they can come back again—with more fluffy lightness than ever before, with all their fruity refreshment, their healthful nutrition, their solid satisfaction. With superheated steam in a pressure cooker, the glub-glubbing can be measured in minutes instead of in hours. Here are a few of our favorite recipes—including that fig pudding we remember from Grandmother, an authentic Indian pudding for a truly American Thanksgiving and an English Christmas pudding, so traditional that it might well have been the one prepared by the Cratchits. These are among the unique pleasures of owning a pressure cooker—pleasures impossible to duplicate with any other kitchen machine.

Practical Notes

The techniques of steaming fruit puddings are almost exactly the same as those for steam-baking breads in Chapter 20. So you should first read the basic notes on pressure steaming on page 206 before trying out any of the following recipes. They are really quite simple, once you take the minimum trouble to learn the rules. We are again involved with a dough that must rise, so the cooking pressure must never be higher than 5 pounds. We prepare our puddings in a 4-cup, metal mold with a watertight, screw-on cover. But you can equally well use any type of metal mold and cover it, completely and tightly, with aluminum foil. It must be of a shape and size to fit inside your pressure cooker with enough space all around and over the top for the steam to circulate without hindrance. There is, first, a period of steaming without pressure, to encourage the dough to rise. We never put more than 3 cups of raw dough into our 4-cup mold. When you are first trying out a recipe, there is no harm in opening up everything at the end of the steaming period. You will find—if you have done the job right—that the mold is now entirely filled by the risen pudding. Put back the lid. Check the water in the pressure cooker. Start the pressure cooking as quickly as possible to prevent the pudding from falling again. When the cooking time is completed, check the pudding for doneness and, if necessary, give it a little extra time under pressure. Carefully note this extra time in the margin of the recipe. Finally, you will know the exact time for your particular mold, in your particular cooker, on your particular stove, and you will get consistently perfect results every time.

Steamed Cherry and Loganberry Pudding

For 4
First steamed without pressure for 15 minutes,
then at 5 lb for 40 minutes

¾ cup (170 g) sweet, whole cherries, fresh, pitted, in season, or canned, drained

¾ cup (170 g) sweet, whole loganberries, fresh in season, or canned, drained

1½ cups (170 g) all-purpose white flour, sifted before being measured

4 Tbs (60 g) butter, allowed to soften in advance

½ cup (115 g) brown sugar

1 whole egg, lightly beaten

3 tsp double-acting baking powder

A fair pinch of salt

⅓ cup (80 ml) light cream

This and all steamed puddings may be served either hot or cold. If hot, the ideal timing is to complete the pressure cooking just as you sit down to the meal. Then, let the pressure reduce gradually inside the pressure cooker while you are eating your main course. When you are ready to serve the dessert, take off the lid and unmold the pudding. It will be beautifully hot.

These puddings are light enough, juicy enough, refreshing enough, to serve as they are, without sauce. But, if you want to gild the lily for a party, you may add, at table, some heavy cream, whipped cream, or custard sauce (or brandy hard sauce).

Since loganberries are sometimes hard to find, you can use, as alternatives, blueberries, huckleberries or raspberries. See also, practical notes for steamed puddings on page 219.

You will need a minimum 2½-quart pressure cooker and a 4-cup, metal, covered mold of a shape to fit easily inside it with about ¾ inch (2 cm) to spare all around. First, put the cherries and loganberries into a fair-sized mixing bowl and gently but thoroughly dredge them with the first ½ cup of the flour. In a second bowl, cream together 3 tablespoons of the butter with the brown sugar, and then add the egg, mixing thoroughly. In a third bowl, resift the remaining cup of flour with the baking powder and a fair pinch or two of salt.

Now begin working this flour mix into the butter-egg mix, alternating the dry ingredients with tablespoons of the cream, until all the flour and cream are in and you have a smooth batter. Gently but thoroughly stir the floured fruit into it.

Lightly butter your mold and, giving the pudding mix a final good stir, put it in, making sure that the mold is no more than ⅔ to ¾ full. Cover it tightly. Pour 2 cups (5 dl) of hot water into the pressure cooker, with its base rack in place, then stand the mold on the rack. Put on the lid, but do not put on the pressure control weight. Leave the steam vent open. Adjust the heat so that a gentle flow of steam blows out of the vent, and keep it going—allowing it neither to blow too hard nor to die down—for 15 minutes.

When the timer rings, put the control weight on the steam vent, bring up the steam pressure to 5 pounds and continue cooking for exactly 40 minutes.

When the timer rings again, turn off the heat and allow the pressure to reduce gradually of its own accord—usually in about 5 minutes. Then open up everything and test the pudding for doneness by plunging into its center a bright, silvery knife, which should come out clean and dry. If not, continue the cooking under pressure for another 3 or 4 minutes. Finally, when the pudding is perfect, unmold onto a hot platter and serve.

Steamed Date Pudding

For 4
Cook under pressure at 5 lb for 44 minutes

4 Tbs (60 g) butter
¾ cup (1.85 dl) heavy cream
1½ cups (3.75 dl) crisp, not-too-fine
    bread crumbs
¾ cup (170 g) dates, stoned and coarsely
    chopped (usually about 1 box or
    package)
½ cup (115 g) brown sugar
2 Tbs cherry brandy

Since this pudding contains no leavening agents, it does not need any advance steaming without pressure. Its final texture is luxuriously fruity and juicy.

See practical notes on steaming on page 219, with serving and saucing advice on page 220.

You will need a minimum 2½-quart pressure cooker and a 4-cup metal, covered mold of a shape to fit inside with about ¾ inch (2 cm) to spare all around. First, melt 3 tablespoons of the butter and stir it into the cream. Then work in the bread crumbs. Next, stir in the chopped dates, brown sugar and cherry brandy. Lightly butter the mold and, giving the pudding mix a final good stir, put it in (filling the mold about ¾ full) and cover it tightly. Pour into the pressure cooker, with its base rack in place, 1 cup (2.5 dl) of hot water and stand the mold on the rack. Put on the lid, bring the pressure up to 5 pounds and cook for exactly 44 minutes.

When the timer rings, turn off the heat and allow the pressure to reduce gradually of its own accord. Then unmold the pudding.

Steamed Cranberry Pudding

For 4
First steamed without pressure for 20 minutes,
*   then at 5 lb for 36 minutes*

2 cups (450 g) fresh whole cranberries,
    washed and very coarsely chopped
½ cup (1.25 dl) unsulfured molasses
2 tsp baking soda
1½ cups (170 g) all-purpose white flour,
    sifted before measuring
½ tsp salt
1 Tbs (15 g) butter
6 Tbs (90 ml) pear liqueur

See practical notes on page 219, with serving and saucing advice on page 220.

You will need a minimum 2½-quart pressure cooker and a 4-cup metal, covered mold of a shape to fit inside with about ¾ inch (2 cm) to spare all around. First, in a mixing bowl, blend together the chopped cranberries with the molasses. In a small saucepan, bring ½ cup water just to the boil and stir the baking soda into it, then work this into the cranberries. Resift the flour with the salt and work these into the main cranberry mix.

Lightly butter your mold and, giving the pudding batter a final good stir, put it in, making sure that the mold is no more than ⅔ to ¾ full. Cover it tightly. Pour into the pressure cooker, with its base rack in place, 2 cups (5 dl) hot water and stand the mold on the rack. Put on the lid, but do not put on the pressure control weight. Leave the steam vent pipe open. Adjust the heat so that a gentle stream of steam blows out of the vent and keep it going—neither letting it blow too hard, nor allowing it to die down—for exactly 20 minutes.

When the timer rings, put the control weight on the vent pipe, bring the steam pressure up to 5 pounds and cook for another 36 minutes.

When the timer rings again, turn off the heat and allow the steam pressure to reduce gradually of its own accord—usually in about 5 minutes. Then open up everything and test the pudding for doneness by plunging into its center a bright, silvery knife, which should come out clean and dry. If not, continue the cooking under pressure for another 3 or 4 minutes. Finally when the pudding is perfect, unmold onto a hot platter and dribble the pear liqueur over it.

Grandmother's Steamed Farmhouse Fig Pudding

For 4
First steamed without pressure for 20 minutes,
*   then at 5 lb for 40 minutes*

½ cup (115 g) dried or semidried figs,
    first softened by soaking for about 10
    minutes in boiling water, then the
    stems cut off and the fruit coarsely
    chopped
2 Tbs diced citron
2 Tbs diced candied orange peel
6 Tbs chopped walnut meats

This is our modernized version of the old glub-glub recipe from Grandmother's country kitchen (page 219). The texture of this lovely pudding is given extra juiciness and smoothness by the inclusion (in addition to the fruits) of grated carrots and potatoes. The serving and saucing notes on page 220 apply equally to this recipe. See also the basic notes on steaming on page 219.

You will need a minimum 2½-quart pressure cooker and a 4-cup metal, covered mold of a shape to fit inside with about

1 cup (115 g) all-purpose white flour,
    sifted
1 tsp baking soda
1 tsp baking powder
¼ tsp salt
3 Tbs (45 g) butter
½ tsp ground cinnamon
¼ tsp ground cloves
6 Tbs brown sugar
1 whole egg, lightly beaten
6 Tbs grated raw carrot
6 Tbs grated raw potato

¾ inch (2 cm) to spare all around. First, in a largish mixing bowl, stir together the chopped figs with the diced citron and orange peel. Make sure that the sticky bits are well separated. Work the chopped walnuts into the fruit.

Into a separate bowl, sift together the flour, baking soda, baking powder and salt. Measure ½ cup of this dry mixture and work it into the fruit and nuts. In a third bowl, cream together 2 tablespoons of the butter with the cinnamon, cloves and brown sugar. When the mixture is nicely fluffy, beat the egg into it, then blend in the grated carrot and potato. Then gently fold in the remaining flour mix. Beat until it is all very smooth and then work it into the fruit and nuts.

Lightly butter the mold and, giving the pudding mix a final good stir, put it in, making sure the mold is no more than ¾ full. Cover it tightly. Pour into the pressure cooker, with its base rack in place, 2 cups (5 dl) of hot water and stand the mold on the rack. Put on the lid, but do not put on the pressure control weight. Leave the steam vent open. Adjust the heat so that a gentle flow of steam blows through the vent and keep it going—neither letting it get too strong, nor allowing it to die down—for 20 minutes.

When the timer rings, put the pressure control weight onto the vent pipe, bring the steam pressure up to 5 pounds and cook for exactly 40 minutes.

When the timer rings again, turn off the heat and allow the steam pressure to reduce gradually of its own accord. Test the pudding for doneness by plunging into its center a bright, silvery knife, which should come out clean and dry. If not, give the pudding an extra 3 or 4 minutes under pressure. When it is perfectly done, unmold it onto a hot serving platter.

Steamed Crystallized Ginger Pudding

For 4
First steamed without pressure for 20 minutes,
    then at 5 lb for 36 minutes

See practical notes for steaming on page 219, with serving and saucing advice on page 220.

6 Tbs brown sugar
¾ cup (1.85 dl) light cream
¾ tsp pure vanilla extract
2 whole eggs, lightly beaten
6 Tbs (90 g) butter, melted
1¾ cups (200 g) all-purpose white flour,
    sifted before measuring
1 Tbs double-acting baking powder
½ tsp salt
½ cup (115 g) crystallized ginger, or stem
    ginger in syrup, or a mixture of both,
    fairly finely chopped
½ cup (115 g) seedless raisins
3 Tbs diced citron

You will need a minimum 2½-quart pressure cooker and a 4-cup, metal, covered mold shaped to fit inside with about ¾ inch (2 cm) to spare all around. First, in a fairly large mixing bowl, blend together the brown sugar, cream and vanilla, stirring until the sugar is dissolved. Then beat in the eggs and melted butter. In a second bowl, sift together the flour, baking powder and salt.

Stir into this dry mixture the chopped ginger, raisins, citron and orange peel. Finally, combine this mix with the cream-sugar mix, at the same time thoroughly working in 2 tablespoons of the rum. Lightly butter the mold and, giving the pudding mix a final good stir, put it in, making sure that the mold is no more than ⅔ to ¾ full. Cover it tightly.

3 Tbs diced candied orange peel
5½ Tbs dark rum
1 Tbs (15 g) butter, firm, for greasing
    mold

Pour into the pressure cooker, with its base rack in place, 2 cups (5 dl) hot water and stand the mold on the rack. Put on the lid, but do not put on the pressure control weight. Leave the vent pipe open. Adjust the heat so that a small stream of steam blows through the vent and keep it going steadily—neither allowing it to blow too hard, thus boiling off the water, nor letting it die down, indicating that the heat is too low—for 20 minutes.

When the timer rings, put the pressure control weight on the vent, bring the pressure up to 5 pounds and cook for exactly 36 minutes longer.

When the timer rings again, turn off the heat and allow the pressure to reduce gradually of its own accord. Test the pudding for doneness by plunging into its center a bright, silvery knife, which should come out clean and dry. If not, give the pudding an extra 4 or 5 minutes more under pressure. When it is perfectly done, unmold it onto a hot serving platter, dribble the remaining ¼ cup rum over it and set on fire as it is brought to the table.

Williamsburg American Indian Pudding for Thanksgiving

For 4

Cook under pressure at 10 lb for 46 minutes

2 cups (5 dl) milk
1 cup (2.5 dl) light cream
⅓ cup (75 g) yellow cornmeal, the
    coarsest grind you can find,
    preferably stone ground
½ cup (1.25 dl) pure maple syrup
2 Tbs brown sugar
¾ tsp ground cinnamon
1 tsp ground ginger
½ tsp salt
3 Tbs (45 g) butter

For a party, we serve this historic, simple, yet memorable dessert with whipped cream, brandy hard sauce or butter pecan ice cream.

You can make it, as we do here, in a single baking dish—good-looking enough to be brought to the table—or in individual custard cups, so that each diner has his own little private Indian Pudding.

You will need a minimum 4-quart pressure cooker and a 5-cup baking dish or pan of a shape to fit inside with about ¾ inch (2 cm) space to spare all around. Take out the base rack and pour the milk and cream into the cooker. Over moderate heat, bring it up almost to the boil, but not quite. Turn down the heat. Now sprinkle the cornmeal, tablespoon by tablespoon, all across the surface of the hot liquid, and at once stir in to avoid lumping. Adjust the heat to keep it just below boiling, stirring almost continuously until it thickens, usually in about 10 to 15 minutes.

The moment the cornmeal begins to thicken stir in, one at a time and in this order, the maple syrup, brown sugar, cinnamon, ginger and salt, and melt in the butter in smallish bits. When everything is thoroughly blended, pour the mixture into the baking dish. Cover it, completely and tightly, with aluminum foil. Quickly rinse out the pressure cooker, put back its base rack, pour in 1½ cups (3.75 dl) of hot water and stand the dish on the rack. Put on the lid, bring the pressure up to 10 pounds and cook for exactly 46 minutes.

When the timer rings, turn off the heat and let the pressure reduce gradually of its own accord. Serve the Indian Pudding very hot with the garnish or sauce of your choice.

An Authentic English Christmas Plum Pudding
For 4
First steamed without pressure for 20 minutes,
  then at 10 lb for 46 minutes

2 Tbs candied citron
2 Tbs candied lemon peel, diced
2 Tbs candied orange peel, diced
1 medium-sized tart Greening apple,
  cored and chopped, not peeled
2 Tbs pitted dates, chopped
¾ cup (170 g) seedless white raisins
½ cup (115 g) small currants
3 large eggs
3 oz (85 g) white beef suet, preferably
  from around a kidney, ground and
  held refrigerated
2 cups (5 dl) dry bread crumbs
½ tsp ground cinnamon
¼ tsp ground cloves
½ tsp salt
8 to 12 grinds of nutmeg, or about ¼ tsp,
  to taste
6 Tbs dark brown sugar
¾ cup (1.85 dl) milk
1 Tbs good brandy
1 Tbs sweet cider
1 Tbs good dark rum
2 tsp butter

In England, it's the old tradition to make the Christmas pudding in August or September, more or less as soon as the family gets back from its summer vacation. Often, several puddings are made—the extra ones as special Christmas gifts for favored friends. Immediately after cooking, each pudding, in its airtight, lighttight and watertight mold, is stacked away in the darkest recesses of a closet, at room temperature, to caramelize, darken, develop flavor, mature, ripen, become altogether better and more desirable. Then, on Christmas Day, all you have to do is to reheat it in simmering water and serve it in flames, decorated with holly, garnished with rum custard and brandy hard sauce. A nice tradition to steal from the British! Now, with the pressure cooker, it all takes comparatively little time.

You will need a minimum 6-quart pressure cooker and a 6-cup, metal, covered mold of a shape to fit inside with at least ¾ inch (2 cm) space to spare all around. The making of this famous pudding is simply an orderly mixing operation, involving several bowls of different sizes. Hold the largest one for the final assembly. Into the second largest, put the fruits: citron, lemon peel, orange peel, apple, dates, raisins and currants, thoroughly unsticking and loosening them. Into a separate, medium-sized bowl, break the eggs, beat them with a wire whisk until they are frothy, then work into them the ground beef suet, breaking up all lumps with a wooden spoon. Now turn to your largest mixing bowl, which is still empty. Make a layer on its bottom with 1½ cups of the bread crumbs, then sprinkle over them, in turn, the cinnamon, cloves, salt and nutmeg. Cover all this with a layer of 6 tightly packed tablespoons of brown sugar, then mix everything thoroughly with a wooden spoon. Quickly heat up the milk, but do not let it boil, then work the first ½ cup of it at once into the spiced and sugared bread crumbs. The final mixture should be moist and soft, but not at all runny. If it seems too stiff, add more of the hot milk. If too runny, add a tablespoon or two more bread crumbs. Give a final stir to the egg-suet mix, then blend it into the bread crumbs. Now pile in all the fruits from the other bowl, but do not mix for the moment. First give the final blessing by sprinkling on the brandy, cider and rum. Wash your hands, roll up your sleeves and plunge into the final blending. No kitchen tool in existence is half as effective for this operation as a set of sensitive fingers. Feel around for lumps of sticky fruit and break them up. Keep it all as light as possible by lifting it rather than bearing down on it. Feel for dry spots. Make sure that the liquids are evenly distributed. When you are finally satisfied, lightly butter the mold and then fill it by hand, so that the pudding can be quite loosely packed in, yet without unnecessary air spaces. When it is quite full, cover it tightly, either with its own lid, or with several thicknesses of carefully stretched aluminum foil. Pour into the pressure cooker, with its base rack in place, 4 cups (1 liter) of hot water, then stand the mold on the rack. Heat up the water just to boiling, put on the lid at once, but do not put on the pressure control weight. Leave the vent pipe open. Adjust the heat so that a gentle stream of steam blows out of the vent and keep it going—neither allowing it to blow too hard, thus boiling away the water, nor letting the stream die down, showing that there is too little heat inside the pot— for exactly 20 minutes.

When the timer rings, put on the pressure control weight, bring up the steam pressure to 10 pounds and cook for exactly 46 minutes longer.

When the timer rings again, turn off the heat and allow the steam pressure to reduce gradually of its own accord.

You can then unmold the pudding and serve it at once, or you can store it away in an obscure closet at room temperature just as it is in its covered mold. The steaming has, of course, completely sterilized the pudding, so there are no bacteria and it could not possibly go bad. After storage of a few days, a few weeks or a few months, you just reheat it in its mold for, say, 20 to 30 minutes at 10 pounds pressure and serve it at once with its traditional flaming ceremonial sauces and accompaniments.

INDEX

Roy Andries de Groot

Roy Andries de Groot, one-time reporter for the *Manchester Guardian* and later on the staff of *The New York Times,* is known throughout Europe and the United States as an authority on wine and food. A European by birth, he now makes his home in New York, where he is a contributing editor of *Esquire* magazine. He has also been published by *Playboy, McCall's, Ladies' Home Journal, House Beautiful,* and *Gourmet.*

Mr. de Groot was born in London during World War I and was educated at Oxford University. While reporting in the streets of London during an aerial blitz of World War II, he received a serious eye injury that resulted in total blindness twenty years later. A U.S. citizen since 1948, he has lived in Chicago, Washington, D.C., San Francisco, New Orleans and now New York.

Mr. de Groot is the author of the classic cookbooks *Feasts for All Seasons, The Recipes of the Auberge of the Flowering Hearth, Revolutionizing French Cooking* and *Cooking with the Cuisinart.*

In addition to all of this, Mr. de Groot is president of the International Gourmet Society.